ENDEMIC

ENDEMIC

Exploring the wildlife unique to Britain

James Harding-Morris

BLOOMSBURY WILDLIFE
LONDON · OXFORD · NEW YORK · NEW DELHI · SYDNEY

For Elara, Falco, Max, Andie and Jude

BLOOMSBURY WILDLIFE
Bloomsbury Publishing Plc
50 Bedford Square, London, WC1B 3DP, UK
Bloomsbury Publishing Ireland Limited,
29 Earlsfort Terrace, Dublin 2, D02 AY28, Ireland

BLOOMSBURY, BLOOMSBURY WILDLIFE and the Diana logo are trademarks
of Bloomsbury Publishing Plc

First published in the United Kingdom 2025

Copyright © James Harding-Morris, 2025

Chapter illustrations © Natasha Foxford, 2025

James Harding-Morris has asserted his right under the Copyright, Designs and
Patents Act, 1988, to be identified as Author of this work

For legal purposes the Acknowledgements on pp. 326–327 constitute an extension of
this copyright page

All rights reserved. No part of this publication may be: i) reproduced or transmitted
in any form, electronic or mechanical, including photocopying, recording or by
means of any information storage or retrieval system without prior permission in
writing from the publishers; or ii) used or reproduced in any way for the training,
development or operation of artificial intelligence (AI) technologies, including
generative AI technologies. The rights holders expressly reserve this publication from
the text and data mining exception as per Article 4(3) of the Digital Single Market
Directive (EU) 2019/790

Bloomsbury Publishing Plc does not have any control over, or responsibility for, any
third-party websites referred to or in this book. All internet addresses given in this
book were correct at the time of going to press. The author and publisher regret any
inconvenience caused if addresses have changed or sites have ceased to exist, but can
accept no responsibility for any such changes

A catalogue record for this book is available from the British Library

Library of Congress Cataloguing-in-Publication data has been applied for

ISBN: HB: 978-1-3994-0567-6; ePub: 978-1-3994-0566-9; ePDF: 978-1-3994-0571-3

2 4 6 8 10 9 7 5 3 1

Typeset in Stempel Garamond LT Std by Deanta Global Publishing Services,
Chennai, India
Printed and bound in Great Britain by CPI Group (UK) Ltd, Croydon CR0 4YY

To find out more about our authors and books visit www.bloomsbury.com and sign
up for our newsletters

For product safety related questions contact productsafety@bloomsbury.com

Contents

Introduction	7
1 Stone Cold Survivor: Northern February Red	13
2 In a Flap: Scottish Crossbill, Red Grouse and Willow Tit	25
3 Celtic Creatures: Celtic Woodlouse and Chater's Bristletail	40
4 Blown Away: False Fen and Bertha's Dandelion	55
5 Just Right: Goldilocks Buttercups	68
6 The World's Unluckiest Plant: Interrupted Brome	83
7 Shrimply Amazing: British Cave Shrimp	96
8 Devon's Galápagos: Lundy Cabbage and its Beetles	115
9 Purple Prose: Purple Ramping-fumitory	134
10 Back from the Dead: York Groundsel	142
11 Roadsides and Seasides: No Parking and Menai Strait Whitebeams	158

12	Berry Good: Great Orme Berry and South Stack Fleawort	175
13	Mantle Peace: False-toothed Lady's Mantle	194
14	Rooting For You: Elms	206
15	By a Single River: Baker's Hawkweed	221
16	Down to Earth: British Earthstar	235
17	Between a Rock and a Wet Place: Derbyshire Feathermoss	250
18	Orcadian Adventures: Scottish Primrose and Orkney Vole	263
19	The Rarest Tree on Earth: Catacol Whitebeam	281
20	Small Wonders: Horrid Ground-weaver and British False Flat-backed Millipede	298

Epilogue	317
Acknowledgements	326
References and Bibliography	328
Index	331

Introduction

Here is a thought experiment for you. Imagine that one day Britain sank beneath the sea and was lost forever. Ireland is safe, as are the Isle of Man and the Channel Islands, but Wales, England, Scotland and their surrounding islands (including Orkney, Shetland, Skomer, Anglesey, the Isle of Wight and the Isles of Scilly) are all gone. Let's also imagine that the human population was safely teleported away somewhere else so that you don't have to dwell on the apocalyptic imagery.

What, from a natural history perspective, would be lost? Of course, the answer is 'everything', so a more insightful question would be: what would be irreplaceably lost? Which species would vanish entirely from planet Earth? This is when you realise that most of our wildlife also exists elsewhere: badgers roam across most of Europe; the range of the so-called 'English' or pedunculate oak stretches all the way to Asia; and purple saxifrage blooms in the Alps, Greenland, and the North American Rocky Mountains. If Britain disappeared, the global populations of these species wouldn't really suffer.

Then there are species like the Eurasian curlew, where Britain holds about a quarter of the world population. The loss of Britain would be a huge blow, but the species would survive elsewhere. Similarly, we have around 50 per cent of the global population of bluebells. An enormous loss if we went the way of Atlantis, but bluebells would still survive in Ireland, France, the Netherlands and beyond. So how many of the approximately 70,000 species that call Britain home are *only* found here?

I first pondered this question in 2017 when I started working on the Back from the Brink project; a grand collaboration of conservation organisations dedicated to saving some of England's most threatened species from extinction. Amongst the 200+ species we were aiming to save were a handful that are only found in Britain: the frosty-looking and highly-endangered prostrate perennial knawel that is only found in a few spots in the Breckland of East Anglia; the interrupted brome, a mysterious grass of arable farms that appeared and very nearly vanished entirely within the span of a century and a half; and the Cornish path moss, a minute baize fuzz of a plant whose entire global population covers $0.16m^2$ – about half the size of a doormat. These, and others like them, are our endemic species.

Let's consider the word 'endemic' for a moment. The term is generally used to describe species found within a defined geographical area. Lemurs are only found on Madagascar – they are Madagascan endemics. The kakapo, a large, moss-green flightless parrot, is endemic to New Zealand. The Devil's Hole pupfish is only found in a single cavern in Nevada in the United States; it could therefore be described as endemic to the United States or to Nevada – or to the single pool in which it is found.

My interest piqued by British endemics, I started to research further – and soon hit a wall. I could find no authoritative document, website or article that laid out a full list of all the species that are unique to Britain. Instead, I found scattered references – to ghostly shrimp in Devon caves, extinct urban flowers, and a lonely tree, the last of its kind, on an island off the coast of Scotland. I started making notes when I came across references like these, aimless lists of sea lavenders and whitebeams with no real purpose in mind.

In 2021, as the Covid pandemic waned, I planned a birthday trip. Every year on my birthday, I try to see a species I've not seen before – a flower, butterfly, bug or anything else. I'm a pan-species lister, you see. Some people specialise in an area of natural history, becoming botanists, birders, coleopterists or mammal-enthusiasts. Pan-species listers instead try to learn how to recognise *everything*, as delighted by seeing a new springtail as we are by a new orchid or a rare bird, and over time we build up a personal overview of the entire biodiversity of our islands. It's not about creating a long purposeless list, though; it involves tackling tricky and overlooked species groups and submitting records to formal recording schemes. This means that I have no single area of expertise but know a little bit about everything.

With the hope of seeing something unusual, I put out a message on social media to gather suggestions on what I could look for this year:

> *Next week I'm in the Yorkshire Dales. Does anyone have any suggestions for interesting species to see in the triangle between Leyburn, Skipton and Ingleton?*

I soon heard from Kevin Walker, head of science at the Botanical Society of Britain and Ireland (BSBI):

> *Where do I start? Those coordinates triangulate a host of British rare plants! How about Sulber Pasture on the slopes of Ingleborough – home to almost the entire*

world population of Yorkshire Sandwort, Arenaria norvegica *subsp.* anglica.

I shot to Google. The entire world population of Yorkshire sandwort (or English sandwort) is found within a stone's throw of Ribblesdale, a place I'd been dozens of times in my life, and I'd never even heard of it.

A week later, on 23rd June, my friend Heather and I started up the gradual flank of Ingleborough, the stepped summit still far in the distance. Heather, an ecologist, and I had originally met when working for the RSPB. She has enormous patience for my adventures; all the walkers around us were here to summit Ingleborough, but she was happy to help me find this tiny, porcelain-white flower instead.

The yellows of mountain pansy mingled with the purples of heath milkwort and we passed stands of cottongrass with their fluffy seedheads nodding gently in the breeze. Skylarks sang overhead, and meadow pipits occasionally flicked up and over the tussocky grassland.

It didn't take long to reach the rough area that Kevin had described to me: a crossroads with tired climbers descending the mountain heading east, and eager walkers full of energy heading west. Backtracking slightly, we explored the pasture to the south, looking for the crisp white flowers and lime-green cushions of Yorkshire sandwort.

We found gone-over early purple orchids with wilted petals hanging like tattered flags, cushions of prickly juniper and – with a flash of white that got my heart beating in excitement for a moment – the fuzzy flowers of mountain everlasting. We criss-crossed the pasture for nearly an hour, hope fading.

Then Heather found it. On the edge of a dried-up stream, near a patch of carnivorous butterwort, were two fist-sized patches of Yorkshire sandwort side by side. A tangle of maroon stems with tiny, thickened, almost-succulent, fresh green leaves made a small, domed mound. This mound was then topped with flowers – some finished, some in bud, but many open stark-white to the sky. Five oval, paper-white petals against the sharp star-shape of the sepals, the flowers larger than the leaves, making each stem look top-heavy.

I gently touched a flower, which nodded softly. It was awe-inspiring to see a plant that exists nowhere else on the planet, and to realise that everyone who has ever seen it must have once visited these same Yorkshire pastures.

After returning to Lincolnshire I read up on the Yorkshire sandwort in more detail and learnt that it is not thriving in its only home. Two outlying populations have vanished since the 1990s, and overall numbers over the past 30 years have seen counts of thousands of plants drop into the hundreds.

How is this not a pressing conservation concern? Have you ever heard of the Yorkshire sandwort, donated to its cause, seen it featured in a nature documentary? Probably not. Unlike the capercaillie, the beaver or the white-tailed eagle, which, having all been lost from Britain have since been reintroduced from abroad, this little plant exists nowhere else on Earth. If we don't save it, then it's gone forever. Shouldn't all our endemics – the plants, animals and fungi that we have total global responsibility for – have the highest conservation priority?

With this realisation, I decided to discover and tell the stories of endemic species in Britain. If these are our most precious species, then shouldn't they have their moment in the limelight? A chance for recognition and acknowledgement as something uniquely British and special?

As no definitive list of British endemics exists, I created my own by pulling together every scant reference I could find online, in books, or by contacting species experts. This revealed that, astonishingly, we have around 700 species and at least another 100 subspecies unique to Britain – animals, plants and fungi found nowhere else on the planet.

From these species and subspecies, I picked 20 to highlight, between them showcasing specialised habitats, conservation successes and species under threat. Sometimes these are tales of a single endemic, sometimes of multiple unique organisms, and occasionally I simply encountered a 'bonus' species that just had to be included.

I chose as wide a range as possible: crustaceans, a moss, insects, a spider, a bird, a fungus, a mammal and a whole range of plants. Some of these are agonisingly rare, others actively threatened – and there are a few that you might be able to walk outside and see for yourself. Think of the featured organisms as figureheads; ambassadors for the rest of our endemics.

I spent 2022 and 2023 tracking these plants, fungi and animals down across the length and breadth of Britain, from the shores of the English Channel to the Orkney archipelago, and meeting the experts and conservationists devoted to their study and survival. This is the story of how I delved into the rich tapestry of Britain's endemic wildlife, and celebrated the uniqueness that makes our natural history so profoundly special.

CHAPTER 1

Stone Cold Survivor: Northern February Red

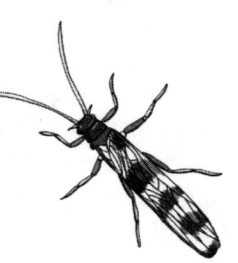

I had spent the winter researching Britain's endemic invertebrates – our unique insects, spiders, snails, crustaceans and their ilk. While Britain is home to more than 40,000 invertebrate species, there is a common consensus that only a small number of these are endemics. Yet, strangely, no one actually seemed to know exactly how many we had. The internet offered up the same few names, combing through books revealed a few more, but I had no idea how comprehensive this information was.

The thing is, the term 'invertebrate' covers an enormous category of life. There are people who specialise in beetles (coleopterists), or butterflies and moths (lepidopterists), but there aren't really people who work with invertebrates as a whole and who are capable of summarising all of the information from across this broad swathe of species. That is, except for Craig Macadam, conservation director at Buglife.

I had contacted Craig because he was – for the first time – trying to draw together information on endemic invertebrates in Britain into a single, useful report; the exact type of document that I had been vainly searching for.

Craig was doing amazing work on clarifying the available information around our endemic invertebrates, but isn't it bizarre that this information had never been collated before? These are, arguably, some of Britain's most important species – the utterly unique and irreplaceable – and until Craig started this work, we had no clear idea of what they all were.

Over an email conversation, Craig told me he had recently completed draft global Red List assessments for all 18 of our endemic invertebrate species. By either sheer coincidence or good research on my part, I'd also compiled a list of 18 endemic invertebrates. We compared. Our lists were not the same.

Craig pointed out that three species on my list were now no longer considered endemics: these were the rove beetle *Meotica anglica*, which is now considered the same as its mainland European counterpart *Meotica moczarskii*; the tumbling flower beetle *Anaspis septentrionalis*, which is now synonymised with *Anaspis thoracica*, found in Sweden and Denmark; and a leafhopper called *Anoscopus duffieldi*, which is now considered a subspecies of the much more widespread *Anoscopus albifrons*. However, my list did include Chater's bristletail (*Dilta chateri*), and a dung beetle called *Psammoporus insularis* that hadn't made it onto Craig's. He said he'd look into them.

This meant we had a combined list of 20 endemic invertebrates, comprising four beetles, five flies, a millipede, a centipede, a flea, two crustaceans, a bristletail, a bug, a spider, two stoneflies and a sea anemone. From this I wanted to pick an interesting suite of species – fascinating creatures found in interesting habitats with intriguing tales of discovery and conservation.

I was immediately drawn to Ivell's sea anemone, a species only ever known from Widewater Lagoon in Sussex, but I discovered that it hadn't been seen in 40 years and might now be extinct. Not that then. What about a bug, the Caledonian planthopper? It would be great to see an endemic Scottish invertebrate. Ah. No one had seen it for 70 years. That's not to say it's definitely extinct, but it seemed a long shot that I'd be the one to rediscover it.

The more I researched, the more I realised that some of our endemic invertebrates either didn't seem to be well known or were faring very badly. Turk's earth centipede, *Nothogeophilus turki*, was described from the Isles of Scilly in 1988 and has never been seen again. The dance-fly *Poecilobothrus majesticus* was discovered in Essex in 1907 but hasn't been found in over a century.

After eliminating all of the possibly extinct and vanishingly obscure from consideration, I made a selection: a woodlouse, a shrimp, a beetle and a spider. What's more, Craig made me an unbeatable offer of showing me another endemic invertebrate to start me off; a species that he is a particular expert in – a stonefly called the northern February red.

As the name suggests, I needed to head north for this species. However, unlike its name suggests, Craig proposed we met in March when the weather is a little more reliable. 'Northern March red' doesn't sound as good though, does it?

I recruited my friend, Robert, an all-round naturalist with a particular interest in flies and whose day job is with the British Trust for Ornithology (BTO). Robert has been my pan-species listing partner in crime for the past decade or so. We've tracked down hundreds of species together in that time: oil beetles, stick insects and lizards, as well as everything else in between. When we first started out, our dynamic was based on the fact that

I could drive and he could read a map. Now, our skills have diversified so that between us you could make one very competent ecologist. He does flies, I do moths; he does slugs, I do snails, and so on. What's more, we could split the driving on our way up to the Scottish Highlands.

The weather was cold, clear and bright as we left England. However, by the time we reached Newtonmore some hours later, it was dark and the wipers were swiping wet sheets of snow from the windscreen as we peered into the murk to spot our accommodation for the night.

Checking into our little hotel and stomping the slush from our boots, I hurriedly checked the weather and my emails. These didn't feel like the sort of conditions in which to go looking for an insect. I had a disconcerting message from Craig:

> *The weather isn't looking too great now for tomorrow. I'm still coming up so we can have a look for Northern February Reds but it might be a bit more difficult than usual!*

But, looking on the bright side, I'd been feeling almost certain that our scheduled rendezvous would be a complete write-off. I supposed northern February reds must be hardy creatures – 'northern' is in the name, after all – and they must deal with snowy squalls pretty regularly. I went to bed with a flicker of optimism.

The next day we awoke to find the car under a mushy blanket of wet snow, rapidly melting in the warm patchy sunshine that the forecast had failed to predict. After clearing the windows, Robert and I hopped in, and the rest of the snow sloughed off as we made our way to Boat of Garten, a village in the heart of the Cairngorms National Park.

We parked in a little pull-in that Craig had described to me over email, just next to a bridge crossing the River Spey, and waited for him to arrive. The forecasted grey and gloom stayed at bay and the high, white cloud and patchy sun felt encouraging.

Not long after we had arrived, a red car parked up ahead of us. Out stepped Craig, who waved to us, and, after an exchange of greetings, led us across the bridge, through a sturdy wooden gate and along a narrow footpath that snaked down to the riverbank. The river was wide and peat-stained a rich tea brown. On the opposite side grew a tangled bank of trees, currently stark and bare, the willows on the edge trailing their twigs in the swirling water.

On our side there was a 5m strip of tussocky grass, gorse and a few trees planted in green plastic tubes, all extending down to the river's edge. Behind that was a wire fence, where we were standing, which separated this bankside vegetation from a field of stout, fluffy sheep.

'This', said Craig, sweeping his arms at the riverside in front of us and the bridge beside us, 'is what I call the "tourist spot" for the northern February red. They're easy to find here, usually, and you can park right alongside.'

He walked forward to the wire at the edge of the sheep field and placed his hand on top of a wooden fencepost. 'These fenceposts are the place to look. Even at this time of year, the side in the sun can reach up to 20 degrees and that's where we find them, basking in the warmth.'

'I guess the fenceposts act as a kind of proxy for riverside trees?' I asked, as I felt the sunny side of the wooden stake. It was warm against the palm of my hand.

'We assume so,' replied Craig, bending to inspect the fencepost through his rectangular, black-framed glasses. 'But based on our surveys, it seems like fenceposts may be preferable to trees – maybe trees shade each other but fenceposts are more often in a neat row out in the sun? We're not sure.'

Craig moved on to the next post to check it, with me keeping pace alongside. Robert had leapfrogged us and was searching further down the fenceline.

'So do they emerge on the riverside and then fly to the posts?' I asked.

'The females probably do,' he replied, scanning the wooden post. 'But the males are short-winged; they literally have stubbier wings than the female and can't really fly. They must crawl here from the river edge.'

I eyed up the 5m of tussocky grass between us and the river. 'That must be quite a slog for a little insect.'

Craig looked down to the river edge. 'Yeah, but they must crawl further than that. At Grantown we've found them on posts 200m from the river.'

Robert called from up ahead, 'I think I've found one.' We hurried down the field edge to join him.

'I'm so good at this,' he said modestly as we arrived at his side, and he pointed out a skinny stonefly sitting happily on the sunny side of the post.

The stoneflies, the order of insects called Plecoptera, are an ancient group. They pre-date the evolution of butterflies (around 100 million years ago), of dinosaurs (200–250 million years ago) and of beetles (295 million years ago), appearing in the fossil record at least 311 million years ago. They perfected their body plan early on and stuck with it.

There are groups of insects that everyone has some sort of mental image of. Everyone can picture a butterfly; everyone can imagine an ant, a beetle, a fly, a bee – a generic image, sure, but some sort of conceptual blueprint of size, shape and maybe even colour. I don't think this is true of stoneflies; I think they exist just outside the realm of general awareness.

The most striking feature of a stonefly is its wings. On a typical stonefly the wings are longer than its body and lie elegantly and tightly folded flat along its back like a cape. These wings are exquisite; dark curving veins, like elaborate wrought-iron, support translucent smoky panes like frosted glass. It's these wings that give the stonefly family its name, Plecoptera, meaning 'braided wing', referring to the intricacies of their wing venation. In front of the wings is a stout, shield-like plate, and in front of that is a wide head with two well-spaced eyes, as round and black as neat drops of ink. From the head sprout two long, simple antennae, which gradually taper away to nothing. They are, in short, beautiful insects.

The stonefly Robert had found looked just like this. The entire body and wing veins were black with a faint brownish hue, the membrane of the long cape-like wings a smoky grey, marked with three distinct charcoal bands.

'A female,' said Craig, peering at her. 'Do you see how long her wings are?'

Her wings extended well past the tip of her abdomen, almost as far as the tips of her outstretched back legs. From head to the tip of those folded wings, she was probably around 14mm long.

'She's fully winged. In the males, the wings are only about as long as the body. Sometimes even a little bit shorter than the body.'

I leant in to take a photo. She shivered her wings slightly as I snapped away but stayed still, gently flexing her mandibles.

'A Scottish endemic,' I murmured as I snapped my picture.

'Well, that's not always been the case.' said Craig. 'They were found on the River Usk in Wales until the 1980s and the River Wye in Herefordshire up until 1992. After that they disappeared – it's not completely clear why. River management might have been part of it; dredging is bad for the larvae. Pollution probably played a big role as stoneflies are particularly sensitive to it. They're a great indicator of river health, though, because of that. If you've got stoneflies, you've probably got a very clean river.'

'I think I've found a male.' called Robert from up ahead. We picked up the pace to join him. 'It's a good thing I'm here,' he said, pointing to a fencepost, 'I'm finding everything.'

On the fencepost was a stonefly that looked simultaneously very much like the female we had just seen, but also distinctly different. Craig nodded his assent to Robert's identification. 'Yep, that's a male.'

The male was distinctly browner than the female, a warm brown that had led to the species being optimistically called the northern February 'red'. It's a beautiful toffee colour but it's certainly not red. Putting that untruth aside, his wings were distinctly shorter than the female's, just cresting the tip of his abdomen, and his legs looked longer and ganglier than the female's. He looked shorter overall, around 8mm from head to wingtip. Perhaps aware of our presence or bothered by the light breeze that had sprung up, he huffily walked a few steps around the corner of the post out of sight and onto the more sheltered side. The motion of his long back legs was almost grasshopper-like, reminiscent of something vaguely mechanical.

I said this out loud and Craig nodded. 'I see what you mean. Did you know that stoneflies make noise? Not like grasshoppers, but they drum with their abdomens.'

He pulled out his phone and, over the rush of the river, we strained to hear the recorded sound of a different, larger stonefly species. It was a strange noise, percussive, rhythmic and sort of hollow, woody and rough. I was impressed. This behaviour was entirely new to me.

Craig explained that he got the recording by putting a male stonefly in a cardboard box and then resting his phone on top so it could pick up their subtle noises. 'I'm going to take a male back with me today to try to get another recording,' he told us. 'The drumming each species makes is diagnostic, and I don't think anyone has ever recorded the northern February red.'

'Is this newly discovered behaviour?' I asked.

Craig shook his head. 'It was discovered in the late 1800s. At the time it was described as sounding like "a mouse chewing at the wainscot". I've got mice and can confirm how accurate that is! It's not just the males – the female, if she's interested, will tap back. In some stonefly species a rival male will mimic the response tap of a female to interrupt and distract another male.'

We spread out again along the fenceline and searched, finding plenty more northern February reds. One female was busily making her way along a strand of barbed wire, threading herself between the spikes. One fencepost held no fewer than seven males, some soaking up the sun, others striding around with their long, jerky back legs.

'How safe is this, as a species?' I asked Craig.

'Well, it's been lost from England and Wales already,' he replied. 'It was first discovered in Scotland on the River Clyde in the 1830s but it's gone from there now. Here on the Spey and along the River Dee we've done volunteer citizen science surveys that have given Buglife a lot of information and show that it's still widespread, but there are patchy records from elsewhere. Climate change is a threat, as that will change the oxygen levels and general composition of rivers, and stoneflies need high oxygen environments. Pollution remains a concern too.'

Despite their extinction in the rest of Britain, the February reds have no legal protection in place. Because they're widespread in Scotland they're classed as least concern, even though their British range is now drastically smaller.

Craig went on to tell me how little we know about the species. As it doesn't exist anywhere else, we can't learn from research in other countries. We don't know much about its egg-laying behaviour – how many eggs it lays or in how many batches – or exactly how and where the larvae live in the river. Considering this is a species originally unique to Britain, and now just Scotland, it's amazing how little we know about what it needs in order to survive and thrive.

To help address this knowledge gap, Buglife are always on the lookout for records of northern February red, especially if these are away from the strongholds on the Spey and Dee. If you want to help, check their website for identification guidance and information on how to submit records.

As Craig was talking, Robert walked up and joined us. He waited a moment for a slight break in the conversation and announced, 'I just saw a man pull a lamb out of that sheep.' He pointed.

We looked. In the field next to us there was a man standing next to a sheep and a very shaky newborn lamb.

'It felt important I tell you,' said Robert, still gazing thoughtfully at the new mother and offspring.

The conversation thus disrupted, we started back along the fence towards the bridge.

We scanned the fenceposts as we passed, seeing all the same stoneflies we presumably spotted on the walk out, but some movement on the one nearest the bridge caught our eyes. One male was fluttering his wings jerkily and rhythmically whilst a female wandered around a few inches away.

'That's the drumming!' said Craig.

Sure enough, the male buzzed his wings again and it was possible to see him repeatedly tap his abdomen against the top of the fence post. Even with our breath held we couldn't hear anything – the river was too loud and the fencepost not particularly resonant – and perhaps the female couldn't either. She didn't appear at all interested in his advances and ambled off the top of the fencepost and away. She may not have been impressed, but I was.

We crossed the bridge and returned to our cars. I thanked Craig and waved as he drove off. Seeing the northern February red had been a treat – my first encounter with one of our endemic species, and one of our very few endemic invertebrates. In a landscape dominated by species shared across Europe, finding this unique, hardy insect felt like a triumph.

Reflecting on Craig's words about the stonefly's tumultuous past and uncertain future, I was struck by how little we still know about it. But today, with the warming sun breaking through the clouds and the stoneflies scattered along the riverside, the northern February red seemed, at least for now, secure.

The northern February red may have been the reason for our visit, but it also afforded an unmissable opportunity to try to catch up with another of my target endemics, this time in the ancient Caledonian pine forests. Here, supposedly, was the home of Britain's only endemic bird.

CHAPTER 2

In a Flap: Scottish Crossbill, Red Grouse and Willow Tit

After setting off from Boat of Garten, leaving Craig and the northern February reds behind, Robert and I drove for mere minutes to Abernethy National Nature Reserve. Abernethy Forest is home to what is considered at the time of writing to be the only endemic bird species in Britain, the Scottish crossbill, *Loxia scotica*.

If you have never seen a crossbill before then you have an absolute treat in store for you one day. The common crossbill, *Loxia curvirostra* – the crossbill species most widespread across Britain – is a thickset, beefy finch, about 50 per cent larger than a greenfinch, with a stout chunky neck and, most remarkably (and as its name suggests), a rather strange beak that is crossed at the end. The tips of this beak don't meet neatly as they do in most other birds; rather the top bends down and the bottom up, curving past each other. This asymmetrical bill is used like a pair of tweezers to extract seeds from the cones of coniferous trees. The males are brick red, and the females a brownish green amber.

The Scottish crossbill, *Loxia scotica*, looks very much like a common crossbill, but is restricted to the pine forests of Scotland. It was originally described in 1904 by German ornithologist Ernst Hartert as a separate subspecies of the common crossbill, but was elevated to species level in the 1970s. Its exact range in Scotland is hazy, the lack of confidence of some birders in identifying it clashing with the overconfidence of others leads to an overall opaque picture. This difficulty is understandable, however, because this species is almost identical to the common crossbill. Even if you were an absolute expert and holding one in your hand, there is no single physical feature that distinguishes the two species.

A paper by Alan Knox in *British Birds* says:

> *There are no known plumage or behavioural differences between [Common] Crossbill and Scottish Crossbill. Compared with the Crossbill, which is more widely distributed and better known, the Scottish Crossbill is on average marginally larger and heavier. There is much variation, and the difference is not particularly noticeable in the field, even when the two forms are seen side by side.*

In that case, is this one of those species that can only be distinguished through genetic testing? Unfortunately not. Genetic testing back in 2001 found no difference between the common and Scottish crossbill – at least not in the regions of DNA sampled (genetic testing typically doesn't involve comparing the *entire* genome of species, rather it looks at specific chunks of DNA where differences might be expected).

This whole situation is complicated further by the fact that there is a *third* crossbill species in Scotland's forests: the parrot crossbill. The parrot crossbill is larger still than the Scottish crossbill, with an even chunkier beak and a neck like a bodybuilder's. These finches are distinctly bigger than common crossbills, and if you are in an area with just parrot and common crossbills, the two species can be told apart by a good view of the shape and size of their beaks. If held in the hand by an expert, then wing and beak measurements would also clearly distinguish them as they do differ in size. The problem is that the Scottish crossbill overlaps with the smaller end of the spectrum of variation in parrot crossbill *and* with the larger end of common crossbill variation. Basically, in Scotland, there is an entire continuum of crossbill sizes ranging from the smallest individuals of the common crossbill, through the intermediate Scottish crossbill, up to the largest individuals of the parrot crossbill.

So if there are no physical features that unequivocally allow Scottish and common crossbills to be separated, or Scottish and parrot crossbills, then how do you identify the Scottish crossbill? And what makes it a different species?

The answer is in the birds' vocalisations. The common crossbill, the Scottish crossbill and the parrot crossbill all supposedly make consistently different calls to each other, and only breed with other crossbills making the same type of call. This means that they are reproductively isolated from each other; they are practising 'assortative mating'. The best way to identify them, then, is either by having a very finely-tuned ear, or by recording the call and turning it into a sonogram – a visual representation of the sound – so that it can be compared with others. Crossbills make a sound known as the 'excitement call', which is vital for ID. Common crossbills make three types of excitement call, known as Type A, Type B and Type E. Scottish crossbills make one excitement call, Type C, and parrot crossbills make the Type D call. That's it. That's the one supposedly certain way of distinguishing the Scottish crossbill from its close cousins.

Robert and I were not equipped with sophisticated recording equipment, but we had read that it was possible to capture a clear enough recording on a humble phone to make a sonogram, provided the birds are close enough and there isn't too much background noise. We walked from the Abernethy car park, crunching along the pine needle-strewn path between the rufous, contorted trunks of Scots pine and hoped we'd get lucky.

Despite the weak March sun, we soon spotted piles of leaf litter and pine needles swarming with busy wood ants dotted along the path. At our approach, the ants ran a little more frenetically and sprayed formic acid in our direction. If you ever encounter a nest heap, then I thoroughly recommend waving a hand low over the nest and then giving it a sniff so you can experience the sharp, vinegary hit of formic acid at the back of your throat.

Then, suddenly, distracting us from the wood ants, we heard it. The overlapping excitable *jypp* calls of crossbills – but of which species? Unfortunately, they didn't land nearby, their red and amber forms passing over the treetops whilst I frantically fumbled my phone out of my pocket, failing miserably to record anything. That said, they didn't sound, to my uncultured ear, any different from the crossbills I'd heard in the pine plantations of Yorkshire.

After an hour of unproductive walking, we returned to the car park, where I paid attention to the interpretation panel I had ignored on the way in. There was a photograph of a male crossbill drinking from a puddle and some information about the different crossbill species. One line jumped out at me: 'The differences between them are very subtle and much debated, so if you see one, take your pick!'

Though it was tempting to take the sign's advice and claim our brief sighting as Scottish crossbills, I'm a bit of a purist, so I reluctantly categorised the birds we had seen and heard as unidentified.

Over the next couple of days, Robert and I wandered through various beautiful fragments of Caledonian forest. We saw red squirrels and crested tits and even, early one morning, a stunning male capercaillie standing right in the middle of the path as we rounded a bend. And we saw crossbills. On one occasion a male and a female sat in the top of the tree dissecting cones whilst we watched from below. We couldn't tell if they looked any bigger than common crossbills, and they utterly refused to call, and so remained mysterious and unidentified. Later, some more crossbills came *jypping* overhead and, phone in hand, I was at last able to set the recorder going. Unfortunately, I discovered later that the sound of them had been completely obliterated by a gust of wind that blew at exactly that moment and turned my recording into a staticky mess. How did anyone manage this?

In my desperation, I wrote an email to a birding tour company, who I had noticed featured Scottish crossbill regularly on their reports, thinking I could maybe pay an expert for their time. They did not reply to me. I was later told (and this is hearsay and rumour!) that some tour companies can be – how do I put this? – 'flexible' with their crossbill identification for the commercial benefits it brings.

I also contacted the bird recorder for Highland, John Poyner, who told me that he hadn't formally accepted any records of Scottish crossbill for well over five years; instead, in their annual summary, they mention 'reports' of Scottish crossbills, or birds 'believed to be' Scottish crossbill.

With no expert advice, and no luck with getting a recording, I ended up leaving Scotland unsure of what species I'd seen in these ancient pine forests.

It was only a few months later that my attention was drawn to an article in *Scottish Birds* about the position of the Scottish Birds Records Committee on the Scottish crossbill. This paper discussed how the Type C call, which was thought unique to the Scottish crossbill, had now been encountered across mainland Europe. Even more puzzling, despite extensive recording between 2014 and 2016, this supposedly diagnostic Type C call *hadn't* been recorded at all in Scotland. The final complication, the cherry on the cake, is that an entirely new type of call from crossbills was discovered in Scotland during this period, but it's unknown which species - or supposed species - of crossbill was making it. The article ends:

> *Because of this current uncertainty, the committee is no longer aware of any plumage, biometric, vocal or genetic criteria that can be used to identify Scottish Crossbill with confidence. As a result, the committee will no longer consider any records of the species.*

The species is now in limbo, with no known means of identification. This is probably not a surprise to many. When I first started researching the Scottish crossbill, I came across forum threads of birders dismissing its existence. When trying to find experts willing to show me one, I couldn't find anyone who seemed confident it was real. Even the Highland bird recorder, John, told me that in his opinion, and in those of many experienced birders, the status of the Scottish crossbill as a true species remains highly uncertain.

I'm not an expert, and so my thoughts on this are worth taking with a great heap of salt, but I wonder if the Scottish crossbill may be a *potential* species. Perhaps it's in the early stages of diverging but hasn't reached a clear point of distinction. This could explain the lack of DNA differentiation; the Scottish crossbill 'form' (or whatever we want to call it) is currently too young to significantly differ from its closest relatives. If this newly discovered call type *is* characteristic of the Scottish crossbill form and these crossbills *are* remaining reproductively isolated from other crossbill species, maybe they will continue to diverge and become clearly and unambiguously different (what is known as a 'good' species) in the fullness of time.

Robert has his own opinion. He thinks the Scottish crossbill was simply made up to attract tourists.

If the Scottish crossbill ends up being demoted from species status then we will no longer have an endemic British bird. This isn't the first time that we've 'lost' an endemic bird; though the first time it was a British *and* Irish endemic.

A few days after returning from Scotland I was driving across the North Yorkshire moors from Rosedale Abbey to Glaisdale. This wasn't a deliberate endemic trip, instead I was spending a day off to stop at regular intervals across the moor to spot populations of a newly arrived non-native plant species, the alpine cotula. First recorded in the 1970s, this Australian species seems to be spreading rapidly in moorland habitats. My strategy for finding it was to pull over in grassy spots at the edge of the road and check the turf for its little jagged leaves, shaped like the snout of a sawfish.

I swung into one likely spot, a grassy rectangle wide enough for four cars, and opened my door. Before even putting my foot on the ground I spotted a tangle of cotula leaves sprawling through the turf. I knelt to take a photo and as I did I heard a croaking, disyllabic call roll across the moor; *go-back, go-back, go-back*, followed by a toad-like chuckle. This was the sound of the red grouse.

Until relatively recently the red grouse was considered a unique species, *Lagopus scotica*, found only in Britain and Ireland. This characterful pigeon-sized, chicken-like gamebird lives in heather moorland and is found from northern England up to Orkney and Shetland. It is also found in upland regions of Wales and Ireland, and was historically introduced to Dartmoor in Devon, where a small number still persist. The species is well known as the quarry in driven grouse shooting; a so-called 'sport' often sustained by the illegal persecution of birds of prey and largely enjoyed by the worst people you can imagine.

The male red grouse has a wonderful warm heather-red colouration with subtle frosty edges to his feathers and dense white fluff covering his legs and feet; these fluffy socks are why they have the genus name *Lagopus*, which means 'hare's foot'. He also has thick, fleshy red 'eyebrows' and a crisp white ring around his eye. The female is more cryptic and camouflaged than the male but no less beautiful; her feathers have a golden base colour, barred with black and liberally scattered with delicate spangles of white. She also has a smaller, more demure, red eyebrow than the male.

In the 1970s the red grouse was relegated to being a subspecies of the willow grouse, *Lagopus lagopus*, becoming instead the endemic subspecies *Lagopus lagopus scotica*. The willow grouse, also known as the willow ptarmigan, is found across northern regions of Eurasia and North America. As you'd expect, it is very similar to the red grouse (or the red grouse is very similar to it), with a couple of key differences. The willow grouse usually has white feathers on the belly and wing during summer, which the red grouse lacks. It also moults to become entirely snow-white during winter, something the red grouse completely declines to do, presumably because staying rufous is better camouflage in our milder winters where our moors often remain reddish-brown with heather.

This makes the red grouse – unlike the Scottish crossbill – physically distinguishable from its closest relative, not that red grouse and willow grouse ever come into contact with each other (it's said that red grouse can fly at over 70mph, but they don't make wide ocean crossings). The fact that they don't ever meet is partly why they are not classed as different species: we do not know whether they would breed assortatively or if there are barriers to them crossbreeding. That said, the fact that there are geographic obstacles preventing them from even trying seems like a significant barrier.

The key reason for the demotion of red grouse as a species is that an unusual population of willow grouse was discovered on a cluster of small Norwegian islands in the 1930s. These birds appear intermediate between 'normal' willow grouse and red grouse; they only turn *mostly* white during winter. These birds lessened the sharp delineation between red grouse and willow grouse, making red grouse look like one end of a spectrum of variation rather than something entirely distinct.

Then, in 2022, a paper called 'The taxonomic status of Red Grouse' was published in *British Birds*.

Summarising genetic research on red and willow grouse, it argued that the red grouse should once again be recognised as a British and Irish endemic species. The paper cited a 2019 study that analysed DNA from willow grouse worldwide: birds from Scandinavia, Russia, Alaska, red grouse from Yorkshire, as well as the intriguing intermediate birds from those Norwegian islands. This genetic evidence was used to construct a family tree, revealing how closely related the different populations are – and the results were striking. All of the willow grouse cluster together, the strange Norwegian intermediates nested *within* the group rather than out on a limb. In fact, this family tree shows that 'normal' mainland willow grouse from Norway are more closely related to these island intermediates than they are to willow grouse from Russia and Alaska, despite looking more physically similar to the latter. And the red grouse? They stood out distinctly. All the willow grouse from across the world form a cohesive group, with red grouse forming their own, separate branch. Closely related, but distinct.

The paper's authors point to this DNA work, and the clear physical differences between the red grouse and willow grouse, as evidence to un-demote (or re-promote) red grouse back to being a full species, *Lagopus scotica*, endemic to Britain and Ireland. This hasn't been adopted yet, but if it is – fantastic!

But then – why is it fantastic? I'm certain I wouldn't be alone in finding it exciting if the red grouse was once again classed as a British and Irish endemic, but it already *is* an endemic. It's an endemic subspecies. The fact is that we simply don't appreciate subspecies (endemic or otherwise) as much as we do species. Perhaps partly it's the terminology; the prefix 'sub' maybe holding unconscious negative connotations.

I looked up after I finished photographing the cotula, just in time to see three red grouse skim low across the heather, wings whirring, plump-bellied. It doesn't matter to them whether we class them as an endemic species or subspecies; the birds themselves aren't changing, only our perception of them.

Perhaps it's time to challenge the focus on species as the primary unit of biodiversity. Often, we overlook the importance of subspecies—especially when an endemic subspecies faces significant threats.

A week after returning from Scotland I took a trip to Carlton Marsh in South Yorkshire's Dearne Valley. This Yorkshire Wildlife Trust site was once a piece of contaminated land beside the Hull to Barnsley railway line, apparently so polluted with diesel that the water didn't freeze in winter, until the site was bought by the council in the 1970s and turned into a nature reserve. This 18-hectare site is now a mix of open water, grassland, scrub and wet woodland with the old railway line, now a footpath, running alongside. This post-industrial site is also now home to one of Britain's remaining populations of willow tits, represented in Britain by a unique subspecies.

I squelched my way down the muddy footpath as I listened for them. Spring is the best time to look for willow tits; they're becoming more territorial and vocal and this makes them easier to find. It was a cheerful spring day, the path edged with bright golden lesser celandines and the unfurling arrowhead leaves of lords-and-ladies. I could hear the *teacher teacher* call of great tits and the twinkling of goldfinches in the treetops, but no sign of willow tits.

The willow tit, *Poecile montanus*, has a few dubious honours. It was the last breeding bird to be discovered in Britain, only recognised as recently as 1897. Most British birds were discovered much earlier than this. The find was made by two German ornithologists who were looking through specimens of what were thought to be marsh tits in the British Museum when they discovered two mislabelled willow tits hidden among them. The marsh tit had long been known from Britain, but the willow tit, despite being discovered in mainland Europe 70 years earlier, had been entirely overlooked here because the two species look so similar.

It is also the fastest-declining resident bird in Britain. Since the 1970s it is estimated that the number of willow tits in Britain has dropped by around 88–94 per cent. Or, to put it another way, for every 100 willow tits we had 50 years ago, we now have about ten, or even fewer. Surveys across Britain in 2020 and 2021 put the total population of willow tits at an estimated 5,700 breeding pairs and the species has now been pretty much lost from south-eastern England. For comparison, the British population of blue tits is an estimated 3.4 *million* pairs.

The endemic subspecies of willow tit in Britain is *Poecile montanus kleinschmidti*, named after Otto Kleinschmidt, one of the German ornithologists who first discovered it. Our birds are supposedly smaller and darker, with a distinct overall brownish hue, compared to willow tits in mainland Europe – though the ones on the near continent do look pretty similar. Behaviourally, our birds are different too. In much of Europe the species is found in boreal and alpine forests of conifers, but in Britain it is largely a bird of wet woodland, riverside trees and scrub. Its common names elsewhere reflect this: in French it's *mésange boréale*, the 'boreal' or 'northern tit'; in Norwegian it's the *granmeis*, the 'spruce tit'; in Italy *cincia alpestre*, the 'alpine tit'.

Those 5,700 pairs that we have are the entire global population of this subspecies. Our rarest resident bird is one that does not exist anywhere else; if it is lost, it is gone. And yet where is the outcry? If you ran up to a stranger in the street, grabbed them by the shoulders, and implored them to name one of our most threatened species, I am certain they wouldn't mention the willow tit. Our willow tit is unique, dramatically declining and largely unrecognised.

That's not to say work isn't done to save them. There was a Back from the Brink project focused on the population in the Dearne Valley, improving habitat, gathering data on how willow tits use the landscape, and establishing key parts of this area as Sites of Special Scientific Interest, including here at Carlton Marsh.

As I followed the path of the old railway line, I listened carefully. Marsh and willow tits may look very similar, with their black caps, white cheeks and shadowy goatees, but their calls are entirely different. The marsh tit lets out a plosive, sneezy *pi-chu!* whereas willow tits give a drawn-out nasal *zee-zur-zur-zur*. I heard neither, just the descending trilling song of chaffinches and the occasional scolding *chak* of wrens.

Two hours later I had lapped the reserve twice. Despite lingering in the spots where I'd seen willow tits only a few years earlier, I saw and heard nothing. For the third time, I passed by a graffitied brick wall, a downbeat painting of Shrek staring placidly at me with the text alongside reading 'It's all ogre now'. I gave up and went home.

It turns out that these willow tits have vanished. According to a 2024 *British Birds* paper, the willow tit population in the Dearne Valley is now extinct. There was a healthy population of 70 pairs surveyed here in 2015. In 2018, when I visited and saw one, a survey revealed 20 pairs. By 2023, despite the designation of the Dearne Valley wetlands as an SSSI and the work of Back from the Brink, the willow tits were gone. No one has any idea why this population declined and vanished so rapidly.

Willow tits still persist just outside the Dearne Valley, and at many other sites across Britain, but without knowing exactly why the Dearne Valley population disappeared the fear is that this disastrous loss could be repeated elsewhere. With only a few thousand of them left, we don't have a lot of time to make sure that this irreplaceable bird isn't lost forever. We need to spread the word: the British willow tit, a subspecies for which we have total responsibility, is threatened with extinction.

Yet, there is hope. We still have the power to change the future for species like the Scottish crossbill, red grouse, and willow tit. For the Scottish crossbill, its current status as our only endemic bird species highlights the urgent need to conserve and restore the Caledonian Forest, a habitat threatened by overgrazing by deer and climate change. By supporting efforts in forest conservation, such as those by the RSPB and Trees for Life, we can safeguard the home of this enigmatic bird and ensure its future, whatever its status.

The red grouse, once thought to be an endemic species to Britain and Ireland, now seems set to return to its former position as a unique species of these islands. In 2024, the International Ornithological Committee (IOC) announced plans to designate it a full species again, in the light of genetic evidence. While not threatened in Britain, we must confront the challenges of habitat destruction and illegal persecution used to artificially boost its numbers for shooting. Is this the legacy we want for a unique bird, or can we secure a future where the red grouse thrives in healthy, protected landscapes? The introduction of licensing for gamebird shooting across Britain – building on Scotland's recent licensing of grouse shooting – offers a promising solution. This measure, advocated by the RSPB, would certainly help curb the criminal practices that threaten other species.

As for the willow tit, the extinction of this bird in the Dearne Valley serves as a stark reminder of what we stand to lose. With the help of the BTO, RSPB, and local Wildlife Trusts, we can better understand the needs of this elusive species, protect its habitats, and fight to prevent further declines. Through citizen science projects, habitat restoration, and donations to these vital organisations, we can give the willow tit a fighting chance to survive – and ultimately thrive – once again.

Together, we can ensure that these birds not only survive but are able to flourish in the landscapes of Britain. The time to act is now.

CHAPTER 3

Celtic Creatures: Celtic Woodlouse and Chater's Bristletail

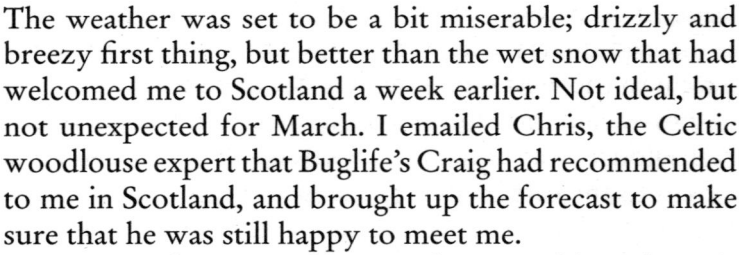

The weather was set to be a bit miserable; drizzly and breezy first thing, but better than the wet snow that had welcomed me to Scotland a week earlier. Not ideal, but not unexpected for March. I emailed Chris, the Celtic woodlouse expert that Buglife's Craig had recommended to me in Scotland, and brought up the forecast to make sure that he was still happy to meet me.

We're used to miserable in Wales, came his reply. Fair enough, I thought.

The morning in question turned out to be beautiful. As I drove from my accommodation in Llantrisant to Ogmore-by-Sea, I spied roadside verges glinting with lesser celandines, taking over from tired-looking snowdrops.

Ogmore Castle came into view, crumbling scenically into the water below, the road following the river down to where it met the sea. I reached the parking area and saw the sand dunes of Merthyr Mawr Nature Reserve on the opposite side of the river.

I pulled into a parking bay and looked at my phone. I was early. I'm persistently early because I always assume that on every journey I make something will go wrong. I had told Chris I'd aim to arrive between 10 and 10:30 a.m., giving myself a whole half-hour of leeway. It was 9:30.

It was a pay-and-display car park but I realised I had no idea how long we might spend looking for our target. I decided to sit in the car and wait for Chris to arrive and advise.

To pass the time, I pulled out my phone and reminded myself of the characteristics of the species I was here to see – the woodlouse *Metatrichoniscoides celticus*. This species was discovered new to science from the Glamorgan coast as recently as 1979 and was only formally named in 1981. Other than a handful of sites on the coast between Ogmore-by-Sea and St Donat's, for a long time the only other known site for the species was a disused quarry near Crwbin, Carmarthenshire, about 50km to the west – making it a Welsh endemic!

However, the alliterative satisfaction of the 'Welsh woodlouse' was dashed in 2020 when it was found some 60km to the east in an allotment in Bristol – great news for this enigmatic species, but 'Celtic woodlouse' just doesn't have quite the same ring to it. As well as this new English site, it has also turned up recently on Anglesey, some 170km to the north of Ogmore, painting a rosier picture of the range, and thus global security, of this special species.

I navigated to the website of the British Myriapod and Isopod Group (BMIG). Myriapods are millipedes and centipedes, and isopods are a subset of crustaceans that are represented by the woodlice and their aquatic relatives, the freshwater hoglice and the marine sea slaters. The BMIG exists to raise awareness of these animals and is a goldmine of information. I started reading the page for the Celtic woodlouse.

'This woodlouse appears to be endemic to the British Isles' – great, that's why I was there – 'It is primarily associated with sparsely vegetated erosion banks occurring just above the supralittoral zone.' I considered this for a moment, staring out through the car window as I mentally translated. I was pretty sure that this meant 'The woodlouse can be found on the short turf just above where it crumbles into the sea.' I continued reading: 'Characteristically, small numbers of specimens are found with extreme difficulty under large stones firmly embedded into damp humus-rich soil.' I scratched my beard and considered the phrase 'extreme difficulty'. I decided not to dwell on it.

The page goes on to say that the Celtic woodlouse, in addition to being extremely difficult to find, is very small, white, and that care needs to be taken to ensure you don't confuse it with other very small white woodlice that you might find in the same places. However, one very helpful clue emerges; in contrast to the other small white woodlice, the Celtic woodlouse is blind – indeed, eyeless. This means if you get a very good view of the head and can be absolutely sure there are no black, red or pink eyes (the eye colours of other species of small white woodlice), then you probably have it.

Trying not to dwell on the 'extreme difficulty' of finding the woodlouse, I decided instead to look out of the window and admire the sparsely vegetated erosion banks instead. A car pulled up in my field of view, a big, grey Zafira. A man got out and looked at his phone. By some sixth sense I knew this must be Christian 'Sparrow' Owen, the man I'd come to see. I got out of the car and, by the same psychic connection apparently shared by naturalists, he saw me and waved. I walked over and we shook hands, speaking over each other as we attempted to greet and introduce ourselves. Chris was lean, taller than me, and younger than I'd expected; he'd mentioned a grandkid in our email exchange and

I'd imagined someone more staid than the talkative guy in front of me.

He gestured at the turf a few metres in front of his car. 'This is the spot,' he said. 'Literally this patch here between the cars and the sea – though you need to turn over the stones stuck in the ground to find them.'

I asked him about how hard it is to tell the Celtic woodlouse apart from other small white woodlice, such as *Haplophthalmus mengii* or *Trichoniscoides saeroeensis*. I didn't add that I could only throw out these names so confidently because I had literally just looked them up them in the car.

'Well I'd be delighted if we found any *Trichoniscoides* species along here,' he replied. 'I've never seen one. So that would make *my* day, but it wouldn't be great for you. We do get *Haplophthalmus mengii* but they're easy to tell apart.'

We'd been slowly wandering towards the sea as he spoke, and Chris suddenly interrupted our chat to point out a cluster of stones jutting out of the turf, the habitat we were looking for. The stones were irregular, about a foot across, and sunk about 2cm into the ground. I eagerly knelt and flipped one over and was immediately confronted with half a dozen small white woodlice. My heart leapt momentarily, but then my brain quickly caught up and I realised these were the delightfully named *Platyarthrus hoffmannseggii*, the ant woodlouse. The ant woodlouse is genuinely beautiful, a glossy, pearly white, shield-shaped creature with thick, characterful antennae – almost like an adorable exaggeration of a woodlouse – and, as the name hints, it is only found in association with ants. Despite being similar to my target species in that it's white and blind, its staggering 5mm length would dwarf the Celtic woodlouse, which is often less than 2mm long.

Chris peered over my shoulder. 'Keep looking,' he said. '*Celticus* can stay still and nearly invisible for a while; after a few minutes, they'll suddenly move and that's when you spot them.'

He flipped over the stone next to mine and stared at it intently. I decided to stare at mine too.

'I read that they're *extremely difficult* to find,' I said, eyes focused on my rock. 'How do you rate our chances of finding one?'

'Oh, not too bad, not too bad,' he replied. 'Oh, hey, look at this!'

He pointed at the surface of his stone. At the tip of his finger, nestled amongst the moist soil clinging to the rock, was a tiny white woodlouse, noticeably smaller than the ant woodlice I had just been admiring.

'Is this it?' I asked.

'Oh no,' he replied, 'this is *Haplophthalmus mengii* – see how it's a sort of dirty white? *Celticus* is a very clean, shining white.'

Haplophthalmus mengii, also known by the surprisingly badass common name spurred ridgeback, was one of the possible confusion species I had read about. I fumbled my hand lens out of my pocket and leant in for a close look. It may not have been the species I was looking for, but I'd never seen a spurred ridgeback before and it was worth savouring the moment. It was a creamy colour or perhaps sandy, and its back was indeed ridged with several lines of raised rectangular bumps. With a squint I could even make out its tiny dark eyes.

I leant back. Chris pointed again. 'There's another one.'

Another spurred ridgeback. Chris had good eyes.

'And another,' he said, pointing.

I was now eager to find one and prove myself so, giving up on my paltry stone, I focused on Chris's instead. I stared at the surface of the rock, attuned for any hint of movement.

'There!' I had spotted another tiny woodlouse, which I now recognised as a spurred ridgeback.

Chris didn't respond, his attention zeroed in on a section of the stone a few inches from my find. After a moment, he spoke. '*Celticus*,' he said, pointing.

It took me a moment to process. 'The Celtic woodlouse?'

He nodded and put a fingertip to the surface of the stone, indicating the most minute woodlouse I had ever seen, smaller even than the spurred ridgeback. Even though it was tiny, it was still possible to make out that it was clean white in colour, distinct from the delicate yellow-white of the spurred ridgeback. I leant in with my hand lens.

Up close it was possible to see that the Celtic woodlouse was largely translucent, lending it an almost gummy bear–like appearance, enhanced by the gently rounded segments of its body. Its stubby little antennae were particularly characterful – four or five chubby sections followed by a longer one that narrowed to a sharp point. As I watched, the woodlouse would gently move them: waving them back and forth, pointing them sideways, and sometimes curling them back on themselves when it sensed my breath. Its head was totally eyeless and covered on top with miniscule blobby growths that terminated in a blunt spine. These stubby blunt peaks extended across the entire length of the creature, lending it the quality of gooseflesh. The body narrowed off at the rear, and terminated in two short conical 'uropods', appendages at the back end of woodlice (and other crustaceans) which in this species stick out like two little tails. It was the most perfect creature I had ever seen. We spent a few minutes cooing over it, photographing it, trying to coax it onto a coin for a sense of how incredibly tiny it was, before letting it continue its meanderings unhindered. It wandered off the face of the stone and disappeared into the soil.

Chris sat back, pleased with himself. The woodlouse was under the second stone we'd turned over, and the first stone that Chris had turned over (he's clearly charmed). The time it had taken to locate this *extremely difficult to find* woodlouse was less than 15 minutes.

He looked at his watch. 'Want to go see another endemic?' he asked, 'And some millipedes?'

I had the time, and I wasn't about to turn down a bonus endemic. Chris gave me directions for a wood 20 minutes' drive away and we both set off.

The endemic that Chris had offered me was Chater's bristletail. This was one of the species I'd read about back in winter and had noticed wasn't on Craig Macadam's list. He'd got back to me since our stonefly trip, confirming that it was indeed an endemic and one he planned to include in his report, alongside the dung beetle *Psammoporus insularis*.

Bristletails, the order Archaeognatha, are an ancient group of insects, older even than the stoneflies and amongst the oldest fossil insects ever discovered, first appearing in the fossil record some 400 million years ago. They've changed little in that time. There is something inherently primeval about how they look – elongated, dusted with glittering scales, long antennae at the front and three long tails at the back. And they 'jump', in a crude sense, when disturbed. There's no elegance to this as there would be with a grasshopper, or neat mechanism as with a click beetle; no, the bristletail 'jumps' by flexing its abdomen and pinging itself off at random.

Archaeognatha is not a particularly species-rich group. More than 2,500 species of moths have been recorded in Britain alone, compared to about 500 bristletails known worldwide. Until the 1990s it was thought that we only had five species in Britain and their distributions are still only patchily known. This is probably because conclusive identification relies on microscopic examination of the hairs on the surface of the male's labial palp (a structure next to its mouth), which takes a lot of effort and technical skill. One person who wasn't fazed by this was Arthur Chater, one of the greatest all-round naturalists of our time. In 1991 Arthur put in the time to microscopically examine the bristletails that he was finding. Upon this close examination he discovered that the *Dilta* species he found was not *Dilta hibernica*, the southern bristletail, supposedly the most common and widespread species, but a species that didn't match *anything*. He sent some specimens off to experts and in 1995 this brand new species was named in his honour, *Dilta chateri*, Chater's bristletail. It has since proved widespread in mid- and South Wales and has more recently been found in Somerset and Cornwall.

I parked up behind Chris's car on the tarmacked oval at the entrance to the woods. This was a damp place, the trees furred with moss and the understory dripping with ferns. Chris hopped out of his car with a battered and taped-up white tray. I grabbed my own from my boot – there's nothing like a white tray for spotting tiny creatures. Drop in a handful of leaf litter, spread it out, and you can spy the various tiny invertebrates plainly against the stark backdrop.

We entered the woods. Chris had a favourite place here where he'd made a number of outstanding finds. As we walked, I asked him why he was known as Christian 'Sparrow' Owen. He grinned at the question. 'I got the nickname back in school – I had skinny little legs in my shorts, like a sparrow,' he said, laughing. I admired Chris greatly. He'd worked as a gardener for years but his absolute zeal for invertebrates and sheer drive had led to him becoming a self-taught entomological consultant.

We shortly came to a sloping bank of beeches amongst a sea of conifers. 'This is my special spot,' he told me.

Chris told me that the best way to find Chater's bristletail was to brush or shake moss over a tray and they'd come tumbling out. I went straight to the nearest mossy beech trunk, pressed my tray against it, and gently swept my hand down the damp furry greenness and into my tray.

Chris, spotting this, said, 'Ah, no, you want to find a tussocky overhang of moss …' but stopped when I held out my tray with a single bristletail in it. 'Oh!' he said, squinting at it. 'Unfortunately it's got no scales left; I can't tell what species it is.'

A bit like a butterfly's wing, the entire body of a bristletail is covered in fine, dust-like scales that easily brush off. The one I had found was almost bald, so I let it scurry off into the leaf litter.

By the time I'd done that, Chris had already found something else exciting. In his tray was, by far, the biggest millipede I'd ever seen in the wild. Glossy black, a full 4cm long and thick with it, its most astounding feature was its bright Ribena-pink legs. Millipedes, when bothered, will often coil into a flat spiral and this millipede did just that, looking like some sort of strange confection; a liquorice swirl with raspberry filling.

Chris was first alerted to a large, strange, pink-legged millipede here by a photo posted online by Emma William in 2017. He, and Steve Gregory of

BMIG, thought it was likely a Portuguese millipede, *Ommatoiulus moreleti*, a species native to Portugal and parts of Spain but never before seen in Britain. Chris came on his next available free day, found dozens, and was able to confirm the identification. It is assumed that this species was introduced to South Wales, possibly with iron ore imported from Spain.

'May I take a pic?' I asked, brandishing my phone.

'Go ahead,' said Chris. I went to take the tray from his hands but he didn't let go. 'Sorry', he said, with a shake of the head and a chuckle, 'lucky tray. I've had a lot of good finds in this.' Instead he sat it down on the leaf litter for me so I could take my pictures. The tray was certainly well used, with taped-up cracks, yellowing places and scratches, but I understood how a piece of kit, even a simple one like this, can become a store of memories.

As I sat up from photographing this pink-and-black wonder, Chris – having been off flipping logs – returned and dropped another millipede into the tray. This one was smaller, thinner and more of a brassy-brown colour, each segment of its body immaculately lined with dozens of narrow horizontal depressions. I recognised it as being one of the *Cylindroiulus* species, a group with 13 members in Britain and whose identification to species level is tricky – to the extent that I often sigh and pretend I haven't seen them. I said as much to Chris.

'Have a look at its back end,' he said, with a grin.

Very carefully, I picked the millipede up and held it so that only the tip of its body stuck out between my fingers. Flipping open my hand lens, I took a long look at its rear end. I momentarily wondered how I came to be squatting in a damp Welsh woodland, intently staring at a millipede's bottom, but I quickly dismissed that and concentrated. This was *important*.

The bodies of some millipedes simply round off at the end; a smooth curve. Others have little 'tails' – a narrow protruding tip extending from the body. These can be rounded, pointed, curved down, angled up, each offering a clue as to which species it is you're looking at. But in this case, it wasn't the shape of the tail that was the clue. This millipede had two tails – one extending from the tip of the body as normal, the other emerging from underneath like an exhaust. Something in my mind clicked. 'Is this the Welsh two-tail?' I asked.

Chris's grin – somehow – got even wider. 'Yep, *Cylindroiulus pyrenaicus*. I found it here on the same day that I came to try and re-find the pink-legged one.'

Chris was being modest. His find of *Cylindroiulus pyrenaicus* was the first confirmed record of this species in Britain (some other millipedes with two tails had been found years earlier in the same broad area but were immature and never conclusively identified).

Like the Portuguese millipede, the Welsh two-tail is originally from somewhere else – in this case, as its scientific name suggests, the Pyrenees – and it was presumably also introduced to South Wales through the same trade routes. The fact that these two species were found at the same site and almost at the same time is intriguing. Was it sheer coincidence? Or does it reflect something about a person like Chris, who deeply scrutinises what he sees?

Over the next hour we slowly wandered up the slope, rummaging through leaf litter and turning logs. Amongst our finds were two other recently identified millipedes: the Welsh silk millipede, *Maurieseuma nontronense*, and Telfer's millipede, *Ceratosphys amoena*. Both of these species were discovered on the same day when a party of ecologists came to visit Chris in the Welsh valleys, and both are assumed to be non-natives accidentally imported into Wales.

Chris has also been instrumental in the finding of three *entirely new* species of millipede – not just new to Britain, but new to science. They have not yet been formally described and named: one is flat-backed, pearl white and a mere centimetre long, known romantically as the 'Celtic ghost millipede'; another has distinct 'shoulders' on each chocolate-brown body segment and has been given the unparalleled nickname of the 'Maerdy monster'; the third species is almost identical to the Maerdy monster, at least to the naked eye, but microscopic inspection of the distinctively different male gonopods (the sexual organs) revealed it to be another undescribed species.

If that isn't impressive enough, Chris discovered that third millipede on the *same day* as he confirmed the identification of the Portuguese millipede *and* discovered the Welsh two-tail. This third new species hasn't even been given a nickname yet (I propose 'Sparrow's spectre', to credit Chris's initial discovery of all three).

Despite being new to science and discovered in South Wales, these millipedes are most likely not native to Britain. In each case, the nearest similar known species (their 'closest cousins') are from Spain and Portugal. Given that so many other Iberian species have been discovered in South Wales, it seems likely that these three millipedes have been introduced by the same route. This puts them in a very strange category: they are only known from Britain, but we strongly suspect that they have come from elsewhere.

There is no classification for organisms like this, so I have invented one. These are 'false endemics'. Like true endemics they are only found in a single geographic area, but they are either known, or are strongly suspected, to have originated from elsewhere in the world.

Chris's millipedes are not the only example of this. There is also a mysterious land nemertine that has been found across Devon and Cornwall. Land nemertines, or 'smiling worms', look a lot like flatworms but have the ability to evert a horrifying, branching proboscis out of their mouths (they are, honestly, a lot more delightful than that makes them sound). These nemertines were thought to be the Australian species *Argonemertes australiensis* until DNA testing showed them to be a different species, currently unnamed, and entirely new to science.

Even more stark is the woodlouse known only as '*Gabunillo* sp. Eden A'. This tropical species is emphatically non-native, found only as an accidentally imported population in the rainforest biome of the Eden Project. Two similar species are known in the wild: one is *Gabunillo aridicola*, known from Brazil; the other is *Gabunillo coecus*, known from caves in Gabon, West Africa. The Eden species is *neither* of these.

Something else we don't know is whether 'Eden A' still exists in the wild. Think about it: an area of rainforest the size of Eden's biome is destroyed every 11 seconds. There is a possibility that this woodlouse was accidentally brought to Europe decades ago. In that intervening time could its natural home have been lost? It is, terrifyingly, quite possible that this is the case.

Eden A isn't necessarily unique in this regard; could Chris' millipedes have been lost from Iberia by the very mining activity that brought them to Wales? It's interesting that – so far – they remain stubbornly undiscovered in their native range.

False endemics like these are organisms that, though non-native, find their only known existence within our borders due to accidental human intervention. This is the paradox of the false endemic; Britain has total global responsibility for them, yet they are not inherently British species. At present, these organisms fall straight through the cracks of conservation. No one is spending any time working out if they need to be conserved – they're *alien* after all – but there is the very real possibility that Britain may be their only home.

We reached the top of the slope without seeing another bristletail. I lamented this to Chris, who was unfazed. 'Ah, we'll go find one now,' he said, marching back down the slope. 'I know a reliable spot.' We returned to the path, rounded a bend, and encountered a section of track with a low overhang on the left-hand side, crowned with hearty clumps of moss. Chris placed his magic tray under a clump, raked his fingers through the moss like he was scratching a shaggy dog, and looked in the tray. 'There you go,' he said, plonking the tray on the ground. In it were three glittering Chater's bristletails.

I crouched beside the tray to admire them. Imagine a prawn – a tiny prawn, a centimetre long – straightened out and covered in iridescent glitter. Give it two big, black and surprisingly charismatic eyes perched pleadingly on top of its head. Beneath these eyes are two shyly folded palps (short, sensory appendages located next to the mouth) and two whiskery antennae that can rotate in any direction. At the other end of the body are three bristle-like tails, from which it gets its name. But I have to return to that sparkle. The entire body is clothed in minute brownish-grey scales that refract miniature rainbows of light as they shift.

I tried to position my phone close enough to one bristletail for a photo, but my looming presence was enough for it to engage its party trick. By sharply contorting its abdomen it sprang away in an uncontrolled hop. Uncontrolled, yes, but a good strategy if you think something is about to eat you. It managed to flick itself entirely out of the tray and into the leaf litter. That's roughly the equivalent of a human suddenly doing a sit-up so hard that they jump over a house. Wild.

I moved my attention to one of the others, admiring the pink and green lichen-like hues that played across its scales.

'Pleased?' asked Chris.

'Very,' I replied, as I gently tipped the tray and let the bristletails vanish back into the woodland floor.

Both Chater's bristletail and the Celtic woodlouse were first discovered in Wales, and both relatively recently. For a time, they were thought to be purely Welsh endemics, exclusive to the soil of Cymru. It's only in the last few years that they have been discovered further afield. In a way it's a shame that there are (as far as we know) no invertebrates that are proudly and exclusively Welsh, but this broader distribution highlights a richer story of ecological resilience, the thrill of discovery, and the intricate, often unseen, connections that thread through our natural world. If a woodlouse once thought to be found exclusively on the Welsh coast can appear in an English allotment, where else might it be?

Like Chris and his millipedes have proved, there's clearly a lot left for us to discover.

CHAPTER 4

Blown Away: False Fen and Bertha's Dandelion

In contrast to my experience of researching invertebrates, for plants I found the document of my dreams: an incredibly valuable paper published by the BSBI called 'List of vascular plants endemic to Britain, Ireland and the Channel Islands 2020' by botanist Tim Rich. Reading this, I learnt that we had an astounding *six hundred and fifty-six* species and subspecies of endemic plants.

Some groups of plants are particularly rich in unique British species; there are tens of whitebeams, more than 50 each of buttercups and elms, and more than 100 hawkweeds, and so I decided I needed to see at least one each from these groups. I also picked a few intriguing singletons; Scottish primrose, Lundy cabbage, the Great Orme berry, and the interrupted brome, an agonisingly threatened grass that had been one of the focus species of Back from the Brink but which I had never had the opportunity to see. Another target was a lady's-mantle endemic to Yorkshire, chosen because it felt right to visit my birth county on at least one of these trips.

Some of the species I've chosen are probably unfamiliar to most people (what on earth does a Great

Orme berry look like?) but I decided to start with a group that everyone can recognise. On Tim's list are 53 dandelions endemic to Britain and Ireland, of which 29 are only found in Britain.

Dandelions fill me with joy, but often lead me to anger. This might seem a powerful response for a cheerful yellow flower but let me explain. After a long, dark winter, there is something immensely uplifting about how grassy spaces, roadside verges and pavement cracks suddenly fill with these profuse shaggy golden flowers. You see that carpet of yellow and you know that winter has passed.

The anger comes a week after this glorious show gets underway, where our apparently cash-strapped local councils send out fleets of men kitted out with high-vis jackets to crop the verges back to a blank, dull canvas of green. Sure, councils are selling their assets to keep afloat, but at least this means they can keep on top of essential services like removing flowers for pollinating insects and stripping the wonder of spring from our lives. To add insult to injury, they leave behind a carpet of clippings that go wet and brown and rot back into the soil, fertilising the grass so it grows back even quicker. It's madness. If councils simply removed the clippings, then over time the grass would grow less vigorously, make space for more wildflowers, and lead to the cheaper option of cutting them less often.

Even worse, in a way, was the time I saw a man spraying herbicide on dandelions on a verge outside his house. To reiterate; not his garden, not his property – a verge that just happened to be near him. I asked him what he was doing.

'Dandelions,' he said, making a face and shrugging, as if he was telling me he'd found a puddle of vomit on his doormat.

'I like the dandelions,' I said, 'and they're good for insects too.'

'Not very tidy, though, are they,' he said, squirting another liberal jet of poison.

I like to imagine that I'm a person who can understand a wide range of opinions and perspectives. I won't agree with everything, but I can appreciate where these ideas come from and respect our individual differences and the richness this brings to the world. I like to imagine this, but it's not true. I actually think anyone that poisons dandelions for the sake of neatness should be tried at The Hague.

There are multiple species of dandelions. In fact, there are around *two-hundred and fifty* species of dandelions that have been recorded across Britain and Ireland, some of which are uncommon, rare or endemic. This is what makes the indiscriminate destruction of dandelions particularly painful; how can anyone be sure they're not killing something special?

I had seen online that Alex Prendergast, senior vascular plant specialist for Natural England, was something of a dandelion expert and so I sent him a message asking if he would be willing to show me an endemic. He immediately agreed, and invited me to join him on his ongoing endeavour to find *Taraxacum palustrisquameum*. I looked it up. It's also known by the English name of false fen dandelion, and is endemic to Britain and Ireland.

In advance of that expedition with Alex I thought I really should try and learn at least *something* about the art of dandelion identification. I bought the BSBI handbook by A. J. Richards, opened up some guides on the BSBI website, and started playing a video on dandelion identification by the knowledgeable and enthusiastic Joshua Styles.

The first thing I needed was a dandelion. Apparently, dandelions get harder to identify as the year goes on, so March to April is the time to get stuck in. It couldn't just be any dandelion though; it ideally needed to be one with both an open flower and a closed flower. Oh, and it couldn't be from a regularly mown lawn as those dandelions wouldn't be growing in their natural, untrammelled state.

I walked out to the edge of my Lincolnshire village until I found some hearty dandelions growing on an as-yet unmolested verge. I photographed the whole thing – flowers, buds, leaves – from multiple angles, then gently slid my trowel under the rosette of leaves and scythed the whole plant off from the root. This may sound like botanical vandalism, especially considering my impassioned plea for dandelion-clemency earlier, but they are hardy plants and can regenerate from the roots just fine – not surprising considering how well they survive being regularly mown to the ground.

Back at home, I opened up the handbook. To make identification easier, the 250-ish species of dandelions are divided into 'sections', which are basically groups of similar-looking species. If you can get as far as working out which section your dandelion belongs to, then you have a much smaller number of species to compare against. Some sections contain very few species, such as *Obliqua* (two species) and *Palustria* (five species), vastly narrowing down the possible candidates.

By answering a few simple questions I would discover which section my dandelion belonged to. Is the flowerhead 3cm or more across? Yes. Do the bracts (the green 'ruff' around the base of the flowerhead) point upwards or curve back to point at the ground? They point down. Are the leaves covered in purplish spots? No. Is the midrib of the leaf a solid green colour? Yes.

And that's it, my dandelion apparently belongs to the section 'Ruderalia'. I opened the key and was immediately confronted with the sentence 'Ruderalia is the largest and most difficult of the dandelion sections in Britain and Ireland.' I scanned ahead and spotted that this section contains more than 120 species. Great. Why couldn't I have found a dandelion from a section with only a handful of species?

I got a cup of tea before I started working through this second key. Are the petioles (the bottom, narrower part of the leaves below the jagged lobes) white to green? Yes. Do the petioles have 'wings'? Yes. Are the midribs green? Yes. And then I was hit with three intimidating options that included terms like 'abruptly acuminate', 'sigmoid' and 'subobtuse', which all made *me* feel pretty obtuse.

After much wrangling and making dubious progress through the key, I gave up. These dandelions were just too similar for me to distinguish, and there was too much terminology that I wasn't familiar with and wasn't sure I was applying correctly. Dandelions are for the minds of geniuses, I decided, and hoped that Alex might be able to clarify some of this for me in the field.

A week later I parked up at a narrow pull-in at Foulden Common, a 139-hectare SSSI in Norfolk about 15 miles north of Thetford. It's a site with varied habitats but it's the fen that we were here to see. The false fen dandelion, our target, had been recorded here in the 1970s. This dandelion appears to have vanished from almost all of its Norfolk locations and Alex had been working his way through all of the known historical sites trying to re-find it – with no luck so far. Foulden Common was the last site on his list.

I sat on a log in the pull-in and waited. The sun came out and I took my jumper off. It then went behind a cloud and I put it back on. A car pulled up slightly down the road. A guy with a lime-green mohawk got out and walked towards me, wearing a big, naturalist-style khaki backpack. This was Alex. He gave me a nod and a quiet 'hello.' I introduced myself.

He got out his phone – in a robust, protective case – and showed me a map of the site, pointing out the wetter areas that he thought looked promising for the dandelion. Route planned, we set off towards the fen areas.

'We're looking for the dandelion in damp or wet grassy areas in and around the Schoenus-fen,' said Alex, as we squished our way across some damp grassland.

'Schoenus-fen?' I asked

'The areas with *Schoenus nigricans*,' he said, gesturing to the tussocks around us.

Schoenus nigricans is black bog-rush, clumps of long green spikes intermingled with little black cat-paw flowers, an indicator that we're in the right sort of habitat.

As we navigated the edge of the wetland, I confessed to Alex that – beyond 'a dandelion' – I didn't have a clear idea of what I was looking for.

'With *palustrisquameum* the bracts clasp the flower, rather than pointing outwards or downwards,' said Alex. 'Look at the bracts.'

I consulted the picture in the book. The bracts pointed upwards, overlapping and looking sort of artichoke-like, rather than spreading sideways or curling over like a mane as they do in most common dandelions. This single feature may not seem like a lot, but it was enough to narrow down the field of candidates dramatically.

That said, we simply weren't finding any dandelions in these soggy fen areas at all. We trudged. Despite the target of the day being a species of wet habitats, neither of us had worn wellies and several times I sank nearly to the ankle in cattle-poached muddy patches. I resorted to stepping on the tussocks of bog-rush and sedge to keep myself from sinking any deeper. And, despite this effort, we still saw no dandelions.

After half an hour of slipping about in the mud, we retreated to slightly drier ground and it was here, as a grey heron croaked overhead, that Alex spotted the first dandelion with those erect, artichokey bracts.

He knelt and I immediately got excited.

'Is this it?' I asked.

Alex tilted the flower head and delicately untangled a leaf from the turf. 'No,' he said.

'Oh,' I said, mildly deflated. 'What is it?'

'I'm not sure, but you could key it out.'

'*I* could key it out?'

'Well, *one* could key it out,' he said, wryly. 'No, I'm sure you could.'

Amused by Alex's touching faith in my non-existent taraxological skills – taraxology being the study of dandelions, which are all in the genus *Taraxacum* – I opened my dandelion book. This dandelion was in the *Celtica* section, which narrowed it down to a near-palatable 45 species. The key began with 'Does the dandelion have pollen?' I checked the flowerhead with a hand-lens. Here, amongst the golden forest of petals (or 'ligules' in dandelion-speak), were the yellow pig's tail-curled styles, which, in this species, were covered in obvious clumps of pollen, dusted like amber sugar on a doughnut. The presence of pollen immediately excluded about 20 species, including the false fen dandelion. I carried on. 'Are the ligules yellow or orange? Is there a strongly marked stripe on the underside of the ligules? Do the leaves have tar-coloured blotches?' I read and answered each question aloud to give Alex a chance to correct me, but he nodded along with my answers. I began to think that maybe this dandelion stuff wasn't too hard.

The key soon spat me out an answer – *Taraxacum bracteatum*, the dark-green dandelion. It may not be the most poetic name, but it is accurate. The leaves were a fresh, shiny dark green and the midrib a rich rhubarb purple. In fact, the overall effect was reminiscent of chard. I can see why dandelions are sometimes used in salad; this was a tasty-looking dandelion!

This was also the first time I've ever looked at a dandelion and known what species it is. It may not have been the endemic I was looking for – the dark-green dandelion is widespread across Britain and Europe – but it was amazing to be able to appreciate the myriad of subtleties that separated this species from every other dandelion.

This reminded me of the dandelion that I had tried, and failed, to identify from my village. I pulled out my phone and showed Alex some pictures.

He shook his head. 'That's one of the *Ruderalia* section; they're really hard. They're also most of the commonest species you see, which is unfortunate. The dandelions of specialised habitats – wetlands, mountains and so on – are often easier to identify because they're a bit more distinctive. And there are fewer of them.'

'Does that mean that all the dandelions on verges and green spaces are probably common species then?' I asked. 'Because I hoped that maybe I could dissuade people from mowing them down if I was able to say that some could be rare or unusual.'

Alex considered this. 'Rare dandelions do pop up in odd places,' he said, and told me how a couple of years earlier he'd identified a photo of an English dandelion, *Taraxacum anglicum*, which someone had posted on social media. This species – which, despite the name, isn't endemic – is usually a species of fens and water-meadows, but instead had popped up in a plant pot in someone's garden. Bertha's dandelion, *Taraxacum berthae*, an endemic species supposedly of acidic moors in the west, turned up on a roadside verge in Oxfordshire. I suppose with those wind-borne parasol-like seeds, dandelions have the potential to end up almost anywhere.

As we weren't having any luck at the first spot, Alex suggested we head over to a different part of the site where there is another area of fen. We left the wetter ground and crossed a meadow covered in cowslips and studded with dandelions. It wasn't the right habitat for the false fen dandelion, but Alex took this opportunity to point out a different dandelion to me. This was the cut-leaved dandelion, *Taraxacum lacistophyllum*, and it is an absolute refutation of the claim that all dandelions look the same.

This plant was the polar opposite of the dark-green dandelion I had just keyed out. The flowerheads of the cut-leaved dandelion are more delicate and at least a quarter smaller. The bracts, rather than reaching up and hugging the bottom of the flower, instead arched away, outwards and downwards. But it's the leaves where the major differences lie. Whereas the dark-green dandelion had those hearty, shiny-green salad-ready leaves with the purple midrib, the cut-leaved dandelion had singularly unappetising leaves. Instead of plump, rounded lobes, the leaves were skeletal, jagged, all toothy sharp angles and with a pale green midrib. I immediately loved this spiky-looking little devil.

We left this dry patch behind and headed back into the fen. Alex and I had split up, each of us checking dandelion bracts, when I spotted something interesting – a dandelion with erect bracts. I heard the clean, bright song of a yellowhammer off in the distance as I knelt and untangled a leaf from the turf. I flipped through the dandelion book with building excitement. It looked, to me, like a good fit for the false fen dandelion. I called Alex over.

He immediately made an approving noise, and dropped down to inspect it further. He disentangled a couple of other leaves from the grasses around it and made another, more downbeat noise.

'The leaf you pulled out looked really good for it,' he said, 'but the rest of the leaves are different, much more jagged and with more triangular lobes. This looks like a Nordstedt's dandelion with one weird leaf.'

I suggested that we just focus on the good-looking leaf and count it as a success, but Alex, quite rightly, wouldn't be swayed. He's a professional after all.

We resumed wandering and, a little later, Alex called me over to a dandelion he'd found. 'Here you go,' he said, with a small smile. 'It's not the false fen dandelion, but it is an endemic.'

At his feet, growing in the slightly squishy turf, was a beautiful dandelion. To my newly taraxologically awakened senses, I could see why this was special: it had erect bracts, purple-spotted leaves, and was clearly different from anything else we'd seen so far.

Purple spots on the leaves are a goldmine for dandelion identification as most spotty-leaved species are in the section *Naevosa*, which contains only 14 species – of which seven are endemic to Britain and Ireland.

The stem was pinkish red and clothed in a cobwebby fuzz of delicate hairs. The golden petals surrounding the flowerhead were striped underneath with a vibrant red-purple band, and the leaves – salad-green with dark bruise-purple spots and supported by a mulberry-coloured midrib – had elegant arched lobes. This was Bertha's dandelion, *Taraxacum berthae*, a British endemic.

Bertha's dandelion was first described in 1984, based on a specimen found in the garden of Chris Howarth, a noted dandelion expert. At that time it was only known from his front garden and he named it after his wife, who in the original description he dryly credits for her 'forbearance with the hoe'.

'Third record for Norfolk,' said Alex. 'I had the first two records last year from fens on the outskirts of Norwich.'

I flipped through the book. The distribution map showed it to have a distinctly western distribution: Cornwall, Devon, Wales, Cumbria. Is it spreading east? Or are there just not enough people with dandelion identification skills to give us a full picture of its range? One thing's for sure: if this is the third one that Alex has bumped into in Norfolk, then it must be more widespread than the maps suggest.

We took some pictures of this unexpected endemic and returned to our original search. We didn't succeed. Despite scouring the damp areas for the rest of the afternoon, we saw nothing that looked like the false fen dandelion. Eventually, faintly dejected, but buoyed by the unexpected appearance of Bertha, we began our walk back to the cars.

'There's a chance we were a bit early,' said Alex as we left the fen behind us. 'This one can flower a bit later than other dandelions; it might be worth visiting again in May.'

'Do you think that's likely?'

Alex wrinkled his nose slightly. 'Not really. It might just be gone; it seems to be gone from everywhere else in Norfolk. It's closely associated with grass fen and *Schoenus nigricans* mire, which is habitat that requires constant irrigation with high-quality and low-nutrient water – and that habitat is being lost across Norfolk.'

That habitat isn't being lost in the sense that it's being built on or intentionally transformed in some way, but because it is drying out, altering the plant communities that live there. The nature reserves and protected sites still exist, but the habitat itself is changing within them. This is because increasing amounts of water are being drawn out from the aquifers that feed the fens for use by people. Groundwater extraction reduces the amount of water that reaches and replenishes fens, and this is probably being exacerbated by climate change, which is leading to hotter, drier summers.

As we got back to our cars, passing through the dappled green shade of the trees at the edge of the common, I was struck by a thought. If the false fen dandelion was a bird, or a butterfly, or a cute fluffy mammal, would it be in such a dire situation? I hadn't even *heard* of it until Alex invited me along – a species unique to Britain and Ireland that looks like it may now be lost from East Anglia, and we only know that because of Alex's dedicated efforts to try and find it.

Conservation, to an extent, is a beauty contest, and in a world where the industrial decapitation and demonisation of dandelions is normalised, how can anyone care about one that's disappearing? After all, there's *loads* of them.

So, spread the word. We have hundreds of dandelion species, many are endemic and rarities can pop up anywhere. We can all carve out a little space in our gardens, green spaces and our hearts for them. And, if we're very lucky, Alex or another dandelion expert might rediscover the false fen dandelion hanging on in a damp corner of East Anglia.

As for me, my next endemic belongs to another familiar, yellow-flowered group of plants with many species – the buttercups.

CHAPTER 5

Just Right: Goldilocks Buttercups

'Are they named after the girl from the fairytale?'

That's usually the first question I'm asked when I bring up goldilocks buttercups – which is relatively frequently because they're a delightful flower and absolutely always worth drawing attention to if you see one.

The answer to that question is 'no'; the bear-bothering protagonist only being given the name Goldilocks in 1904 after decades of being variously named Golden Hair, Silver Locks and everything in between. In fact, 'goldilocks' originated at least half a millennium ago as a nickname for fair-haired folk, and was soon applied to this cheerful yellow flower.

The scientific name for the goldilocks buttercup is *Ranunculus auricomus*. *Ranunculus* means 'little frog' and is the genus that includes all the buttercups and the closely related water-crowfoots, and *auricomus* means 'golden-haired' – one of those neat situations where the common name matches the scientific name. Or … it would be neat, but the name 'goldilocks buttercups' actually represents lots of closely related but subtly different species. Fifty-eight different goldilockses have been named in Britain so far, not a single one of which has ever been found anywhere outside this island.

It was with these 58 endemics in mind that I tried to organise a day out with Alan Leslie, the former BSBI plant-recorder for Cambridgeshire and author of what must be the most thorough, mammoth and simply best county flora ever written, the 2019 *Flora of Cambridgeshire*. His PhD in the 1970s was the foundational work in describing British goldilocks buttercup species.

However, when I rang Alan, he demurred.

'There are other endemic species that might be a more interesting alternative', he told me down the phone, 'like *Sorbus* or *Rubus*.' Alan is the sort of consummate botanist who speaks in scientific names, here suggesting I should consider whitebeams or brambles instead of goldilockses. It's also remarkably humble; he's described every goldilocks species in Britain and yet didn't seem eager for acknowledgement.

'But *I* think they're fascinating,' I replied. 'I'm hooked on the idea.'

He relented, and we agreed on a date in mid-April to meet.

Very kindly, I was offered a bed for a couple of days by my friends, the Jones family, who live in Bedfordshire. This was doubly useful – easy access to Cambridge and my meeting with Alan, but also very close to a site where one of these species of goldilocks was first described.

And so, the day before my scheduled meeting in Cambridge, I decided to try to get my eye in by searching for the endemic Pertenhall goldilocks buttercup. I had seen goldilockses before but had never appraised them critically. This would be a perfect opportunity to start.

I offered the Joneses the opportunity to join me and see the incredible species that was basically on their doorstep and Emma Jones agreed to come along. The endemic Pertenhall goldilocks buttercup was located 10 minutes up the road in the village of – unsurprisingly – Pertenhall. Many of the goldilocks buttercups have geographic common names like this; aside from the Pertenhall goldilocks, there are also the Risely, Comberton, Gransden, Stradishall and Kedington goldilocks buttercups and even more besides, reflecting where each species was first found.

Pertenhall is a small, green village with only a few dozen leafy homes, a church and a village hall, outside which we parked up. Opposite, a public footpath sign pointed through a gap in the flowering blackthorn hedge and down a green lane that led to the church. Churches, or churchyards more specifically, are good hunting grounds for goldilockses as they are often less intensively managed than the countryside around them – isolated islands of habitat in a sea of change.

The footpath was wide and wild. Spikes of lords-and-ladies thrust up beneath the hedge, the occasional dainty pink cuckooflower trembled in the breeze, and everywhere there were yellow stars of lesser celandines. Emma, walking alongside me, asked what she should be looking for. My mind went blank.

'It's a buttercup, it's yellow …' I said, lamely.

Emma pointed at a celandine. 'Is that it?'

'That's a lesser celandine. It is in the buttercup family though …'

Before I had a chance to continue, she pointed at another. 'How about that one?'

I started to politely tell her that it was another celandine and she laughed and told me she was now just doing it to annoy me.

My brain now in gear, I tried to describe a goldilocks. 'They have fewer petals than celandines, five at most, and they're taller, maybe up to 30cm tall, with the lobes of the stem leaves narrow, almost grass-like, I suppose, but sticking out sideways.'

We continued walking, crossing a rickety wooden bridge over a sparkling beck waving with weed, the churchyard now only a couple of hundred metres away. That was when I suddenly spotted them – a swathe of goldilockses on a slight bank to our right. Or maybe swathe isn't the right word; with those strap-like stem leaves jutting out at right angles and entwining with the throng of other goldilocks around them, it was more of a tangle. A tangle of fresh green leaves extending for a few metres along the bank, all topped with cheerful golden flowers and joyfully jumbled up with the emerging leaves of docks and cow parsley.

I knelt to get a closer look at a single plant. In my opinion, a goldilocks has four key parts to it: leaves that grow from the base of the plant; a stem that steadfastly straggles upwards; those strappy stem leaves that radiate out almost in whorls at regular intervals; and all this topped with a flower. The two most important parts for identifying a goldilocks, I had read, are the basal leaves (the leaves at the base of the stem) and the flower. The basal leaves aren't strappy like the stem leaves, instead they are ... variable. They all follow the same basic blueprint – a leaf with three lobes that are toothed around the edges, like the picture at the start of this chapter, or a little like the maple leaf on the Canadian flag – but the plant produces leaves with variations on this shape throughout the year. This means that across the season there is a spectrum of shapes on a single plant. However, the shape of these basal leaves also varies between the different species. Identifying goldilockses, in the main, involves comparing the continuum of variation in these basal leaves between the species.

I parted the damp vegetation around the plant in front of me in search of these basal leaves. My plant had a whole range of leaf shapes, some clearly fresh and new, others older and slightly yellowing. Most of the leaves had jagged toothing around their edges; on some the two basal lobes were split almost to the mid-vein, making the leaf look like it had five lobes; and on a few these split basal lobes were so large they reflexed around the leaf-stem and overlapped each other. I dutifully took pictures.

The other key feature in identifying goldilockses is the flower. Goldilockses are known for their weird flowers – some grow with a full complement of golden petals, some have a mixture of normal petals and strange, stunted petals. Some might grow one or two normal petals and leave it at that, and others still produce a flower with no petals at all. This can often give goldilocks a scruffy sort of attractiveness, a certain raffish air.

This tangle of goldilocks seemed to have the entire range. At first glance it looked as though most had a complete set of five petals, but the more I looked, the more oddities I found. One had four petals and a conspicuous empty gap, the next one had three, another only two. Then I realised that many of what I thought were flowerheads in bud were actually flowers with no petals at all; only close inspection revealed that the stamens and carpels were open to the air. I was describing this variation to Emma, pointing to each of the flower variations, when she asked me about the ones with green petals. Green petals?

I had a look. Emma had found a flower with five fully formed petals, but one of them had a broad green stripe from base to tip. Odd. Oh, and nearby another one. And another. These must be examples of the 'strange' petals that goldilocks occasionally produce.

So was this the endemic Pertenhall goldilocks buttercup? I had no idea. Just because this was a goldilocks at Pertenhall it did not necessarily make it the Pertenhall goldilocks – many sites may have more than one species present. The other problem was that there isn't an easily accessible guide to goldilockses. The only book that includes them is Sell and Murrell's *Flora of Great Britain and Ireland Vol 1*, a book that costs more than a car I once bought. The best easily accessible resource available is the Flickr page of Brian Eversham, CEO of the Bedfordshire, Cambridgeshire and Northamptonshire Wildlife Trust. He has been building up a photographic reference collection of goldilockses based on the sites they were originally described from. I opened this up on my phone and started flicking through the photographs of the characteristic basal leaves.

And ... yeah. Brian's photographs of the leaves of the Pertenhall goldilocks did seem to approximately match the real ones in front of me. One looked five-lobed with toothy edges, one was three-lobed but with the front lobe incised with two deep slits, and another was compact and kidney-shaped, with the three lobes barely distinct from each other. But as I scrolled, I started seeing photographs of other goldilocks species – the Risely goldilocks, the Gransden goldilocks – and I realised just how much overlap in shape there is. My tentative confidence that this was *the* Pertenhall goldilocks began to evaporate.

I scrolled back up to the Pertenhall photos and spotted something I had missed before. Mixed in with the close-ups of flowers and leaves were some wider shots of a sloping bank of Pertenhall goldilocks buttercups with a fence in the background – the exact view that was currently in front of me. This must be them! I excitedly told Emma, who seemed faintly unimpressed.

'You haven't really "found" it then, have you?' she pointed out.

She was right. Matching a photo to a location so you know you're looking at the right thing? That's very poor form, botanically speaking. Still, it was the only option I had.

I took a few photos to ponder over later, hoping that Alan could help clarify goldilocks ID for me the following day.

The next morning I got up early and drove to Allan's house in Cambridge. Alan offered me his parking space (he doesn't have a car) and ushered me through his beautiful garden, which heaved with various ornamental and native species, a number of which were interesting forms or varieties. He pointed out a white-flowered bluebell with tremendously long bracts, and a privet whose berries never turned black and instead remained a pale pearly green.

His sitting room was similarly plant-rich; floor-to-ceiling bookcases heaved with botanical books and the walls were hung with plant artwork. The side of one bookcase was decorated with a full set of playing cards arranged in suit order, each with a photograph of a different variety of snowdrop.

I thought that by having an entire shelf of plant books at home, as well as a few orchid prints on the walls, my house was developing quite a botanical theme. Compared to Alan's collection it showed me as the rank amateur I am.

On his table lay a vast tome, Alan's copy of his own *Flora of Cambridgeshire*. At 900 pages long and covering over

2,300 species and hybrids, it truly is a masterpiece. I said something to this effect and Alan immediately brushed the compliment away. He's incredibly self-effacing.

He flipped open the Flora and riffled through the pages, landing on an artwork of our target for the day: the Backs goldilocks buttercup, *Ranunculus cantabrigiensis*, a buttercup known only from the Backs of St John's and Trinity Colleges (the 'Backs' being where these college grounds back onto the River Cam). This flower is therefore not just a British endemic or a Cambridgeshire endemic, but a Cambridge endemic. The artwork takes up a full page and shows three plants with half a dozen flowers between them. Most are petalless but a couple sport a single petal. Below that are those spreading, strappy leaves, and at the bottom of the illustration are the all-important basal leaves.

I ran a finger across them. 'Are these lower leaves drawn true to life?'

'They are,' he said, flipping over a couple more pages and pointing out a sentence to me: '*Isobel Bartholemew has provided original paintings ... and I am grateful to her not only for her artistry, but her patience in dealing with the problems in capturing some critical taxa and with a demanding client!*'

Alan got his hat and led me through his house, past a shelf with a delicate glass sculpture of some snowdrops, to the front door and out onto the street. As he locked up, I admired the fern-leaved corydalis growing as an escapee at the edge of the pavement.

I excitedly pointed it out to Alan, who obviously already knew it was there, but seemed to quietly approve of my enthusiasm. I'm a big fan of urban botany, exploring towns and cities for the plants that escape gardens and carve a life for themselves in untended edges and harsh stony edifices. It turns out that Alan is even more of an enthusiast, having a seemingly encyclopaedic knowledge of the Cambridge flora drawn from his in-depth investigations. In 2001, within the city, he made the first British record of *Betula pendula x utilis*, a hybrid between the native silver birch and the planted ornamental Himalayan birch. A few years later, he made the first record of a hybrid alder, *Alnus cordata x A. incana*, a cross between two non-native trees often planted in parks and urban areas.

As we walked the green streets of Cambridge, Alan pointed out a few things to me: the invasive few-flowered garlic on a verge by the side of the road, and a tobacco plant, *Nicotiana sylvestris*, which has been popping out of the vertical brickwork of a wall of Magdalene College, just above the surface of the river, year after year.

It was obvious that Alan was a tremendous botanist, which was handy as I hoped he could explain something to me. Of the 656 endemic plants in Britain, the vast majority of them – including the goldilocks buttercups, but also some brambles, whitebeams and dandelions – reproduce 'apomictically', but I didn't have a completely clear idea of how this style of reproduction worked, or why it was employed by so many of our endemics.

I asked this of Alan, who explained it to me as we walked. Put as simply as possible, some groups of plants have evolved to forgo traditional sexual reproduction. At school we all learnt that pollen from one flower reaches the stigma of another, genetic material is combined, and a seed is subsequently formed. However, with apomictic plants, the seeds only contain genetic material of the mother plant, and so they grow into identical copies – these species are essentially cloning themselves through their seeds.

'So there's no pollen required?' I asked. 'A plant grows, flowers, and then sets to work on developing little clone seeds completely solo?'

Not quite, it turns out. Some plants *can* apomictically reproduce completely by themselves, and this process is called autonomous apomixis, but other plants still need pollen to stimulate seed development. The genetic material of the pollen is ignored, but the arrival of pollen from another goldilocks essentially serves to tell the plant that it's time to get to work on growing those clone seeds. This method is called pseudogamous apomixis – from pseudogamy, meaning 'false marriage'. Goldilockses use the latter sort – they need pollen, but promptly ignore it (to be *strictly* accurate, they ignore the genetic material from pollen, but it does contribute to the development of the seed's 'endosperm', the nutritious part that feeds the developing embryo).

This style of reproduction leads to populations of essentially identical plants. However, this cloning is not always 100 per cent perfect, which means that a parent plant, like a goldilocks buttercup, may very rarely produce a subtly different offspring. Through either random drift – as in, by sheer chance a genetic change becomes the norm in a population – or if the mutation is beneficial, this new 'form' could come to dominate a local population. Imagine this happening thousands of times, over thousands of years, and you can easily imagine how goldilocks buttercups in different places can end up looking quite different from one another. No wonder Alan has named 58 different species.

'There's probably a lot more than that,' Alan told me as we followed the path along the river. 'I only looked at the goldilocks in detail in this part of the country – Bedfordshire, Cambridgeshire, Suffolk, a few from elsewhere – and they were all endemic. I expect there could be at least another 200 undescribed species out there.'

I had sort of assumed that discovering and naming new species of plants in Britain was ... done? Complete? Sure, new species being found in rainforests and tropical islands makes sense, but in Britain – which must be the most studied place on Earth from a natural history perspective – it feels so *strange* that there could be, and likely are, hundreds of undescribed species out there waiting to be named. If you spot a goldilocks buttercup anywhere other than where Alan studied them, then there is a very good chance you're seeing an unnamed species.

Alan undertook his study on goldilockses in the 1970s as his PhD under Max Walters, who – aside from being an expert in lady's-mantles, another group of apomictically reproducing plants – was at various times the curator of the herbarium at Cambridge, director of Cambridge Botanic Garden and a president of the BSBI. It's fitting then, that one of Alan's 58 described goldilocks species honours him: *Ranunculus waltersii*, Walters' goldilocks buttercup, so far found only in a single wood in Cambridgeshire.

Alan and I had now deviated from the course of the Cam and were walking down Queen's Road. There were short, black iron railings to our left, but as the road crossed Bin Brook the railings came to an end and the footpath forked, defining a large, grassy triangle of green space studded with mature trees. This green space extends down to a bank and a stream, which separates this publicly accessible space from the North and South Paddocks of Trinity, the distant yellowish walls of the college visible beyond them.

In mid-April these green spaces were surrounded by temporary fencing; plastic posts with grey plastic ribbon looped symbolically between them, encouraging people to keep off the flowers. There were plenty of flowers here: blue drifts of Balkan anemones, white cushions of wood anemones, the green lion's-mane ruffs of gone-over winter aconites and, if you looked closely, the diffuse growth and inconspicuous flowerheads of goldilocks buttercups scattered amongst their bigger, bolder and brasher cousins, the bulbous buttercups, which towered over them.

Alan and I knelt side by side in front of a spread of goldilockses, an airy green thicket of stems and leaves topped with a bright constellation of flowers. The first thing I noticed was that I couldn't see a single flower with a full complement of petals. A few had three or four, but they were vastly outnumbered by flowerheads with only one or two petals. An individual flower, close up, could look a bit dishevelled, but in profusion like this they formed a cheerful harmony.

'Are there any species that have a full flower as standard?' I asked, angling a scruffy bloom with a single petal between my finger and thumb.

'Some do', replied Alan, 'but most have some missing or misshaped nectaries.'

'Nectaries' is the technically accurate name for buttercup petals, each having a small nectar-producing gland near the base to attract pollinators. For a moment I thought I had an epiphany: of course goldilockses can afford to lose their petals, they don't need to be pollinated to reproduce! But then I quickly remembered that although they don't *use* the pollen, they still need pollen to arrive in order to stimulate seed growth. In which case, wouldn't you think the nectaries would be important? I said this out loud, as coherently as I could muster.

Alan listened carefully. 'They don't need to receive pollen from another plant,' he answered, 'they are self-compatible – within each flower their own pollen can serve to stimulate their own seed growth.'

He had tested this himself experimentally, bagging individual flowerheads so that they couldn't receive pollen from another source and showing that they still developed seeds in isolation. However, when he removed the stamens (the source of pollen) from the flowerheads and bagged them, they didn't develop seeds – a conclusive demonstration that each one could essentially fertilise itself. It's pseudogamous apomixis contained within a single flower.

Goldilocks buttercups *can* afford to lose their attraction to pollinators. They're doing all of their own reproduction in-house.

We turned our attention to leaf shapes, preening through the basal growth to untangle a range of basal leaves. As with the Pertenhall buttercups of the day before, there were a variety of shapes, ranging from sort of kidney-shaped and blobby with scalloped edges through to those which are large and dissected, and split into five deeply serrated lobes.

'These are *Ranunculus cantabrigiensis*,' said Alan. I stared at them. To my uncultured eyes they looked like they exhibited a similar sort of variation to the Pertenhall plants. I opened my phone and flipped through my pictures from the previous day. Similar, yes, but not the same. The biggest and blousiest leaves from the Pertenhall plants were larger and more jagged than the most ostentatious leaves of the Backs buttercup, and one leaf type on the Backs buttercups – where the leaf was divided into five narrow lobes – was totally unrepresented at Pertenhall. Still, it was clear that telling them apart required a keen eye, familiarity and expertise.

'Is the Backs buttercup the only goldilocks species here?' I asked

Alan shook his head, telling me that whereas the Backs buttercup is the most common species here, the Toft goldilocks buttercup has also been found in the area. The Toft species lacks petals entirely, but so do some of the Backs buttercups, so it's down to careful scrutiny of the leaves to identify it.

'There's also another one I've seen in the Trinity Fellows' Garden,' he said, pointing behind us, 'not far over there. That one is undescribed.'

'There's an undescribed species just over in that college garden?' I asked.

'Oh yes,' said Alan. 'As I said, there are many more unnamed than named.'

We spent some time wandering amongst the goldilocks, admiring the fuzzy golden haze of them on the banks of the stream. I asked Alan if I could take a photo of him with 'his' buttercups, which he politely declined, and then I remembered something.

'I saw that one of the goldilocks buttercups is named after you,' I said. '*Ranunculus leslieanus*. How does that feel?'

Alan shifted his shoulders uncomfortably. It is against the rules of biological nomenclature to name a species after yourself, and so the honour of having a species named after you has to be bestowed by someone else – a tremendous sign of respect and admiration. In this case, Alan named one of his 58 buttercups *Ranunculus multidens*, the Tandridge goldilocks buttercup, but it was subsequently noticed by German botanist Franz Dunkel that this scientific name had previously been used for a buttercup species in Italy. As such, Franz renamed it in Alan's honour.

'I thought I had checked all the proposed names very carefully,' he said, characteristically more concerned with his oversight than with the prestige of having a species named after him.

As we walked, leaving the Backs buttercups behind us, I was filled with admiration for Alan. He deserves that buttercup named after him. The only botanist ever to tackle this complicated group in Britain, his work will lay the foundation for all that follows. And I hope more botanists do follow in his footsteps – there are probably hundreds of undescribed species of goldilocks waiting to be discovered, hidden in remote and unexpected places. Even in the heart of Cambridge, as it turns out. Someone out there needs to continue what Alan has started, and uncover the hidden stories of hundreds of our undescribed endemics.

Despite hundreds of years of research, the British flora is far from fully mapped, and it's not just the delicate nuances of our buttercups that demand our attention. There are other plants, often less conspicuous, whose presence and distribution are just as complex and intriguing. Take, for example, interrupted brome – my next target species – an enigmatic grass with its own mysteries.

CHAPTER 6

The World's Unluckiest Plant: Interrupted Brome

I had only visited Ranscombe Farm once before, on a 30°C+ summer's day a few years earlier. The site was a veritable wonderland of rare arable plant species. Arable plants are the fastest declining suite of plants in the UK; the red swathes of poppies and pheasant's-eye, blues of cornflower and yellows of corn marigold and corn buttercup have largely been lost from our countryside. Ranscombe Farm was acquired by Plantlife in 2005 to try to slow this trend by creating a reserve for arable plants and a place to trial management techniques that could then be rolled out elsewhere. It is a soothing oasis of farm biodiversity.

It's also home to our only known endemic grass, interrupted brome. During my time at the Back from the Brink project, my job, essentially, was to try to get people to care about endangered species by telling them just how amazing they are: how fly orchids deceive male digger wasps into thinking their flowers are alluring female digger wasps in order to be pollinated; how northern dune tiger beetles may be one of the world's fastest insects; and how narrow-headed ant queens can live for at least 27 years.

But despite this, the Back from the Brink species that most strongly captured my heart was this grass. I think what I admired about it was its scrappy, underdog nature. The world threw every possible negative scenario at this species and it scraped by, clinging to existence by the skin of its teeth. It has the dubious honour of being, as far as I can tell, the only plant species to be declared globally extinct *twice*.

I pulled off the road and into the farm's public car park on a bright May morning. Clumps of fluffy green fennel billowed gently on the verge next to the tarmac. I didn't park here though; I'd been given me permission to carry on through the gate and drive up onto the reserve proper. I swung round a bend, young cherry trees on one side, a scramble of hawthorn and blackthorn on the other, and carried on straight. To my left, over a wire fence, was a rolling field carpeted with a red blaze of poppies.

Ranscombe hadn't actually been my first choice when deciding to track down this species, but purely for reasons of geography I thought it would be easier for me to see it in Cambridgeshire, where the species has a long pedigree. Unfortunately, though, fate intervened in my plans.

The first known record of interrupted brome was made in 1849 in Cambridgeshire. It was initially described as a variety of a similar grass species, soft brome, but was elevated to full species status in 1895. This was a fantastically late discovery of a native plant species and so, for a very long time, it was thought that interrupted brome was probably an alien species that was undiscovered in its native range – a false endemic.

That native range has never materialised, and it is now thought that interrupted brome evolved in Britain at some point: mutating from its close relative soft brome, finding its own niche amongst crops of sainfoin grown as fodder, and from there spreading to arable fields across the country. At its peak, it was found north to Lincolnshire, west to Somerset, east to Lowestoft in Norfolk, and south to Brighton. Other than two records in the 1930s in the Netherlands where it was almost certainly accidentally imported from England, this was the extent of its entire global range.

By the 1960s its distribution had shrunk to a single site in Cambridgeshire, about 15 miles away from where it was first discovered around a century earlier, and by 1972 it had disappeared. Efforts to manage the site and encourage its re-emergence from the seed bank failed. Interrupted brome never reappeared here, or at any other native site, ever again. Thankfully we got a second chance. Seed from the dwindling population had been collected and stored at the Cambridge Botanic Garden some years earlier, and in 1975 this precious seed was planted out and ... didn't grow. It was bad seed. Just 124 years after it was first discovered, interrupted brome was pronounced extinct.

Luckily, the story didn't end there. A year later, at a BSBI conference in Manchester, Dr Philip Smith, an expert in bromes, revealed a pot of living, breathing interrupted brome. He had collected seed from the last Cambridgeshire site in the 1960s and had been growing it on his windowsill ever since. After the conference, he sent seed to various botanical gardens where it was safely stored.

In the early 2000s, there was a growing appetite for reintroduction attempts. The first, in 2003, was at Whittlesford in Cambridgeshire, a mere mile or so from the last native site. The second was in Oxfordshire a year later, with seed sown at Aston Rowant National Nature Reserve. Both were announced to great fanfare, both were positive steps to right the losses of the past, and both failed. In Oxfordshire, management of the site was delayed due to poor weather, and any surviving plants were eaten by escaped sheep. In Cambridgeshire, after four years, the population succumbed to a now-banned herbicide called simazine. When the field adjoining the population was ploughed it spread soil containing the still-active chemical, which killed off the nascent population.

Interrupted brome was extinct – for the second time.

Ten years later, wiser from previous failures, ecologists attempted new reintroductions. These were at College Lake in Hertfordshire, Ranscombe Farm in Kent, and once again at Whittlesford in Cambridgeshire. Throughout my time working on the Back from the Brink project I'd been told positive stories about how these reintroductions were doing, but I never got the chance to go out and see this endemic grass for myself. This was the perfect opportunity to finally make my acquaintance in person.

I emailed Ashley Arbon, who farmed and managed the Whittlesford site, thinking that seeing the grass thriving again so close to its last native site would come with a real sense of continuity. However, Ashley's reply caught me by surprise:

> *I am very sorry to say that we have had a disaster this year. The interrupted brome has been growing very well here for the past nine years. This year, due to a communications failure, the headland that has the population was cultivated and drilled with spring beans by mistake. It is a long story.*

Eek. Interrupted brome may well be the world's unluckiest plant. This may not mean that it's (once again) lost from this spot; Ashley assured me that some seeds or seedlings would likely survive, but they weren't going to be ready for me to visit this year.

So, instead, I chose Ranscombe Farm. I emailed Richard Moyse, who had been the manager of the farm until his retirement a couple of years earlier. He warmly offered me an opportunity to join him on a survey, and sent me directions of where to park and meet him.

I found the spot described to me by Richard and parked up. He was already there and shook my hand warmly, introducing me to his partner, Kathy Friend, who was surveying with us today. Two experts! I was being spoiled.

'Eager to see some interrupted brome?' he asked, with a twinkling smile.

'Absolutely,' I replied, and told him how I'd been desperate to see it for years now, all through my time on Back from the Brink. Richard had been involved with Back from the Brink too, but this was the first time we'd ever actually met.

'Well in that case I shouldn't keep you waiting any longer,' he said, gesturing for me to follow, a white quadrat clamped under his arm.

We walked for all of 30 seconds, reaching a flower- and grass-rich margin at the edge of a field bordering the track. Richard paused for a moment, scanning through the botanical riches, and then leant forward.

'There you go', he said, 'easy.' He gently pulled a tall stem of grass towards me. 'There's loads of it right here,' he said, letting go of the grass stem, whose heavy flowerhead swung back and forth like a weighty pendulum. 'There's another, and another ...'

It was now I had to admit to my fatal flaw; my iffy skills in identifying grasses. How would Richard judge me?

Kindly, it turned out. He gave me a quick run-down of the four key grasses in this margin. Great brome, *Anisantha diandra*, sterile brome, *Anisantha sterilis*, soft brome, *Bromus hordeaceus*, and, of course, interrupted brome, *Bromus interruptus*. Both great and sterile brome can grow to around a metre tall, have inflorescences (flowerheads) that sweep to one side, and have dangly 'spikelets' (essentially the flowers of grasses) that are sharply wedge-shaped. Soft brome and interrupted brome are different. They can grow equally tall, but they hold their flowerheads upright, their spikelets don't dangle, and they're a gentle oval shape rather than an acute wedge.

Richard carried on, showing me the difference between the common and widespread soft brome and the vanishingly rare interrupted brome. The flowerhead of soft brome is airier and more elongated, each spikelet on a longer rachis (the 'stalk' of each spikelet). In contrast, interrupted brome is clumpier, as if all the airiness had been removed from soft brome. Have you ever had someone try to tickle your neck and so you've crunched your head down straight into your shoulders? Yeah, it's like that, only with spikelets instead of your head. As the spikelets are nearly stalkless they crowd together into a dense flowerhead, often with one or two slightly lower down the stem, creating the gap or 'interruption' in the flowerhead for which it was named.

I felt I had it. I walked along the verge a few steps, pointing out the different bromes to Richard, who agreed encouragingly with my tentative IDs.

'I think you're ready to help with the survey,' he said, dropping his quadrat into the patch in front of us. A quadrat is a simple, square frame used as a standardised way of counting or estimating the population of a species. A number of counts are taken, allowing comparisons between sites or the same spot in different years.

Our task was to count interrupted brome, and as we did so Richard told me a bit about its history on the farm. With each drop of the quadrat, Richard, Kathy and I would gather round and try to count every stem of the brome, sweeping the swaying heads of brome into one corner of the plastic square one-by-one as they were counted, Richard clicking away on a shiny metal tally and recording the counts in a notebook.

'The first formal reintroduction attempt was elsewhere on the reserve', said Richard, gesturing, 'over on the chalky fields. That was in 2012 or 2013, with seed from Kew's Millennium Seed Bank, and it's still doing quite well there.'

He paused as we shifted the quadrat to the next spot a few metres along.

'There was some seed left over from that reintroduction attempt and I wanted to put in some trial plots – where we are right now – on the clay-with-flints to see how it would cope in that compared to the chalk.' He brushed his hand through a clump of interrupted brome inflorescences in front of us. 'It's come up every year since.'

A green woodpecker yaffled as we finished up surveying this strip. As Richard and Kathy totted up figures – of 2,764 flower-spikes, it turned out – I crouched to take some photographs. At this time of year the inflorescences of interrupted brome were green with russet anthers peeking from the edges of each oval spikelet. As they bent in the breeze – and it took very little breeze for these top-heavy grasses to sway dramatically – the spikelets shone a silvery green. My photographic attempts were poor; the slightest movement in the air setting the heads swaying like metronomes, and I gave up and watched them instead.

Kathy and Richard finished up their counting and we set off across the reserve to the original reintroduction spot. As we walked, passing fences with traveller's-joy opportunistically spiralling up them, I asked Kathy and Richard what their favourite species on the reserve were.

'The clustered bellflower,' said Richard. Clustered bellflower is a stunner; a stout stem supporting a dense cluster of royal purple flowers. It's a species mainly found on the chalk, and there's not a lot of it in Kent outside the landscape of Ranscombe Farm.

'I think mine is the ground pine,' said Kathy, after a moment's thought. Ground pine is now an astonishingly rare species, found in only 17 hectads (10km squares) in Britain over the past 20 years. The name is astute; it looks like a tiny conifer seedling and even smells like pine resin when crushed. The big giveaway to its real identity as a member of the dead-nettle family is that it sports a bright canary-yellow flower. 'Oh,' she added, 'Or the poppies.'

Richard chimed in, 'Yeah, actually, maybe it's the prickly poppy for me.'

There are five species of poppies that can be found in arable habitats in Britain. There is the common poppy, the one associated with Remembrance Day, which is our most familiar and widespread species. There is also the slightly scarcer long-headed poppy (whose seedhead is much longer than it is wide, unlike the round seedhead of common poppy), and the more unusual yellow-juiced poppy, which looks a lot like long-headed poppy but 'bleeds' a yellow latex when damaged. Then there are the rarest two, prickly poppy and rough poppy, both of which have been lost from large swathes of Britain but can still be found at Ranscombe.

The chalky path we're walking along brings us high above the landscape. Richard points, 'That's Ladd's Farm over there; it's about four miles away, and in the 1930s that was where the last Kent record of interrupted brome was made.'

'Until the work here,' added Kathy.

'Until our work here,' agreed Richard.

We stood for a moment, taking in the gentle undulations of the North Downs. A skylark sang its burbling song somewhere overhead.

Arable plants have seen a precipitous decline over the past century or so. Increased herbicide use has played a part; killing off everything other than the desired crop, as has increased fertiliser use, which changes the soil itself, as well as meaning that less-competitive arable species get overwhelmed by more vigorous plants. It also used to be the case that seeds of some of these species would be accidentally gathered with the crop; corncockle, for instance, would be inadvertently harvested along with the wheat and sown along with it when planting for the next year's crop. Improved seed-cleaning techniques mean that this doesn't happen anymore. There is now only one site in Britain where corncockle survives in farmland – here at Ranscombe.

I asked Richard what made Ranscombe such a good place for arable plants. How have traditional farmland species here persisted whilst being lost elsewhere?

'It's possibly because the field boundaries haven't changed in centuries. There's been a farm here since mediaeval times, possibly even since Domesday. This means that the field edges – where arable plant diversity is highest because the plough is more likely to miss or the herbicide spray not quite cover them – have had centuries to build up and retain their diversity. The seed bank can survive.'

Many arable plants have seeds that can survive years or even decades buried underground, waiting for the right disturbance to bring them to the surface. It's easy to imagine that a thorough ploughing in one year can bury a lot of seeds, and a thorough ploughing a decade later may unearth them again. Sometimes arable plants can reappear like this. The countryside is full of tiny time capsules of a flower-rich landscape, waiting for the right conditions to re-emerge.

'Is there any chance that interrupted brome could still be in the seed bank somewhere?' I asked.

'Interrupted brome has basically no seed bank,' said Richard, as we reached a gate, 'at least compared to other species. It might *possibly* last a couple of years.'

The field we entered was rouged red with common poppies and smudged yellow with charlock. Kathy almost immediately hunched down and pointed something out to me, 'Narrow-fruited cornsalad.'

This was a plant I'd never seen before. It's another chalk-loving arable species whose range has halved over the past century. It's strangely geometric in shape; its stem forked a couple of inches above the ground, then each of those forks symmetrically forked again, and again, and again, terminating in tiny clusters of pure white flowers, their shape reminiscent of forget-me-nots.

By the time I'd finished appreciating it, Kathy had found something else to show me. 'Stinking chamomile,' she called over.

The name seems almost oxymoronic, the word 'chamomile' almost defined in the popular consciousness as a soothing scent and taste. It had chunky, cheerful daisy-like flowers perched on top of fluffy green foliage.

I pulled a few fronds off, rolled them between my fingers and gave them a sniff. Ugh. It was overpowering, sickly and with a hint of rot.

'That's awful.' I grimaced, shaking the vegetation from my fingertips.

'It's called that for a reason,' said Richard, wryly, as he set out the next quadrat.

The plants of interrupted brome here were much shorter than the margin we'd started at earlier. Half the height, or less, with much smaller inflorescences.

'It's thinner soil here,' said Richard, 'and no fertiliser added in years.'

We gathered around the square and counted the brome, Richard clicking away. Ninety-five plants in this square.

There were long pauses in the conversation because I didn't want to throw off the brome-counting, transcribing of numbers, or the directions to the next quadrat location. Instead I admired the minute pink flowers of field madder and the dainty cream and yellow flowers of field pansy.

'One hundred and sixty-four,' said Richard, straightening up and writing the number down.

Kathy, a few metres away, called over to us. 'Rough poppy!'

I scampered over. I'd only ever seen rough poppy once before, on the Bedfordshire chalk. It gets its name from its seedhead, which bristles with upward curving spines. In flower it is perhaps, at a glance, similar to a common poppy, but its petals are narrower with clear gaps between them, giving it a slightly cruciform shape. The colour is deeper and more intense than in a common poppy, which has petals of a more translucent, tissuey red. The rough poppy is red like the waxen seal on an envelope.

'It's crimson rather than scarlet,' said Richard, admiring it.

'And that blue pollen too,' added Kathy.

The dark centre of the poppy was thronged with stamens, each topped with a fuzzy blob of cerulean pollen.

We continued surveying across the field. Richard and Kathy intent as I meandered, sometimes helping but often distracted by the unmatched array of painfully rare flowers on display.

Two hundred and sixty-three was the highest count of interrupted brome individuals from a quadrat here, but that was an outlier. Overall, the average number of plants per square metre was broadly similar to the margin where we'd started out, though as the field is a lot bigger it held a much larger population. They may be smaller, stubbier plants, but there sure are a lot of them.

Survey complete, Richard and Kathy planned to head over to the other side of the reserve to check out the population of man orchids that Ranscombe is also home to. The day had warmed up, the breeze had died down, and I wanted to try to photograph the tall, elegant interrupted brome in the margin near where I'd parked up. I thanked them both, bid them farewell, and walked back along the paths lined with the scrambling lilac flowers of bush vetch.

The original field margin we surveyed was now still and unruffled and I crouched to take a photo, the weighty heads of the brome steady at last, gleaming silver-green in the bright sunshine, a view impossible anywhere else in the world. Their story of survival against all odds resonated deeply with me. This journey, of double extinction to cautious rebirth, is testament to the efforts of hundreds of people across more than half a century: the botanists tracking its distribution, the scientists preserving seeds, the collaboration between conservationists and farmers. It's a powerful reminder of our interconnectedness with the natural world but also the interconnectedness between people; there is no one single person, or one single discipline that could save our endemic interrupted brome.

A species, twice extinct and yet, improbably, luckily still here.

CHAPTER 7

Shrimply Amazing: British Cave Shrimp

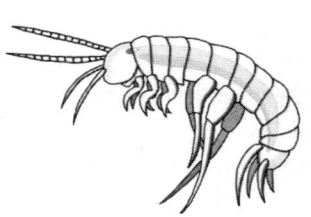

'How big are you?'

Earlier in the year, as I began planning trips to track down some of Britain's rarest endemic species, I reached out to various experts, fielding the usual questions about dates, times, and locations. This, however, was not a question I had expected to be asked.

After a brief pause I replied with a vague and unsatisfactory, 'Errr, I am ... normal-sized? Not skinny, but, you know, normal.'

Lee, on the other end of the phone, considered this, and said, 'Because if you're planning on going to Lundy there's a cave on the North Devon coast that has *Niphargus* in, but it's a bit tight.'

Lee Knight is a freshwater ecologist, the national coordinator for the Hypogean Crustacea Recording Scheme (hypogean essentially meaning 'subterranean'), and the world expert on an endemic, cave-dwelling creature that I was desperate to see.

I didn't much like the idea of a cave that was a 'bit tight' and so, under the guise of being helpful, suggested to Lee that he shouldn't go out of his way to meet me on my trip to Lundy and that I should come and see him in south Devon first. We settled on a date in June, and I was instructed to bring wellies and old clothes, with Lee providing the rest of the caving gear.

I asked Lee if Heather, my friend with Yorkshire Sandwort-spotting powers, could come caving too and Heather, having adventure in her blood, eagerly took me up on the offer. So, on a bright day in early June, the two of us walked from our Devon campsite, past steep hedgebanks of hawthorn illuminated by the bright yellow spathes of lords-and-ladies, down to the edge of the road.

Lee sprang out of his car to meet us. The first thing that struck me was how entirely ageless he was. Lean, wiry, with tightly cropped hair and tattooed arms, he was wearing a gilet vest covered in pockets. As he shook my hand, I took in his round-rimmed sunglasses that had an almost steampunk vibe.

We hopped into the car and Lee immediately handed me a hand lens and a tiny glass tube, magicked up from out of one of his many pockets.

'There you go,' he said, triumphantly, '*Niphargus glenniei*!' He started the engine.

I held the lens to my eye and squinted into the tube. Drifting in the alcohol were a number of tiny, leggy, white creatures, swirling in the liquid as Lee's car navigated the twists and turns of country roads. It was hard to get a sense of the tangle of preserved creatures with us all swaying, and of course these specimens were long dead, but neither of these facts took away from the thrill of holding in my hand what is almost certainly our oldest endemic species.

Niphargus glenniei, the British cave shrimp, is a tiny crustacean found – as the name suggests – in caves.

Until 2000 it was only known from Devon but has since been found in Cornwall too. As for its status as oldest endemic? The majority of Britain's unique species have diverged from their continental counterparts either since the end of the last Ice Age or since Britain became an island, so somewhere between 7,000–11,000 years ago; these are pretty young species in evolutionary terms. *Niphargus glenniei*, however, sheltered underground and weathered the Ice Age. Weathered several ice ages, in fact. Buglife say on their website that it may be the oldest continuously present species in Britain, having been here for nearly 20 million years.

I passed the tube and the lens over the back of my seat so that Heather could have a look, and asked Lee about the site we were heading to.

'It's the Pengelly Cave Studies Trust,' said Lee. 'There's an old quarry with several cave entrances right next to the centre.'

As he spoke we turned off a nondescript road through a village and headed up a steep narrow lane. At the top of the track there was a sharp bend past some old lime kilns before the road was blocked by a bollard.

'Just a sec,' said Lee, getting out of the car. I watched him unlock the bollard and heft it out of the ground. He returned and pulled the car into the little parking area near a cluster of old, stone buildings, and we got out.

'The trust', said Lee, gesturing, 'is named after William Pengelly, who was a Victorian geologist and caver in this part of the world. It was founded in the 1960s when they bought the quarry there.' He pointed to a gate between the trees.

He rattled the gate, which was locked. No one else was here yet.

'Let's hop over and have a look,' said Lee, vaulting the gate. Heather followed, and I went last, clocking the 'Danger of Death' sign attached to it as I did so.

The quarry hadn't been worked since the 1930s and was now a shady sheltered basin full of young trees and a luxuriant growth of ferns, giving it a primeval air. A series of boardwalks and steps ran around the base, leading to the different cave entrances we could see gated and locked with dungeon-like bars. Lee pointed at the different caves and reeled off a list of names. Spider's Hole, Disappointment Cave, Reed's Cave, Partition Cave, Rift Cave.

I stopped at a display board that mentioned greater and lesser horseshoe bats. I remarked on this but Lee didn't seem to share my excitement. 'If I leave the window in my spare room open for a few days a lesser horseshoe bat will get in. I've found them hanging from the lampshade.' Clearly, the bats were not as interesting to him as the shrimp.

However, he added that he often finds horseshoe bats not far from the entrances in some of the caves, sometimes even into early summer. 'We'll probably see one,' he said. I couldn't help but feel a little excitement. I'd never encountered one.

We followed the boardwalk over to the far point of the quarry and up some steps that led under a large rocky overhang. Here was Joint Mitnor Cave. Lee told us it is also sometimes called the 'bone cave' because when it was explored there was an enormous heap of bones inside – hyena, straight-tusked elephant, bison, hippo.

'Most of it's still there,' he said, 'they didn't excavate all of it – there's an elephant tooth and bison bones just lying there as you walk in.'

He must have seen my jaw drop.

'Do you want to have a look inside?' he asked, before marching off across the boardwalk and returning in short order with Rich Vooght. Rich had a precise, calm manner that I immediately warmed to. He worked at the Pengelly Trust and had the key to the cave.

This cave was behind a thick, steel door with hefty locks that opened with a satisfying groan. Rich flicked some switches in a rusted metal box and the cave lit up in front of us. Almost immediately inside the door, illuminated by the orangey lights inside, was the sloping edge of a heap of bones and detritus.

'It's called a talus cone,' said Rich. 'Thousands of years ago the only opening into this cavern was a hole in the ceiling, and occasionally animals would accidently fall in. Over hundreds and thousands of years this built up into this conical shape and eventually blocked the hole in the ceiling.'

Lee led us round to the side where the cone and floor of the cave had been neatly excavated, showing the layers and layers of bone; short-tusked elephant remains jumbled with disarticulated skeletons of bison and hyena in a towering heap whose ancient origins defied my human concept of time.

It was an astounding feeling, to stand and see the bones of these long-extinct species in situ, in the warm amber glow of the cave lights, exactly as they were left thousands of years ago by the forces of nature.

On the slope of the heap was the craggy tooth of a short-tusked elephant, which I cooed over.

'It's not real,' said Lee, bringing me back to Earth with a bump. 'There was a real one there but it was stolen in ...'

'... 2015,' finished Rich. 'Someone broke through the door and took a number of the fossils, including the tooth. They probably thought they'd be valuable, but unless treated very carefully they'll crumble.'

'That', said Lee, pointing at the tooth, 'is a 3D-printed replacement. But most of the bones are real,' he added, quickly, as if to assure me that the cave was still full of magic.

At the other side of the cave Lee pointed out a series of troughs. 'I used to keep *Niphargus* in here,' he said, 'Both *glenniei* and *aquilex*, to try and understand them better.'

Niphargus aquilex is another cave shrimp; larger than *glenniei* and more widely distributed across Britain as well as north-western Europe.

'Do you want to see *aquilex* too?' asked Lee

'Absolutely,' I replied. When would I ever get a chance like this again?

'Which way round do you want to do it, *glenniei* or *aquilex*?'

'*Aquilex* first,' I said, after a brief pause. 'Save the most exciting until last?'

'Baker's Pit it is, then,' said Lee.

As Lee had instructed, Heather and I were wearing tatty old clothes and wellies. He flung open the boot of his car and threw us each a boiler suit. After setting us up with helmets and lights, Lee led us up a twisty lane and into a sheep-filled pasture. The sheep barely paid us any attention as we entered, no doubt accustomed to cavers. In the middle of the field there was what looked to be a vacant plinth, a round dais supporting a narrower cylindrical column. As we reached it, I realised it was a hatch. It matched my imaginings of what the access to a secret nuclear bunker would look like in almost every way, except for the grilled door.

'For the bats,' said Lee, unlocking it and swinging the doors open.

I peered over the edge at the smooth cylindrical tunnel running down into the darkness, a narrow ladder fixed to one side.

'Right,' said Lee. 'You go first, James. Go all the way down until you reach a platform and then find the next ladder to take you down into the actual cave. Heather next, and then I'll follow up.'

I looked down the tunnel, flicking on my helmet light, but it didn't illuminate any further than the sun already did.

'Err, okay,' I said.

I clambered over the edge of the hatch and inelegantly manoeuvred myself onto the ladder and began to descend.

This is probably a good time to tell you that I am *not* claustrophobic and wouldn't describe myself as being particularly worried about exploring caves. That said, a couple of days earlier when I was talking to my youngest sister about my upcoming trip, she decided to tell me in great and horrifying detail about a video she'd watched about someone who got stuck whilst caving and died horribly and slowly over several days. I wouldn't say the thought of it was bothering me, but it was certainly on my mind.

Above me I could hear Heather coming down the ladder. Looking down – my torch now illuminating the darkness – I could see the platform. It was only a couple of metres wide with another ladder at the other end. As I descended, I left behind the concrete walls and entered a proper, real cave.

Waiting at the foot of the ladder, I shone my light around. Wet, muddy boulders glinted back at me. Heather soon joined me, followed swiftly by Lee.

'This is First Chamber,' he said, his voice loud in the cave's silence. 'We're going to head over to Boulder

Hall, through into Boulder Hall Extension, and then into the Crystal Corridor where there should be a pool with *Niphargus aquilex* in it.'

I wish *Niphargus aquilex* had a good English name, I thought, as I slipped over the boulders after Heather, but no one has ever given it one. 'Common cave shrimp' would be appropriate, if a bit dull. I resolved to try and invent one.

Lee, a little ahead of us due to his honed cave-traversing skills, called us over to look at something. At one side of the cave the clay-coloured stone gave way to a milky, terraced crust spreading over the surface of the rock. Water sporadically dripped into a little depression in the centre. Lee explained to us how the dissolved calcium precipitates out of the water and, over thousands of years, creates this smooth coating of calcite. Where tiny puddles form, the calcite is deposited at the edges, leading to this miniature terraced effect.

Heather, off in the gloom, let out an 'Oooh!' at a puddle that glinted in her torchlight. I scrambled over to look, half expecting a ghostly shrimp, but instead found that the little hollow was filled with a neat cluster of smooth, alabaster-white pebbles.

'Cave pearls,' said Lee. 'Instead of the calcite sticking to the floor and building up into a stalagmite, it covers tiny pebbles or grains of sand. The water movement stops them sticking together, so they just get bigger.'

I had never heard of them before. I'd been caving with school as a kid but the most we ever saw were stubby stalactites.

'Well, you'll have been caving in something that's been thrashed by thousands of schoolkids,' said Lee. 'When hundreds and hundreds of people visit a cave all the good stuff gets ruined. Usually there's a sacrificial cave that schools and outdoor retreats use that's utterly knackered but saves the good systems from being destroyed.'

The pearls glowed in the collective light of our torches.

'We'll see even better formations when we go look for *glenniei* in Reed's Cave,' said Lee, carrying on through the maze of sloping boulders.

I slipped every few steps. Often we were walking on a 30-degree surface and I'd slide and thump my calf, knee or thigh on a rock. I cracked my helmet against the ceiling repeatedly, realising I would have rapidly knocked myself insensible without it.

We passed strange amorphous flows of stone, looking almost soft and rippling in the warm light of the lamp, but cold and hard to the touch. It was as though the rock had melted and seeped before solidifying mid-ooze.

Lee kept up a stream of information as we followed him through the dripping dark. Baker's Pit had once been connected to Reed's Cave, whose entrance we'd seen in the disused quarry below and where we'd head next to see the British cave shrimp. The connection between them was blocked up with concrete to protect the much more beautiful features in Reed's Cave, but to but allow cavers to continue to enjoy Baker's Pit.

I tried to take in everything Lee was telling me, but I found I needed a lot of concentration to navigate the terrain. We were half walking, half sliding across sloping boulders and my boiler suit was increasingly slathered with a cold wet mud that chilled my flesh. The helmet strap dug into my chin, and my breathing was loud in my ears. I'd also lost all sense of time. Had we been down here half an hour? An hour?

Heather was filthy too, but seemed utterly unfazed by it all. As I said before, she has adventure in her blood.

'We're at the crawl,' said Lee, his voice floating back from up ahead. 'This leads into the Crystal Corridor.'

The passage shrunk down. At first it was manageable with an awkward stoop, the back of my helmet and my spine scraping the ceiling above, but soon it became a hands-and-knees job. The floor of the crawl alternated between cold, wet mud and awkward rocky sections that dug into my kneecaps. My hands slapped through the slime and I gritted my teeth at the discomfort. The crawl just kept going.

'Nearly there,' called Lee from up ahead. I sped up, reasoning that it would be over sooner despite the pain. After some unknown number of minutes, the crawl opened out into a larger, muddy chamber. Taking a moment to catch my breath and to let the pain fade from my knees, I noticed that areas of the walls sparkled with crystals of gypsum in our torchlight.

Lee pointed at a puddle on the cave floor, bracketed by two damply glistening, grey, craggy boulders. 'This is where I'd expect to find *aquilex*,' he said.

I'd anticipated deep, clear, underground rocky pools, perhaps with stalactites dangling dramatically above limpid waters. I hadn't imagined we'd be examining a puddle that looked like it belonged in the muddy corner of a cow field.

Lee knelt by the edge and Heather and I joined him, the cold mud soothing my battered knees. The puddle was still and clear, the bottom covered in a fluffy layer of silt. It looked completely empty. Our three headlamps flashed on the surface as we scanned, sending strange reflections across the low dripping roof above us.

'There,' said Lee, pointing, holding his finger just above the still surface. Directly below it, a skinny, blinding-white shape slowly trundled through the silt. It was a smidge under a centimetre long, making its way through the shallows at the edge of the pool. As we watched, it flopped onto its side and trudged around in a small circle, seemingly aimlessly.

I realised, looking closer, that it wasn't simply white, it was translucent – like a grain of rice boiled far too long. It had stopped moving at this point and was just lying there, with only a couple of limbs – the pleopods – moving rhythmically, keeping water flowing across the gills tucked under its body.

At the head end, behind two pairs of long filament-like whiskery antennae, I could see a short dark line actually *inside* its body.

'That'll be the digestive tract,' said Lee. 'You should be able to see it going all the way through.'

The dark line looked to be only a millimetre or so long, but on closer inspection it traced right through the curving, slender croissant shape of the shrimp, fading from dark brown to pale yellow. The shrimp was totally eyeless, its head as pale, clean and translucent as the rest of its body, as though it was minutely constructed of frosted glass.

It began moving again, first waving its many pairs of long, gangly legs and then flexing the banana curve of its body, rapidly curving its tail-end (the 'telson') under its body and surging forward through the water. After a couple of loops, it was as though it had warmed up and, reorienting its body straight in the water, it scooted off, narrow and sleek.

Whilst I'd been focusing on this one Lee and Heather had found others meandering through the silt, the trick being to simply sit and wait for movement to catch your eye.

I had seen other amphipod species before, in streams on the surface world. Those were *Gammarus* species: turn over a rock in some streams and dozens of greyish shrimpy things will squirm away. This cave species, in contrast, was skinnier, the legs and antennae markedly longer. This is an adaptation to their subterranean existence; those long slender limbs evolved to feel around in the darkness for food washing in from the outside world. Their ancestors would have had eyes, but what use are eyes here in the inky blackness? Bothering to grow them is a waste of precious resources and so, over countless generations, those shrimp that didn't bother were actually at an advantage. They were a sort of Gollum shrimp. Maybe that's a decent common name for *aquilex*? The Gollum shrimp? Grown pale and strange from their time in the endless blackness.

Thinking about the darkness, I asked Lee if we could turn off our lamps and experience it for ourselves.

'Go ahead,' he said, immediately flicking off his light. Heather, grinning at me with an artful smudge of mud on her cheek, turned hers off next, leaving me to plunge us all into stygian murk.

How often have you experienced true darkness in your life? When you open your eyes in the middle of the night at home you still see vague shapes, don't you? Even outside on a cloudy night there is usually a dim haze from a light source somewhere.

Here, in the cave, there was no light. I waved my hand in front of my face, bringing it closer until my fingers grazed my nose. I saw nothing. Heather and Lee were quiet and, other than the steady drip of the cave, I became very aware of my own heartbeat.

'Pretty dark, eh?' said Lee, switching his lamp back on.

'Don't you worry about your lamp packing in when you're caving?' asked Heather. It was an awful thought. Imagine being lost in the utter blackness with no way of finding your way out.

'That's why I carry a spare light, and why you always tell someone where you're going caving,' replied Lee, sternly.

Lee led us on a different route back through Baker's Pit, giving us a tour of the chambers, passages and tunnels that made up this three-dimensional maze. We crawled through muddy slots and slid down slippery rocks until eventually we made it back to the base of the ladder. Lee sent me up first.

As I climbed, I found myself feeling oddly lightheaded. I became very aware of my heart pounding and my face felt like it was tingling. Was I feeling faint?

Above me I could see daylight and so I picked up my pace, scurrying up the ladder. After endless minutes with the end of the shaft seeming no closer, I was suddenly at the gridded hatch. I flung it open, clambered over the edge, and flopped full length on the grass, relishing the sun on my face and trying to fight the feeling that the world was spinning around me. The sheep, as before, ignored me.

Heather hopped out of the hatch next and laughed at my theatrical sprawl. I laughed back, lamely, pretending that this was indeed just hilarious exaggeration on my part. The world still felt like it was merry-go-rounding.

Lee climbed out of the shaft, locked up the hatch and made to head back to the centre. I was not ready to stand, and too embarrassed to admit it, so I stalled by asking about the next cave.

'It's called Reed's Cave,' said Lee, sitting on the grass. 'It's got some of the best formations in Devon; the entrance is back down in the quarry where we were earlier.'

'And we've got a good chance of seeing *glenniei*?' I asked.

'We'll find it,' said Lee, confidently.

At that very moment the idea of entering another cave was not particularly enticing, but I needed to see the British cave shrimp. That was why I was here!

With a burst of determination I got to my feet and we walked back down the hill.

After a restorative cup of tea and a biscuit at the Pengelly Trust building, we returned to the lush fernery of the quarry. Rich came with us this time, unlocking the grid that barred entry to Reed's Cave.

'We keep them locked to preserve the delicate features,' said Rich, swinging open the grate. 'Well, that and to protect people from themselves. People who'd trespass to explore the caves and get lost or stuck.'

Heather asked if there might be horseshoe bats in this cave.

'Maybe,' said Rich. 'There's sometimes one or two that linger on this late in the year.'

We entered the cave. For the first few dozen metres it was a decent size, walkable with only a slight stoop. I swung my light across the low ceiling in the hope of seeing a bat, but with no luck. The passage began to narrow.

'We're coming up to the squeeze,' Lee called back, as the tunnel shrank down to something that was barely wider than the drum of a washing machine.

Dragging myself along on my forearms, knees protesting at the hard, uneven floor and slipping in the slick mud, I followed them in. The ground turned into a shallow, sludgy pool that we squirmed through, followed by an expanse of muck. How far had we crawled? 15 metres? 30? Longer? Or did it just feel longer? We kept going.

Eventually we reached an awkward right-angled turn that went up and over a ledge. As I clambered onto the higher platform I looked down. Below me there was an undisturbed patch of mud with what looked like a tuft of dry grass resting on it. This incongruous sight caught my attention – how would grass get down here? – but I rationalised that it must just have dropped off someone's boot.

I made my way onto the ledge and into the next section of tunnel. This section was, thankfully, not as tight and not as long, and after only a few minutes of awkward crawling it opened out into a grotto.

Lee grinned at me. 'Did you see the bat?'

'No!' I answered, irritated to have missed it.

'Well, it was a dead bat,' said Lee. 'You'd have crawled right over the top of it. It was by the ledge. There were only bones left.'

It hadn't been a tuft of grass at all; it was a heap of fragile bat bones.

Heather joined us, crawling out of the tunnel behind, and Lee gestured to the space around us. 'This is Shark-fin Grotto. Named after this feature over here.'

He stepped across the chamber and shone his lamp through a hanging, undulating blade of translucent stone. It changed the tone of the light to a warm yellow, and strange shadows formed in the stone as Lee angled the torch. It was essentially an elongated stalactite, a curtain of calcite rather than the standard icicle shape.

'The Shark-fin Grotto is linked directly to the Easter Chamber, where we should find *glenniei*.' Lee turned and followed Rich into the larger cavern beyond. I hurriedly followed.

The British cave shrimp was first discovered as recently as 1948 by Brigadier E. A. Glennie and Mary Hazelton. They were visiting Pridhamsleigh Cave – a cave not very far from where we were at the Pengelly Trust – where they collected cave shrimp that were smaller than the typical 'Gollum shrimp', *Niphargus aquilex*. These specimens were named as a new species four years later, in 1952. The British cave shrimp is still found in Pridhamsleigh Cave but is now much harder to see there; Pridhamsleigh has become one of those school-trip caves where everything has been scoured away by visitors.

Easter Chamber was large, torchlight barely reaching across its full span. Heather and I walked round part of the perimeter, seeing more glossy-white cave pearls in divots in the rock and great molten-looking seeps of flowstone, like craggy pipes of church organs. In one sloping corner, the ground was covered in a spreading mat of glittering crystals, gleaming bronze in my lamplight. Lee was crouching over a small pool, focusing intently, and I went and joined him. Like those in Baker's Pit, these pools were mere muddy puddles.

'I'd imagined that the shrimp would have been in something more permanent, like pools in the rock,' I said.

'These aren't their real home,' said Lee, still staring at the puddle. 'Their real habitat is in water-filled solutional voids and fractures – tiny wet fissures in the rock, millimetres wide. They just get washed out of it sometimes and end up in puddles like this.'

'Do they ever manage to get back into the fissures?' I asked

'I think so,' said Lee. 'I've sometimes, after heavy rainfall, seen pools in caves with loads of them in. Then, days later, they're gone – migrated back into the fissure network. The humidity in caves is high enough that I assume they can move across the wet rock when they want to.'

There were a few moments of silence as we scanned the pool.

'I think that *some* cave pools must provide decent habitat as they do seem to hold established populations', Lee added, 'probably topped up occasionally as more wash in after wet weather.'

He suddenly leant forward sharply and pointed. 'There's one!'

A tiny snow-white shrimp was navigating the silt. Lee scooped it out of the water with a little petri dish and carefully handed it to me. 'There you go, there's your endemic.'

I watched it wriggle in the dish. Blind, eyeless and with gangly limbs, it was the spitting image of *aquilex*, only scaled down. Whereas *aquilex* can get to just over a centimetre long, *glenniei* is more petite, maxing out at 4mm. I peered at it through a hand lens. It was like looking through frosted glass, immaculate and exquisite, every detail, internal and external, crisp and perfect. Its only colour was the narrow topaz thread of its digestive tract, arcing from head to telson. The shrimp stopped swimming for a moment, still, other than the whirring motion of its pleopods as they churned oxygenated water over its gills.

Holding the dish in my hand, I marvelled at how this tiny, delicate crustacean is, as far as we know, the oldest British endemic. In fact, its origins are so deep in history that it feels almost simplistic to describe it amongst our other endemics. Whereas most of our endemics have diversified and become new species within Britain, with *glenniei*, Britain instead formed around it. It was here for around 19 million years before we became an island.

Until 2000, *glenniei* was only known – worldwide – from 13 sites in Devon and was added to the Red List (a list of global conservation statuses of species and their extinction risks) on account of its endemic status and insufficient knowledge of its requirements. In 2000 it was discovered in a farm's well water in Cornwall and Lee began investigating, subsequently finding 9 more sites in Cornwall and a staggering 40 more sites in Devon. That means Lee is responsible for discovering more than three-quarters of the known range of this entire species. In 2007 *glenniei* was added to the British Biodiversity Action Plan list, largely due to Lee's efforts, as very little is known about its ecology, population size and the true extent of its range.

One unanswered question I had was how it had managed to get into so many different cave systems across the South West. Had it got into them millions of years ago when they were all linked up and was now isolated in each system? Or do the shrimp sometimes, somehow, make their way to new caves and colonise them? I put this to Lee.

'You're thinking of caves wrong,' he told me. 'You're thinking of caves as holes in the ground big enough for a person to get into, but that isn't the end of it. Tunnels get smaller and smaller until they're too small for people but plenty big enough for shrimp. These things have evolved to live in those wet fissures and narrow cavities in the rock, and these fissures might link up caves miles apart.'

I considered this.

'And', added Lee, 'think of a river. The riverbed might look like the bottom, but the water is flowing underneath that too, through all the gaps and cracks in the rocks below it. Interstitial habitats. The shrimp could be moving along underneath rivers. All these things are joined up.'

Until this point I had thought of caves almost like islands, with lonesome communities of species separated from other suitable habitat by hostile terrain. I now realised that the subterranean world was a lot more porous than I had imagined, the shrimp perhaps less fragile and isolated than I had pictured. And, thanks largely to Lee's efforts, we know that the British cave shrimp is more widespread than ever imagined. Perhaps one day soon he'll even find it in Somerset, some recent discoveries in North Devon being close to the county border.

I gently lowered the petri dish back to the puddle and let the water lap over the edge. My shrimp, feeling the movement of water, arched its back and propelled itself into the pool.

Maybe down here they're safer than the rest of our endemics. Maybe in another 20 million years they'll still be here whilst the sunlit world is completely unrecognisable, Britain itself a forgotten concept.

I looked around the cave, crystals glittering in my torchlight.

'You happy?' asked Lee.

'Yes,' I replied. 'Very.'

CHAPTER 8

Devon's Galápagos: Lundy Cabbage and its Beetles

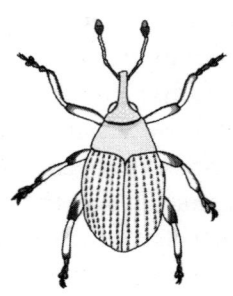

The weather had been beautiful when I set off. As I stood in the harbour at Ilfracombe waiting to board, the sun had made the bronze Damien Hirst statue *Verity* gleam against a clear, glittering sea filled with jellyfish.

But as the *MS Oldenburg* chugged towards Lundy island, drizzle began to whip our faces. A pink-faced man in stout wellies walked around the deck with a sheaf of sickbags. There were several takers. A few minutes later he returned, this time with a folded stack of beige blankets. These proved even more popular than the sickbags; the blue skies and sunshine had stayed behind on the mainland and we now ploughed through pewter-grey seas under a matching sky.

As we approached two hours of sailing, Lundy rose on the horizon. It's not a big island, about three miles long by half a mile wide, but it's steep-sided, and as we approached it seemed to grow inexorably taller. As the island swelled in front of us, the weather really began to turn. Plump raindrops fell, and Lundy seemed to loom out of a growing bank of fog.

The Oldenburg surged along to the south end of the island, pulling up alongside the landing bay beneath a rocky pinnacle topped with a lighthouse. We slowly began to shuffle our way off the ship. There was a wooden building at the top of the shore and a green 4x4 parked nearby. Two ranger-type people with polo shirts and healthy tans were greeting visitors off the boat and dealing with queries. I thought about making myself known to them – I'd been in contact with Rosie Ellis, the Lundy warden, to help organise my trip – but they were in the rain and surrounded by tourists with questions and so I stole around the welcome party and began the long climb up the sloping road to the small settlement where I'd be spending the next two nights.

Rain had properly set in, and I stopped for a moment to wrangle my waterproof out of my bag. I was just about to continue trudging when I spied a tangle of lupin-like flowers to the left of the path. On closer inspection I discovered that the plant was a vetch – but a big, exuberant vetch with flowers in a delicate shade of pale lilac, the top two upturned petals veined with a delicate tracery of bold purple. This was wood vetch, a flower widespread in much of the west and north of Britain but entirely new to me. I snapped a quick photo, then hunched my shoulders and continued up the steep path.

There aren't many buildings on Lundy, and most are clustered together around the Marisco Tavern at the south of the island. There's a church, a shop, a small museum, the farm, homes for the tiny population – just under 30 people – and the rest of it is largely holiday accommodation for tourists. I was staying at the campsite.

When you get on the ferry in Ilfracombe your luggage goes in the hold. This is unloaded on Lundy and a tractor comes and collects it and drops it off at the various holiday cottages. That's where my tent was; among the bags on this slow-moving vehicle as it made its way up the island's steep flank. Without having it to retreat to, I went looking for somewhere to avoid the rain.

I walked south, through the whipping wind, out to the church of St Helen's, a late-Victorian building that would have seemed proportional in a town but here, on the open ground of Lundy, it seemed a towering structure. In the porch was a sign: 'Swallows nesting – please do not linger', so I hastily walked through. Inside I found most of the other tourists from my boat, sitting on the pews and keeping dry. An entire school party was here, eating from plastic lunchboxes. Much of the space inside the church had been turned over to an array of displays about Lundy, its geography, history and wildlife. I gravitated towards them and found myself looking at a poster entitled *All Creatures Great and Small*.

This display gave an overview of the wildlife of Lundy: the feral goats and Soay sheep, the sika deer, the pygmy shrews, fungi, lichens and flowers. But given pride of place were the species I was here to see: the endemic Lundy cabbage and the two insects that live on it, the Lundy cabbage flea beetle and the Lundy cabbage weevil.

Lundy has been described – with perhaps more than a dash of hyperbole – as 'Britain's own Galapagos', but to be fair, it is probably our best contender. A number of our offshore islands have their own endemics: Arran has its whitebeams, Orkney has its own subspecies of vole, Shetland has Edmondston's chickweed, but only Lundy has an endemic that is itself host to *other* endemic species.

After reading all the displays I decided to brave the weather again. The fog had deepened, and as I walked south from the church, I knew that I *must* be close to those steep cliffs with the ocean far below, but the visibility was too poor and the wind too loud for me to have any real idea of where I was. I backtracked, thinking that falling off the edge of Lundy in the fog and dying in the sea might be a bit of a shame, especially as I hadn't even seen any of the endemics yet.

I checked back at the campsite and found that my tent had arrived, wet from sitting out in the elements. I set it up quickly, showering droplets of water over myself, and hoped that it would be reasonably dry inside. There was a sign at the campsite that I hadn't spotted earlier. It began 'SEVERE WATER SHORTAGE' and went on to recommend 'only flushing toilets when <u>absolutely necessary</u>' and 'wash dishes only when absolutely necessary'. I read this, dripping with rain, appreciating the irony.

The Marisco Tavern was my next stop, and I was delighted to find that an entire wall was dedicated to books of natural history, texts about the island and a few novels. There was also a poster advertising a talk that evening from Rosie, the aforementioned warden of Lundy, about the local underwater life. I got a drink from the bar, curled up in a corner with a Gavin Maxwell book I'd found on the shelf and slowly dried off for the next couple of hours, waiting for the talk to begin.

Rosie, wearing a plaid shirt and with sun-bleached brown hair, gave the talk in the back room of the tavern to an assorted group of overnighting tourists. We were given a potted history of the island – how it was formed 59 million years ago and has been connected to the mainland at various points since then. We were told why the water around Lundy is so special; it's home to a number of species at their northern limit due to the sea being warmed by the Gulf Stream, and

Lundy is isolated enough to be safe from mainland pollution.

A marine reserve was set up in 1971, a proposal first made by the Lundy Field Society. This was followed in 2003 by the establishment of Britain's first No Take Zone. In 2010 the island became Britain's first Marine Conservation Zone. Rosie highlighted some of the special species to us: the delicate and slow-growing pink sea fan, the acid-yellow sunset cup coral and, of course, the seals and cetaceans that spend their time in Lundy's waters.

Afterwards I introduced myself to Rosie. She'd been looking out for me when the boat arrived but hadn't been worried about not spotting me.

'You soon bump into everyone on Lundy,' she said, with a laugh. 'You can't help it.'

I asked about Alan Rowland, who I'd been emailing about the cabbage and its endemic entourage. He'd been out on a boat today surveying Lundy cabbage from the sea, the best way to count it on the steep flanks of the island. Rosie told me that he'd come to the tavern at some point and that she'd point him out to me. She went off to sort a few things out, promising to join me in the bar shortly.

I got a drink and a table and waited, watching as occasional newcomers entered the tavern. Maybe one of them was Alan, but without Rosie to point him out I had no idea. It's not as though you can tell that someone has been surveying endemic cabbages all day just by looking at them.

Just then the door of the tavern opened and a couple entered. The woman was wearing jeans, a leaf-print top and a blue cardigan. The man was wearing a light blue t-shirt with a picture of a Lundy cabbage on it. Underneath, in bold letters, text read: KEEP CALM

AND COUNT CABBAGE. I surmised this was Alan Rowland and his wife Sandra and introduced myself.

Alan is the chair of the Lundy Field Society and Sandra is the membership secretary. The society is a voluntary group, established in 1946, with a focus on studying the archaeology, history and natural history of Lundy. Lundy probably has some sort of claim to fame as one of the most intensely scrutinised areas of land on the planet, with a page on the Lundy Field Society website listing every species ever recorded here. Twenty-four species of slugs and snails, 26 millipedes and centipedes, 423 beetles ... the detail is astounding.

Alan and Sandra joined me at my table just as Rosie returned, carrying a small, glass-fronted wooden box and a brass hand lens.

'Thought you might want to see this,' she said, placing it on the table.

Inside the box was a meticulous collection of a dozen carded beetles against a white background, each labelled. Contrary to the popular conception of an insect collection comprising specimens pinned through the body, the modern approach is to glue the beetle to a tiny piece of card which is then pinned in place. Above this collection was the heading *Beetles most commonly found on Lundy Cabbage*. There at the top were the headline acts, the two I was hoping to find: the Lundy cabbage flea beetle and the Lundy cabbage weevil.

There is some slight confusion around Lundy's endemic beetles. Some sources claim only one endemic beetle, some three. The truth is that there are *possibly* two; the story is not quite resolved. We'll start with the easy one. The Lundy cabbage flea beetle, *Psylliodes luridipennis*, was first discovered on Lundy in the 1840s and named as a new species. Everyone agrees it's endemic.

There is also another flea beetle that can be found on Lundy cabbage, *Psylliodes napi*, which was informally nicknamed the 'blue Lundy cabbage flea beetle'. This flea beetle is not endemic, but the ones on Lundy are unusually short-winged and so for a time were mooted as an endemic island subspecies. This short-winged form was then subsequently discovered at other sites in Britain and Europe and so is *not* an endemic anything, despite what some online sources might say.

The Lundy cabbage weevil – which comes in black-legged and yellow-legged forms – was named as *Ceutorhynchus pallipes* in 1866. It was subsequently lumped with the mainland brassica-feeding *Ceutorhynchus contractus*, which has all-black legs. The sometimes-yellow-legged form found on Lundy was instead named *Ceutorhynchus contractus* var *pallipes* – a variety of beetle endemic to Lundy. However, genetic work suggests that all the Lundy weevils – be they black- or yellow-legged – are genetically distinct from the mainland *C. contractus* and so could be split back out as a different species. This hasn't happened yet, but if it does it will probably end up being called *Ceutorhynchus pallipes* again.

Squinting through the hand lens, I tried to get a feel for what I'd be looking for the next day. The flea beetle comes in two colour schemes, dirty yellow and metallic bronze. There are several bronzey flea beetles on Lundy, whereas the yellowish non-metallic form is obviously distinct from other flea beetles on the island so was the one that I hoped to find. The black-legged form of the weevil is similar to the non-endemic cabbage seed weevil and cabbage stem weevil and so I needed to find the yellow-legged form to be sure. All I needed to remember was that I needed the yellowest version of each beetle.

Scrutinising complete, I chatted with Alan, Sandra and Rosie. I learnt about the various introduced animals on the island: goats, sika deer, Soay sheep – the largest feral population away from St Kilda – as well as a near-century-old population of golden orfe in a pond on the island.

Some hours of conversation later we made our formal plans for the next day. Sandra and Alan were doing day two of their cabbage surveying – land-based, this time – but before they set off, they'd show me some easily accessible cabbage that they judged would be best for my beetle-hunting.

We left the tavern late. The rain clouds had finally cleared and the sky was lit with a thousand stars. The bright smudge of the Milky Way was clearly visible here, away from the bright lights of mainland civilization.

I met Alan the next morning outside the tavern and we walked together into the sheltered hollow of St John's Valley, down from the white facade of Millcombe House, which gleamed in the bright sunshine. We stopped by a stream – Alan being an expert on the freshwater species of the island – and after turning over a few stones we found a tiny translucent-white flatworm called *Phagocata vitta*.

There was a footpath that ran north from here and along the eastern flank of the island, halfway up the steeply sloping cliffs. This was where Alan and Sandra were surveying, counting the cabbages they could see from the path, most of which are on the steep slopes below it.

'That's going to be the main trouble you have,' said Alan. 'The majority of the cabbage is in places that you simply can't reach. We count the plants with binoculars but that's going to be no use to you looking for beetles.'

He led me along the footpath to a small flattish area surrounded by steep, brambly slopes. In this small area were a dozen or so Lundy cabbages.

If you have been picturing a neat, spherical, ball-type cabbage, the sort you'd see in a supermarket, then I'm sorry to disappoint you. The cabbage family is very diverse, and the Lundy cabbage is instead a metre or so tall with stout, grey-green stems. It has large leaves around the base, bigger than your hand – 20cm or so long – and lobed. Some have quite rounded lobes (think oak leaf) and some are a bit more toothy. It also has occasional leaves up the stem, which get smaller and more sharply dissected the higher up the plant you get. These stem leaves emerge from under each branch, and each branch terminates in a loose cluster of butter-yellow flowers. Each flower has four broadly rounded petals, as all members of the cabbage family do. This is why the cabbage family is also known as the 'crucifer' family, because their four equally spaced petals are reminiscent of a cross.

When I looked up from examining my first ever Lundy cabbage, I saw that Sandra had appeared, kitted up for her cabbage survey with Alan. They bid me good luck in my beetle search and set off along the footpath.

'There might be a few scattered plants along this path, just in case you don't have any luck there,' Alan called back to me as they rounded a bend and out of sight.

I plonked myself in this cabbage patch and began my search. Flea beetles, as the name suggests, are famous for their ability to jump. They do it so quickly that it's almost like they vanish – one second you're looking at one, the next it's pinged away before you've had time to even process it. Even walking near flea beetles can cause them to spring, so I thought that by sitting and waiting I might spot them before they spotted me. It was a theory.

I sat next to the cluster of cabbages and waited. I idly brushed a stem with a finger and found that their grey-green colouring was partially due to a powdery coating that easily rubbed away, leaving the stem shiny and green. The Lundy cabbage was formally discovered very late for a British plant. It was named less than a century ago, in 1936, as *Brassicella wrightii* (now *Coincya wrightii*), after Frederick Elliston Wright, who was the first to notice that this plant was something different and potentially unique. Subsequently, Victorian herbarium specimens from Lundy, supposedly of the wild cabbage, *Brassica oleracea*, were checked and found to represent the Lundy cabbage instead, pushing back the first record of the plant to 1884. Oddly, the Lundy cabbage flea beetle was discovered *before* the cabbage itself, being collected in 1845 and named in 1864 – though obviously it didn't gain its common name until much later.

There was some suspicion over the endemic status of the Lundy cabbage to begin with. Herbert William Pugsley, who, until his death in 1947, was one of Britain's greatest botanists, seemed resistant to the idea. In a paper written a few months after the announcement of this new species, he wrote, 'This addition to the British flora seems somewhat surprising' and that the 'significance of the association of beetles with [Lundy cabbage] can easily be overstated.' He reluctantly concedes that 'Until it can be identified with some form at present unidentified, probably from the Mediterranean region or the Canaries, [Lundy Cabbage] must apparently be treated as a new endemic species.'

And yet, nearly a century on, the Lundy cabbage hasn't been shown to be a hitchhiker from the Mediterranean or anywhere else. It is utterly unique to Lundy, along with its companion beetles. The real mystery is how and where it evolved. Was it here, on Lundy? Perhaps it split off from a similar species since the last Ice Age, maybe from *Coincya monensis*, the Isle of Man cabbage? (Which, despite the name, is found across western coasts of Britain.) Would the time since the last Ice Age be enough for it to evolve and develop its own suite of endemic beetles? Or were the Lundy cabbage and its beetles formerly more widespread, reaching Lundy (somehow) after the Ice Age and then subsequently lost from everywhere else?

A clue comes from the Lundy cabbage flea beetle. Genetic work has shown that it seems to have diversified from its nearest flea beetle relative quite recently, perhaps only since the last glaciation ended around 10,000 years ago. This nearest relative feeds on sea rocket, another member of the cabbage family with a liking for sandy dunes. Sea rocket isn't found on Lundy today, but it's possible that it was once present before it dwindled away to extinction. Could the beetle have made the literal leap onto Lundy cabbage as a substitute host plant and found it to its liking? That, plus a few thousand years to diverge, and suddenly you have a brand new endemic species.

I rubbed a Lundy cabbage leaf between my fingers. It was thick, leathery, but also floppy. I gazed up from my seated position, up through the sinuous glaucous stems towards the flowers, and spotted something. A tiny weevil gently plodding its way along the upper stem.

I didn't have to worry about weevils jumping away from me, so I stood and carefully peered closer. A long snout like an elephant's trunk curved down from its face, a feature that lends all weevils a faintly ridiculous air, and two elbowed antennae projected out in front like little antlers. Weevils have an inherently unserious energy; they don't walk, they stomp, snooting their way through the world with their goofy noses in front of them.

This weevil was about 2mm long and a matt, metallic green. Most importantly, it had distinctly yellow legs that were dark at the joints, giving them a faintly banded appearance. This was it – the ambiguously endemic Lundy cabbage weevil.

I leant in close, hand lens held to my phone. The weevil paused, understandably alert to the enormous mass looming at it out of the sky. I took a few shaky pictures and then pulled back, allowing the weevil to carry on its plodding path.

Over the next hour I spotted several more weevils meandering up and over the Lundy cabbages but saw no sign of any flea beetles whatsoever. I decided that there was little to be gained from staying put, so bade farewell to the cluster of cabbages and the weevils that had kept me company so far, shouldered my bag and walked north along the cliff path.

The sea below was sparkling sapphire. Three grey seals swam along the base of the cliffs, their bodies clearly visible through the crystal waters, and a shag, as black as oil, flew over them. The path I followed was a level track on a steep slope. Above and below me was a tangle of bracken and honeysuckle interspersed with pink spikes of foxgloves. A wheatear *chacked* ahead of me, flashing its bold white tail-sides as it flickered from rock to rock as I walked. And, far down the steep slope below me, I saw cabbage. Lots of cabbage.

Through binoculars I estimated dozens and dozens of plants, but it was hard to tell where the tangled flowering stem of one plant ended and the next began. These cabbages were impossible to reach; trying to traverse this slope without a rope would likely be lethal. It's no wonder that the survey of the lower cliffs is done by boat.

Frustratingly, this is where I expect the Lundy cabbage flea beetle spends its time. Before coming to the island I had emailed Dr Roger Key, who had spent a quarter-century monitoring the endemic biota of Lundy, and he told me that in some years he never saw the flea beetle at all, yet in other years it could be almost abundant.

I assume – and this is purely a theory – that it has average years and boom years. In an average year the flea beetle sticks to the main, out-of-reach, populations of Lundy cabbage. In a boom year the beetles overflow onto the scattered small clusters of cabbage higher up the cliffs where people can reach them. Certainly that would explain how, *six hours later,* after sneaking up on every Lundy cabbage I could access, I hadn't seen a single flea beetle.

I'd seen a lot of other things: a flowering bramble covered in chunky, emerald-coloured rose chafers that buzzed heavily from bloom to bloom, a cluster of wind-curved oaks that bent over the path like a living tunnel, and a rufous sika deer that watched me warily from a sloping patch of bare cliff. There were several distinctly bare patches, a sign of the ongoing effort to eradicate rhododendron.

Rhododendron was introduced to the gardens of Millcombe in the nineteenth century and subsequently escaped, smothering the eastern cliffs of Lundy and reducing the habitat available to the Lundy cabbage. With great effort, this non-native onslaught has been fought back, and the last substantial rhododendron was removed in 2013. However, on my walk I'd also spotted occasional bamboo canes – one with a stonechat perched on it – staked out to mark rhododendron seedlings in need of removal. Without continuous effort to keep removing these, the cabbage, and their endemic beetles, could get pushed out. One benefit of a small island is that an eradication like this is possible – on the British mainland rhododendron there is barely a 10km square where it doesn't now occur, and in places it forms dense thickets excluding native species.

Unfortunately, despite this enormous effort and fantastic conservation story, the eradication hadn't been met with total approval. The night before, at the tavern, Alan told me that some regular visitors missed the dark tunnels through the rhododendron thickets and their blousy purple blooms. For me, the choice between an alien invader and a cluster of utterly unique species is not a hard one to make.

I eventually followed a side path that led me up the cliff and onto the flat top of Lundy, meeting a band of Soay sheep, and then walked back to the campsite, exhausted. I'd try again before the boat arrived tomorrow.

Five more hours of searching the next morning yielded nothing. I tried sweeping plants with my net, sneaking up on them to try and catch any theoretical beetles off guard, and scratching my legs to a bloody mess fighting my way through brambles to new patches of Lundy cabbage off the beaten track. None of this worked, and I gave in and headed back to my tent to get some lunch.

I crossed the green in front of the tavern back towards the campsite, passing Rosie walking in the opposite direction holding an angle grinder.

'Did you hear about the boat?' she asked, pausing.
'No?'

'There's high winds at Ilfracombe, apparently. They've not been able to get the day trippers on to the boat safely. They're not sure when it'll get here.'

'Will it get here today?'

'Oh, probably,' Rosie replied, looking calmly out to sea. I expect on islands you get a lot more used to the vagaries of the weather than you do on the mainland. 'Head down to the jetty at 4pm anyway and hopefully it'll turn up.'

She made to continue on her way, and then paused. 'You don't want to see a Manx shearwater, do you?'

We rattled along the steep road down the flank of Lundy in a 4×4 with me bouncing about in the back. Pulled up by the jetty, we tiptoed our way past sleeping seals and along the rocky beach known as the Devil's Kitchen. Rosie was carefully carrying a cardboard box.

Eventually we reached a spot that Rosie liked the look of, and she sat and carefully opened the box. Inside, in the shadows, sat a Manx shearwater, who looked at us with dark eyes from its gentle face. The Manx shearwater has a body about the size of a collared dove but with much longer wings. At sea, it flaps them occasionally, holding them stiffly, one above, one below, belly sideways, presenting either its bright white underside or black upperside to onlookers. It skims just above the water, banking, turning and shearing.

This individual had turned up, disoriented, around the buildings the night before and had been safely scooped up for release today. Rosie picked it up out of the box, and I admired its long, slightly hooked beak and high, tube-like nostrils. I had seen hundreds, thousands, of Manx shearwaters before, but all at high speed as they zipped past boats or coastal headlands. This was the first time I had seen what one *really* looked like.

'They're doing much better on Lundy since the rat eradication,' said Rosie, jotting down some of the bird's vital information as she ringed it. Non-native rats – which will eat chicks and eggs – had been eradicated from Lundy nearly 20 years previously. In the early 2000s around 200 Manx shearwaters kept trying to breed on Lundy, with limited success. Puffins, too, were struggling, with only 13 birds recorded. Now, nearly two decades on, the Manx population had rebounded to over 25,000 and 1,335 puffins were recorded at the last count. Even storm-petrels have started breeding on Lundy, with more than 150 pairs. This island is now a safe haven for seabirds.

'It's not just the seabirds,' Rosie continued. 'Skylarks, meadow pipits, wheatear ... they're all doing better since the rats have gone.' The eradication was an enormous project, but it paid off. The Isles of Scilly and Lundy were the only Manx colonies left in the South West, and now Lundy's is rebounding strongly. Around 80 per cent of the world population is found in Britain and Ireland, breeding on offshore islands around the entire coast; so, whilst it is not endemic, we do have international responsibility for this species.

That said, it does play a key part in an endemic story. Scotland's Isle of Rum is home to tens of thousands of Manx shearwaters, some 30 per cent of the world population. It was here in 1963 that a species new to science was discovered; that most loveable of creatures – a flea. Some fleas are generalists – the moorhen flea, for instance, has been found on woodcock, robins, goldcrests, treecreepers etc. – but this flea has only ever been found in the nests of Manx shearwaters, and only on the Isle of Rum. It was named the Manx shearwater flea, *Ceratophyllus fionnus*, and after last being recorded in 1966 it has never been seen again.

This doesn't mean it has vanished. In fact, it says a lot more about the lack of conservation interest given to fleas. For more than 50 years no one has tried to find it, despite it being a species with one of the most restricted ranges on the entire planet. The shearwater colony on Rum covers around 50 hectares of the island. That's less than half of a square kilometre, or 0.19 square miles. That is a *minute* range. And, of course, the flea isn't living across that entire area, it's restricted to Manx shearwater burrows. *And* it's probably not found in every single burrow. With these considerations the global range of the Manx shearwater flea combined might be ... well, who knows? Some tens of square metres?

This species is incredibly vulnerable to anything that affects its host. There are non-native rats on Rum; they aren't impacting the Manx shearwater colonies anywhere near as severely as they did on Lundy, but if circumstances change – and in a changing climate they might – maybe they could push the Manx shearwater flea over the edge and into extinction.

I'm sure some people would question the importance of saving a flea. It's a parasite after all, right? To which I say: why be prejudiced against any one species? What makes a red squirrel any more valuable or important than a flea? We're all just distant cousins who've walked different evolutionary paths for a few million years. Should the fleas' journey through the universe be allowed to end simply because we don't find them appealing? As for being a parasite – so what? We care about the conservation of predators who kill their prey – tigers, eagles and bears – but if a species drinks a bit of blood, then it's fair game for extinction?

Perhaps you're wondering if this flea plays some vital ecological role on Rum, an indispensable cog in its food web. The truth is, we don't know. Maybe it does, maybe it doesn't. But does that really matter? Some species exist simply because they do. Not everything needs a grand, human-defined purpose to justify its right to life. Biodiversity has value in and of itself, regardless of our perception of beauty or usefulness.

I was stirred from my thoughts by Rosie, who had finished ringing the shearwater. 'Time to let this guy go,' she said, releasing her hold on the bird.

The shearwater, immediately realising it was free, flapped, paddled its feet against the smooth boulder in front of it, and was airborne. It shot over the short stretch of beach in front of us, veered sharply right and was lost from view behind a rocky crag. Then, it reappeared, shearing strongly to the left, flashing its white belly towards us as it skimmed over the waves.

At quarter to four I was wandering around on the goat-walks on the vertiginous slopes above the jetty. These narrow paths, worn by the nimble feet of the feral goats, wove meandering paths across the cliffs and, in places, intersected with small clumps of cabbage I hadn't yet investigated.

I scanned the horizon – no sign of the *MS Oldenburg* yet – and focused on my goal: scrambling to the next patch of cabbage. A tiny beetle on a stem briefly got my heart beating, but it was 'just' another Lundy cabbage weevil, which had proven to be widespread and abundant. I took a moment to appreciate it, realising how quickly I'd gone from excitement at seeing them yesterday to being blasé about them today. I watched it rhythmically stride like a little clockwork toy, a dull green-bronze pinprick on the glaucous cabbage stem.

A seal far below let out an *awoooo*, which echoed up the cliffs and, looking up, I spotted the *Oldenburg* chugging into sight in the distance. I also spotted a final patch of cabbage, three plants on a small outcrop below me. My last chance.

I scrambled down, past the yellow flowers of kidney vetch and the blue tufts of sheep's-bit, reaching the cabbage. I approached slowly, scanning the leaves and stem. No sign. I got closer, angling my head to check the undersides of leaves, the opposite sides of the stem. Nothing. The universe did not provide me the narrative satisfaction that I craved. Resigned, I scrambled down the slope to the jetty. Despite not finding one of Lundy's special beetles, I had still seen the other in a pairing unique in Britain, our only example of co-endemism: the cabbage and its weevil.

Later, as the *Oldenburg* groaned its way out to sea, I looked back at the island, appreciating the yellowish wash of Lundy cabbage along the lower cliffs that I hadn't spotted on the way in. I knew that I'd return one day, the island and my unfinished search for the unique flea-beetle drawing me back.

CHAPTER 9

Purple Prose: Purple Ramping-fumitory

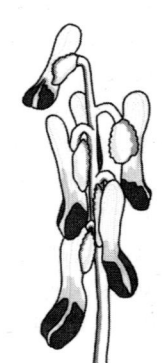

After returning from Lundy I lugged my bags through the streets of Ilfracombe to my accommodation. Before collapsing into bed I checked my schedule for the next few days. Tomorrow was blank. This was originally planned as a rest day, but now, facing it, it felt like a wasted opportunity. I searched through my files of endemic research on the off chance there was something nearby. Bingo. I pinged off an email and fell straight asleep.

The next morning I had a reply from Bob Hodgson, the BSBI recorder for North Devon:

> Fumaria pupurea – *The best populations are on the road south from Mortehoe to Sunnyside Road, Woolacombe. Best of luck with your searching.*

That was only about 10 minutes away. I packed my stuff, picked up a potted plant that the accommodation owner had been looking after for me, and hopped in the car.

It wasn't long later that I was following the winding road into Mortehoe, a village of quaint stone houses complete with a National Trust tea room opposite a squat Norman church. The churchyard was beautifully lush and filled with wildflowers. That's the kind of place to be buried in, I thought, not those sad, sterile bowling-green cemeteries.

I continued through Mortehoe and round to Woolacombe, the landscape of fields giving way to tumbling green hills leading down to the bluest of seas. This seaside town was heaving with tourists, the beach crammed with holidaymakers and the sea dotted with swimmers. I didn't need the seafront, though. I wanted the backstreets.

I parked up away from the beach, up in the residential streets, and – after watering the potted plant in the footwell and leaving my car with a window ajar so it didn't overheat – set off walking down Springfield Road.

I think that people often imagine botany as a pursuit of wild spaces – the countryside, nature reserves, mountains and rivers – but, like Alan Leslie in Cambridge, one of my favourite hunting grounds is in urban streets. These are prime places to search for oddities and aliens, species from across the world that have jumped the garden fence and are making a living in pavement cracks, basking in the extra warmth an urban area brings. Towns and cities are often 'heat islands', places that are noticeably warmer than the surrounding countryside, and so can provide homes for species from warmer climes who couldn't survive in cooler rural areas. I wasn't in Woolacombe with the purpose of searching for urban aliens, but I was going to enjoy them whilst I was here.

As I walked I saw bushes of fuchsia, *Fuchsia magellanica*, with their dangling, hot-pink ballerina flowers growing by the road. They're originally from South America but are now widely naturalised in the west of Britain. Garden walls were obscured by marshmallow-coloured swathes of both the pink and white forms of red valerian, *Centranthus ruber*, a species originally of the Mediterranean but now found across the majority of Britain. A patch of disturbed soil held the wispy fronds and watery-blue flowers of love-in-a-mist, *Nigella damascena*, a species from southern Europe, as well as the startlingly blue flower of dwarf morning glory, *Convolvulus tricolor*, another Mediterranean beauty.

But of my target species? No sign. Purple ramping-fumitory, *Fumaria purpurea*, is a member of the poppy family but it looks nothing like the 'classic' poppy of Remembrance Day. None of the fumitories do. Instead they have delicate, divided leaves that grow from slender, forking, twining stems topped with clusters of minute, elongated flowers in shades of white, pink and red through to blackish purple. The name fumitory comes from a combination of the Latin *fumus* and *terrae* meaning 'smoke' and 'earth'. I have always assumed that this is related to their airy, cloudy tufts of flowers, and have heard that other people have the same interpretation, but I've also read that the roots supposedly smell smoky. Not having dug one up to sniff, I can't comment.

Fumitories in Britain are split into two groups. Four are the 'fumitories' and are smaller plants, typically of arable habitats. The other six are the 'ramping-fumitories', which grow elongated stems, allowing them to twine and straggle through other vegetation. Of these six species, two are endemic: western ramping-fumitory, *Fumaria occidentalis*, whose entire global range is found between Cornwall and the Isles of Scilly; and my target of the day, purple ramping-fumitory, *Fumaria purpurea*, which is a species that favours coastal regions in the west of Britain, from Cornwall north to Orkney.

I reached the end of Springfield Road and turned right up Sandy Lane. The left-hand side of this road was a low cliff of grey stone and at its base, running along the edge of the tarmac, was a narrow strip filled with plants. It was mostly Alexanders, their flowerheads gone over with their seed ripening to black. Between them, though, were the lilac flowers of common mallow, the cheerful yellow clusters of nipplewort and the solid pink of red campion. This verdant tangle of vegetation felt like exactly the sort of place that a ramping-fumitory should be ramping its way through, but despite a careful search I found nothing.

Further up the road the stony cliff gave way to billowing hedgerows filled with a froth of cow parsley and the purple spears of foxgloves, all overhung with the straggling stems of traveller's-joy. I was beginning to leave Woolacombe behind me and, feeling that I was straying from the search area, I turned back. It was only a couple of minutes later that I spotted a small ramping-fumitory growing from the edge of a formal flower bed by a driveway.

This wasn't a full-sized straggling example – it only had a few stems and the longest of those was around a foot long, twisting through the rest of the intentionally planted flower bed – but it was big enough to have flowers, a few dense tufts of pale pink flowers. I knelt for a closer look.

The flower of a fumitory is really quite unlike any other familiar plant. Imagine the head of the alien from the film *Alien*, complete with protruding internal mouth, but entirely made from delicate petals. In the case of the fumitory I was looking at, the majority of the 'head' of the alien was a light rosy-pink with the 'mouth' a deep wine-red with a thin green stripe on top. The second protruding 'internal mouth' of the alien is also rosy pink with a green link up the centre. From each of the alien's 'cheeks' grows a large oval-shaped, tissue-thin petal (really a sepal) with toothed edges, extending halfway to the 'mouth'. If you haven't seen *Alien* then I am very sorry about this description. In fact, I'm sorry about it even if you have seen it.

I thought that this looked like a good candidate for purple ramping-fumitory, but when I opened up my phone to check an ID guide from the Back from the Brink website, one feature immediately stood out – of the six ramping fumitories we have in Britain, only two of them, including the purple one, have drooping seeds. I let go of the perfect flowerhead I was holding and hunted around for one that was a bit past its best. Found one! There were a couple of flowers still looking fresh at the top of the stem and below them the gone-over flowers had been replaced with a little spherical seed on a short stalk. Those short stalks all bent to point downwards. That meant this was either purple ramping-fumitory, my target, or … I checked the guide, white ramping-fumitory, *Fumaria capreolata*.

Well, these flowers aren't white, I thought to myself, so they must be purple ramping-fumitory. But a smaller, wiser and more fastidious voice in my mind pointed out that they weren't really purple either. They were an incredibly pale pink, a colour in between the two illustrations of the species in the guide. I scratched my beard, thinking. I decided to take lots of photos, send some of them to better botanists and carry on with my walk to see if I could find something more convincing.

I sent my messages and set off back down the road. I had barely reached the junction with Springfield Road when my phone chirped. Tristan Norton, the BSBI recorder for South Hampshire, had already replied to me:

> I'd go with white ramping-fumitory there. Big, ovoid toothy sepals, and they do turn pinkish after pollination.

Ah. Damn. But I'd learnt something: white-ramping fumitory can be pink, and purple ramping-fumitory should have less toothy sepals (those alien 'cheek petals').

Opposite Springfield Road was Sunnyside Road, the location suggested by Bob in his email, so I had high hopes of success here. I was getting closer to the sea, seeing bright sapphire glimpses in between the houses as I walked. Clumps of the fluffy pink seaside daisy had escaped gardens and were growing merrily by the road, aromatic waterfalls of prostrate rosemary studded with blue flowers tumbled over walls, and the icy foliage of silver ragwort dotted my route.

As I walked, the sides of the road became a little less tended; more bramble and less formal planting. A smudge of pink caught my eye. From amongst the prickly thicket of bramble to my right emerged half a dozen pyramidal flowerheads of a deep pink fumitory. For a skinny, delicate plant it had managed to grow surprisingly tall; some of its stems must have been a metre long, using the dense mesh of bramble to clamber towards the light.

It was clearly a ramping-fumitory, but which one? I looked for gone-over flowerheads to see if it had those drooping seeds. No luck – this plant was in full, perfect flower. I reopened the guide on my phone. Three of the ramping fumitories have big sepals – those 'cheek petals' – and the other three have smaller ones. I checked my plant. The sepals were enormous.

The three big-sepalled fumitories are the purple ramping-fumitory, white ramping-fumitory, and the western ramping-fumitory. The western ramping-fumitory, being endemic to Cornwall and the Isles of Scilly and never recorded in Devon, was highly unlikely to be the plant in front of me. That left the same two species as before, white and purple.

Thinking of Tristan's message and cross-referencing with the guide, I saw that the sepals of white ramping-fumitory were toothy all the way around. In contrast, purple's sepals are only toothy at the back end. I checked. The sepals were smoothly rounded at the front, a little jagged at the back. Bingo! And they were a deep pink. Not purple (though perhaps poetic licence would allow them to be described that way), but certainly not white or a light rosy pink like the last one I'd seen. This was it! The endemic purple ramping-fumitory, flourishing amongst the bramble on this suburban seaside backstreet.

I took some pictures and posted them as an update to my messages earlier. As I was tapping away on my phone an old man in a blue shirt and sweater vest trudged past me.

'Checking the weather?' he asked.

'Pardon?' I replied, thrown off by the question.

'Checking the weather?' he repeated, nodding at my phone, grinning. 'It's going to be sunny for a few days yet.'

'Oh, I was actually just sending someone a picture of this flower,' I replied, gesturing to my find.

He took a few steps forward and squinted at it. 'What is it?' he asked.

'Purple ramping-fumitory.'

'Purple ramble-what-now?' he repeated back to me, taking off his straw hat and cupping his ear.

We repeated variations of the name back and forth until he was happy he had nailed it.

'Is it special then?' he asked.

'Yes,' I said, and gave him the overview: how it's one of only a pretty small group of species that are only found in Britain; how it's a species that likes being near the west coast and that it's great that there are little untended spaces like this that allow it to survive.

'Well,' he said, leaning in so closely to look at it that I worried he might scratch his face on the brambles, 'I've never heard of that and I've lived here most of my life.'

He told me that his dad had been born in Woolacombe but had moved the family to Bournemouth for a better outlook.

'I grew up and moved back,' he said. 'I like to say that I had a look at the rest of the world, didn't like it as much, and came back.' He let out a bark of a laugh. 'Can I take a bit to show my wife?'

'Sure,' I said. There was plenty of fumitory.

He snapped off a sprig with a couple of leaves and a tuft of flowers.

'Purple ramping-fumitory?' he asked.

'Purple ramping-fumitory,' I replied.

He set off walking, occasionally waving the sprig in the air and calling over his shoulder back to me a triumphant, 'Purple ramping-fumitory!'

CHAPTER 10

Back from the Dead: York Groundsel

A couple of days after finding the purple ramping-fumitory in Devon, and a day after stopping off to look for an endemic whitebeam with a fantastic name (which I'll tell you about later), I was in Wales, navigating my way along twisting country roads. The species I was looking for was a bit different this time; it was an endemic that no longer existed in the wild.

As I drove, my eyes kept flicking to the rear-view mirror. Part of this was the typical due-care-and-attention such meandering routes require, but part was to keep an eye on my precious cargo in the back of my car. You see, for the past few months I had been the guardian of one of the rarest species on the planet, an endemic plant found only on a single roadside on the outskirts of Cambridge – or, at least, it *had* been found there.

Well, I say 'species'. In fact, this plant is a hybrid – an organism formed by the crossbreeding of two different species. What's more, it was a hybrid that had emerged in the wild and had never been found anywhere else on the planet other than this single unprepossessing suburban verge. It is thus an 'endemic hybrid'. What's more, no one knows what it is a hybrid *of* – its parentage shrouded in mystery like that of an illegitimate prince.

It's worth reviewing the whole story. About 20 years earlier a strange-looking comfrey was spotted on the verge of Barton Road in Cambridge. Comfreys are a delightful group of plants, some ankle-height, some head-height, often with soft, felty leaves. The flowers are arranged in an ammonite-like spiral with open bell-like flowers at the outer edge and tight buds at the centre. They come in a wide variety of colours depending on the species: snowy white, rich cream, sky blue, blackcurrant purple. In some species the colour changes as the buds mature; the inner whorls of the 'ammonite' in Russian comfrey can be a deep wine red that end up opening into flowers of watery violet blue.

Most of the comfrey lining the footpath on Cambridge's Barton Road is the white comfrey, *Symphytum orientale*, a species introduced to Britain from Russia as an ornamental plant in 1752 and first recorded as escaping into the wild in the mid-1800s. It grows to hip height and has, as the name suggests, clean white flowers that have a certain tissue-like airiness to them. It was amongst the white comfrey that the unusual comfrey was spotted – similar in shape and stature, but with flowers delicately tipped and streaked with gentle flushes of mauve and baby blue. The flowers remind me of that old chromatography experiment that everyone did at school where you dipped paper in ink and saw how far the different pigments would rise and separate out. In this case, the petal tips retained the mauve, with the blue extending above and subtly graduating into white.

It matched no known species of comfrey and, when some of it was grown in cultivation, it was noted that it never produced any seed (sterility is a common symptom of hybridity). As it grew amongst white comfrey and was structurally similar, it seems very likely that white comfrey is one of the parent species. The other comfrey parent, however, remains a mystery.

This year I was inspired by Alan Leslie to visit the site again. Back in April, after our day of searching for goldilocks buttercups, he'd asked if I knew about it. I told him I did. He asked if I was going to write about it and said, 'Today's endemic hybrids are tomorrow's endemic species.' Keep this quote in mind; we'll come back to it later.

In May, when the comfrey should have been flowering, I returned to Barton Road with my friend Lisa Jones, whose sister Emma had joined me a couple of months earlier on the hunt for the Pertenhall goldilocks. Lisa and I met while we were both working at the RSPB and, despite our radically divergent opinions on the beauty of certain flowers (I've been known to go on long impassioned descriptions of the wonder of a species to which Lisa will flatly reply 'it's a tiny white flower'), but she's always up for joining me to look for a species, especially if it involves a long walk.

I had seen the Barton Road comfrey once before, in 2021, when a single clump was flowering merrily near a bench and a rickety garden fence swathed in ivy. As we pulled up it was clear that something was dramatically different. The ivy-covered panels, the tangled verge with its swathe of white comfrey, all gone. Instead, there was a brand-new fence, so new that the air still held the sharp tang of freshly cut wood. The vegetation had been strimmed down to bare earth. I walked the full length of the new fence, trying to remember exactly where the Barton Road comfrey had been, a fruitless exercise as it was clear that there wasn't a single comfrey left standing, white or otherwise. As I walked back, I found Lisa jumping on the spot, vainly trying to see if by some chance an offshoot of comfrey was growing beyond the fence. No joy. If it truly was gone, it meant that the Barton Road comfrey now no longer existed in the wild.

We were downcast, but thankfully this isn't the end for the comfrey. Directly across the road was the red-brick building of St Mark's where, deliberately planted in the shrubbery opposite the glass entryway to the church, grew what was, as far as I knew, the only Barton Road comfrey left on the planet.

Here some conservation-minded soul had cultivated a piece of the mystery comfrey, accompanied by a sign:

> HYBRID COMPREY
> symphytum x perringianum
> Only known site in the world
> **PLEASE DO NOT DESTROY**

It could perhaps have done with a proofread, but the sentiment was beautiful.

With the permission of the church, and as delicately as possible, I divided the clump with a trowel and planted part of it in a terracotta pot, leaving the rest in the church flowerbed. I named it Connie, Connie the Comfrey.

Over the next few months Connie toured the country, spending a week with Lisa's family in Bedfordshire, a week with my parents in Yorkshire, and the rest of her time in Lincolnshire with me. I obsessed over this plant. To begin with she looked a bit sad and wilted, and it was with my heart in my mouth that I trimmed away a few leaves that were dying off. Thankfully, after a few weeks, she put out a couple of new leaves and I could sleep easy again. My plan was not to keep Connie for myself – my nerves couldn't stand the pressure of having such a rarity in my constant care – but instead get her to an expert.

And so, here I was in mid-June, Connie in the back of the car as I navigated to Andy Shaw's plant nursery. Alex Prendergast had put me in contact with Andy after our dandelion day, telling me that he had just performed a botanical near-miracle: reviving an endemic species from total global extinction.

I'd been on the road with Connie for over a week at this point. When I was slithering around underground looking for shrimp, she was sunbathing on the porch of a caravan; when I was on my voyage to Lundy, she was left in the care of a very kind Airbnb Host; as I explored the back streets of Woolacombe for fumitories, she sat and waited in the footwell. In all that time she had only fallen over in the car twice (on tight bends) and I didn't begrudge her the soil she'd left matted into the footwell.

Squinting at the road ahead I spotted the turn-off I was looking for and bumped down a track between verdant hedges that led towards a sprawling farmhouse. Before I got there, I encountered a polytunnel and a man, Andy, standing alongside and waving. I wound down my window and he cheerfully and loudly directed me into a pull-in.

Andy founded and runs the Rare British Plants Nursery where he grows and conserves some of our rarest and most threatened species, securing them for the future and for use in scientific research, habitat restoration schemes and reintroduction projects. He's also interested in preserving oddities, like Connie. I knew she'd be in safe hands with Andy as he is something of a horticultural genius.

Once parked I got out, shook Andy's hand and thrust Connie at him. 'This is your responsibility now.'

Andy laughed and looked her over. 'So this is the Barton Road comfrey. What is there, one plant on a roadside?'

'Not anymore. One in a churchyard shrubbery and this one right here, as far as I know.'

Andy didn't seem fazed. He put Connie down by the hedge and said he'd deal with it later. I wasn't paying full attention, however, as I was distracted by a tall elegant blue flower straggling out of the hedgerow. It took me a moment to place it – Jacob's ladder! A species I was more used to seeing on limestone in the north of England. I commented on it to Andy, who smiled and said that the nursery collection often overspilled into the garden.

'I sometimes find plants – incredibly rare plants that would take a botanist's breath away to see in the wild – just growing like weeds in the flower beds.'

In fact, so many of Andy's rare plants have escaped into his garden, some so efficiently and in such quantity, that it's hard to understand why they are so rare in the wild.

He led me to his sprawling farmhouse and started making me a cup of tea. I was trying to maintain conversation as he rattled mugs and spoons, but I was incredibly distracted by a taxidermied wallaby staring blankly at me across the room. Eventually, unable to continue without acknowledging it, I said, 'Andy, there's a stuffed wallaby in your kitchen.'

Andy looked up from the kettle to the wallaby and laughed. 'He doesn't say very much,' he offered, before returning to the tea. No further explanation was forthcoming.

Near the window there was what looked to be a tree in a pot. At a second glance I realised it wasn't a tree at all, but I had no idea what it was. Andy came over and thrust a mug of tea into my hands and looked at the plant.

'*Titan arum*,' he said. 'You know, the one that grows those huge smelly flowers? I want to be the first person to get one to flower outside a botanic garden.'

Andy's passion for nature clearly wasn't limited to British plants, a fact driven home when we went outside to drink our tea. As we sat in front of the farmhouse, we enjoyed a rambling conversation that went off at tangents every minute or so. Andy asked me about my endemic trips so far and I mentioned a few species. When I got to Celtic woodlouse Andy responded with a story of his own about spending seven hours searching for the rare woodlouse *Armidillidium pictum*. And then about how woodlice are now bred as 'fancy' woodlice in the pet industry. And how he had a giant deep sea isopod (basically a foot-long underwater woodlouse) preserved in a jar in his house. He had an unbelievable energy and enthusiasm for everything, it seemed, each conversational topic another opportunity for fractal tangents.

In a flash, an hour had passed, vanished in conversation about moth pheromones, the taxonomy of birches, breeds of chicken (a blind silkie sat in a hutch alongside us clucking warmly), before Andy got us back on topic.

'Right, you probably want to see the collection.'

We stood up, but our attention was captured by the meadow that was Andy's front lawn. It was thick and bright with herbs, yellow-rattle, eyebrights, patches of knapweed and the occasional purple smudge of an orchid. As I admired it, Andy pointed out that the yellow-rattle was actually greater yellow-rattle, a rare introduction in Britain, persisting in only a few sites. This was a harbinger of things to follow, the distinction between wild plants, garden plants and Andy's rare plant collection a delightful and colourful blur.

We stopped by a polytunnel which was filled with racks of white and pink flowers. The white was rock cinquefoil, a plant that I have never seen in the wild and in Britain is only found at four sites. The pink was sticky catchfly, another plant I had never seen, which only has around 18 populations across Britain. I cooed over them. There was something both utterly delightful and mildly frustrating about seeing these rarities laid out like this: delight in seeing something so rare and special, frustration that I wasn't seeing these plants in the wild. It's a strange feeling to be literally looking at, smelling, touching a plant and yet to be thinking, 'I wish I could see one of these ... ' – the silent word being 'properly'. I didn't voice this aloud, but I'd find out later that Andy had a similar view of such things.

Outside the next greenhouse was a flower bed with an eclectic mixture of plants – the cheerful pink blooms of thrift jostling with the wine-red flowers of some sort of woundwort, a tuft of creamy saxifrage amidst a sprawling growth of what looked to be herb-robert. I asked Andy to talk me through it. The thrift was 'tall thrift', a different subspecies to the thrift found on the coast and which, in Britain, is only found in and around a single cemetery in south Lincolnshire. The saxifrage was Irish saxifrage, but this plant was a descendant of the extinct Welsh population. The woundwort was limestone woundwort, found at only three sites in Britain. What I had thought was herb-robert was actually its smaller, rarer cousin, little robin.

'In fact', said Andy, delicately angling one of its cheerful pink flowers towards me, the anthers in the centre bright yellow, 'this one is probably of interest to you; this is the endemic subspecies.'

Little robin has two subspecies in Britain and Ireland. One is the common one found across southern Britain, Ireland and across Europe. The other, the endemic subspecies, is different in that rather than growing *up*, it grows *sideways*, hugging the ground. It is now only found, in the entire world, at the top of shingle beaches in Hampshire, having been lost from Sussex, Cornwall and Guernsey and never found anywhere else.

'Speaking of endemics', said Andy, brushing some vegetation aside, 'have a look at this.'

He pointed to a scrambling clump of a tiny-leaved plant, which, on closer inspection, had minute green flowers. I recognised this as rupturewort, having seen smooth rupturewort before, but I guessed that this must be fringed rupturewort, which in Britain is represented by the endemic subspecies *ciliolata* found only in Cornwall and Guernsey.

'That's right,' said Andy. 'If you looked at the leaves through a hand lens, you'd see a little fringe of hairs along the end of each leaf.'

I could go on to describe in lavish detail each and every plant in Andy's collection: the purple coltsfoot that grew like a weed on the floor of one of his greenhouses; the pot of darnel being used as a host by field cow-wheat; the tank of Jersey fern; the alpine blue sowthistle ... each an amazing species with its own fantastic backstory, often perilously rare and with an additional chronicle of how Andy came to have it growing in his collection. Suffice to say, his nursery is enough to leave a botanist in paroxysms. But I will restrain myself, and instead move onto the reason for my visit. I wanted to see the endemic that had returned from the dead.

Andy led me to another greenhouse and solemnly ushered me inside. My glasses misted briefly in the humidity, turning my view to a frosted blur of green and yellow. I wiped them on my shirt and put them back on. In front of me, on a workbench, sat a tray of plants that had been extinct – globally extinct – for the past 20 years. No one, other than Andy, had seen these flowers in the flesh since the turn of the millennium. This was a botanical *Jurassic Park* moment.

For a species that had been revived from the dead they looked tremendous; luxuriant glossy-green, jagged-forked leaves spilled over their pots, and several dozens of small sunshine-yellow flowers strained upwards. Some flowers had finished and turned into tiny fluffy pom-poms of feathery seeds, like miniature dandelions. Andy started gently plucking these and placing the seeds into a screw-top pot.

These were York groundsel, *Senecio eboracensis*, a plant species that probably evolved in York and was weedkillered to extinction within a single human lifespan. However, the real beginning of the York groundsel story starts in Sicily, in the early 1600s.

The Oxford Botanic Garden was founded in 1621, and in the following years received plants from across the known world. Amongst them was a cheerful yellow flower from the slopes of Mount Etna in Sicily. This plant seemingly lived happily in the gardens for a century or more but eventually jumped the fence and was recorded growing on walls around Oxford by 1792. It became known, despite its Sicilian origins, as 'Oxford ragwort' and was named by Linnaeus himself, the father of taxonomy, as *Senecio squalidus*. Over the next century and a half, aided by the industrial revolution's expanding railway network, it spread to most parts of England and became established in Scotland in the 1950s. The first record of Oxford ragwort in York came in 1938, where it is now an established part of the city's flora.

Here, it met up with our native groundsel, *Senecio vulgaris*. These plants look very different from each other. Oxford ragwort has banana-yellow flowers with sprays of petals like a little marigold. Groundsel has much more subtle flowers that are petalless; they look like a short, neat green tube with a tiny fluffy dome of yellow at the tip. It is generally smaller overall, and, while its leaves are a bit dissected and jagged, Oxford ragwort's are much more so. These species are different enough as to be difficult to confuse. Despite that, when they meet up, they occasionally hybridise and produce something broadly midway between them – something that grows small flowers with petals and leaves of intermediate jaggedness. And, like the Barton Road comfrey, this hybrid, *Senecio x baxteri*, is sterile.

Hybrids are often unable to reproduce because their parents have different numbers of chromosomes. Let's take humans as an example of the process working properly; we have 23 pairs of chromosomes for a total of 46. Half of these come from your mum (the egg cell), half from your dad (the sperm cell). If you have a child, you'll give half – 23 – of your chromosomes to them.

Oxford ragwort has 20 chromosomes, of which it gives 10 to its offspring. This is fine if its partner is another Oxford ragwort also giving 10, but if the other partner is groundsel, which has 40 chromosomes and provides 20 of them to its offspring, then you end up creating a hybrid with 30 chromosomes. The offspring, *Senecio x baxteri*, can live like this, but it can't reproduce itself because – and this is where it gets very science heavy and so I'll simplify – the 30 chromosomes can't neatly pair up and split to produce sex cells, the pollen and ovules.

However, in York, something unusual must have happened when these species hybridised. One theory is that the Oxford ragwort parent *didn't* split its chromosomes in half, instead providing the full 20. The groundsel parent still provided half of its chromosomes, which is also 20. The result? Fertile offspring with 40 chromosomes. The plants were intermediate between their parent species and began breeding amongst themselves rather than with either of their parent species. In essence, a new species evolved in a few simple – but incredibly unlikely – steps.

This new species was first spotted in 1979 on waste ground by York railway station by Richard Abbott and Andrew Lowe, who later described it. In 1991 the population across all the York sites was estimated at 250 individuals, and in 1993 a peak count of 56 plants was made at one location. At this point it seemed that this brand-new endemic species was gaining a foothold, but this unfortunately wasn't to last. Two of the sites were built on and redeveloped, and the city in general was liberally dosed with shameful amounts of weedkiller. In 2000 only 11 plants were found – the last individuals of York groundsel ever seen in the wild. Thankfully, a number of seeds were collected and sent to the Millennium Seed Bank, and by sheer bewildering coincidence the year chosen to revive the species was the year I was exploring endemics.

This method of speciation (the process through which new species split off from existing species) happens more often than you might think. Britain has historically been home to small cord-grass, *Spartina maritima*, a grass of tidal mud flats. Some 200 years ago the American smooth cord-grass, *Spartina alterniflora*, was accidentally introduced to Britain. This species hasn't spread or become invasive and it is pretty much found in the same places today as when it first arrived two centuries ago. However, it does hybridise with our native small cord-grass, producing a sterile intermediate known as Townsend's cord-grass. At some point one of these hybrids must have mistakenly duplicated its genome, allowing it to regain fertility and become a species in its own right, common cord-grass, *Spartina anglica*, which went on to become vastly more widespread in Britain than either of its parents. It was also, for a time, endemic to Britain, but has since been planted widely across Europe and beyond.

This is what Alan Leslie meant by 'Today's endemic hybrids are tomorrow's endemic species.' What looks like a quirk, a dead end, like the sterile Barton Road comfrey, could, one day, by some fluke, produce a fertile seed leading to an entirely new endemic species.

Andy was still collecting seeds, pinching those fluffy seedheads between his thumb and forefinger and popping the resulting tuft of seeds into a half-full pot.

'I do this twice a day', he told me, 'morning and evening. I must have 100,000 seeds by now, all earmarked for reintroducing it back into York. I'm working with local landowners to find sites, little scraps of waste ground, that I can sow the seed on. I hope that it'll then naturally seed itself, spread by the wind and passing traffic, in suitable habitat around the city.'

I held a flowerhead between my fingers, narrower and more delicate than that of Oxford ragwort. I grew up in Yorkshire, less than an hour from York, and so this endemic in particular had caught my attention. A plant that evolved in York, was named after York, never found anywhere else but York, and yet lost before I got a chance to see it. I was desperate to see it returned.

'Can you let me know when you're doing the reintroduction?' I asked.

Andy slapped me on the back. 'Absolutely! You need to come *write* about it! Now, do you want to see my collection of endemic whitebeams?'

After admiring Andy's grove of endemic whitebeams – composed of 16 species and an endemic hybrid, Motley's whitebeam, which is now thought to be extinct in the wild – I tore myself away. My appetite was now well and truly whetted for finding my own endemic whitebeams in a few days' time, and I was ready to head off.

What I'd thought would have been a visit lasting a couple of hours to see Andy's York groundsel had turned into a full-day experience that surpassed any actual botanical garden. Kew Gardens? Eden Project? Nah, Andy's nursery had them all beat, not least for it concentrating on tangible, local (as in British and Irish) plant conservation.

As I'd been leaving, Andy had given me a bit of valuable information. A week earlier he had been to Chirk and had checked up on another endemic species, the Welsh groundsel. Perhaps I'd be interested in seeing it on my way home? I checked my route. It barely added any distance, and so I jotted down some notes as Andy gestured at a map.

The Welsh groundsel is, in a sense, a cousin to the York groundsel. Remember earlier when I mentioned that Oxford ragwort and common groundsel can hybridise to produce the sterile *Senecio x baxteri* with 30 chromosomes? Well, at some point, probably a little over a century ago, one of these sterile hybrids must have made a mistake and somehow produced seeds with double the number of chromosomes – a full 60. These then grew into plants that were fully fertile, their chromosomes able to neatly pair up into 30 evenly matched sets.

It has the same parents as York groundsel, but has different amounts of genetic material from each, resulting in a plant that, though similar to York groundsel, is distinctly different. Taller plants, bigger flowers with more petals, and leaves less dissected and more lobed at the tip. The first herbarium collections of it – at the time not recognised as a new species – were made in 1925 but it was 1948 before it was acknowledged as a new species and 1955 that it was formally named as *Senecio cambrensis*, acknowledging its uniqueness to Wales, it having only ever been found in Denbighshire and Flintshire.

In 1974 a new population was discovered in Edinburgh that – and I, quite frankly, find this utterly bizarre – had *independently* evolved. As in, the Edinburgh Welsh groundsel population hadn't come from Wales, but had instead arisen in exactly the same way from a hybrid between Oxford ragwort and common groundsel that then underwent chromosome duplication. The *same* species evolving *twice* in *two different places*. Unfortunately, the Edinburgh population was ill-fated, and this lineage went extinct by 1993 for similar reasons to the York groundsel – sites being built on and general over-tidiness – meaning that the Welsh groundsel is once again a solely Welsh species.

I arrived in Chirk, a town that touches the border with England. Despite this, no Welsh groundsel has ever been seen just over the boundary in neighbouring Shropshire, even though it's only half a mile from where plants are regularly found.

I pulled up on a quiet lane called Wern just off the main road, the B5070, and walked north. Andy had told me that along the base of this hedge, bordering the path by the side of the main road, he had seen Welsh groundsel a week earlier, growing up from the patchy bare earth rich with the other wildflowers of disturbed urban places – Jack-by-the-hedge, cranesbills, dandelions and speedwells.

As I walked, my hopes sank. Instead of a verdant hedge bottom filled with flowers all I could see was curling, yellowing foliage. Some heartless maniac had sprayed weedkiller along the verge. I walked further, hoping to find an edge to this pointless carnage, but the entire length of the hedge had been sprayed, the flowers at the base crisped yellow and dead. I crossed the road, vainly trying along the unscathed verge on the west of the road but found nothing, this shadier side perhaps less suitable for the Welsh groundsel.

Despite an hour's search I saw no sign of the Welsh groundsel, one of Wales' utterly unique species. This modern obsession with tidiness, the sloshing of literal poison to curtail the growth of ambitious flowers, was part of what led to the loss of the York groundsel. It seemed that the people of Chirk were unaware of their own special flower and the uncertain future it faced. Perhaps, if they knew, they might feel more protective of this unique part of their natural heritage.

I left with a heavy heart, but reminded myself that if Andy can bring a species back from the dead, then surely we can inspire people to cherish and protect both of our unique groundsels.

CHAPTER 11

Roadsides and Seasides: No Parking and Menai Strait Whitebeams

I don't think I'm meant to have favourites. I *shouldn't* have favourites. Every endemic species I see is unique, special and with their own individual storied history filled with discovery and excitement. That said, if I *were* to have favourites, *theoretically*, then they might be the whitebeams.

Whitebeams are a group of trees in the genus *Sorbus*. They are small- to medium-sized, the largest growing to around 15m, with many others staying as compact bushy trees. The number of accepted species is in flux, with at least 100 and perhaps even 200 found across the northern hemisphere, occurring in temperate Europe, North America, Asia and North Africa. There are 40-something species in Britain, depending on whether you count ornamental whitebeams escaping into the wild, plus a number of hybrids.

Tim Rich's list of endemic species included 34 whitebeams found only in Britain. Despite the number of them, they are not evenly spread across Britain, whitebeams seemingly preferring areas of beautiful scenery – Bristol's Avon Gorge, Cheddar Gorge, the North Devon coast, the Wye Valley and the Isle of Arran.

With so much choice, how was I ever going to pick one of these as my target? Still, the decision needed to be made. I picked two species that I went and visited in June, one that I saw in Devon the day after seeing the purple-ramping fumitory, and one in Wales the day after meeting Andy and his York groundsel. That was meant to be it… but I found whitebeams so fascinating that I ended up making a third trip, which I'll come back to in a few chapters' time.

I'm a sucker for a species with a bizarre name, and so when I first learned about *Sorbus admonitor*, the 'no parking whitebeam', I knew that I had to see it one day. There are herbarium specimens of this tree from the Watersmeet area of North Devon all the way back from 1865, but it was only named as a distinct species in 2009.

The reason it took such a long time to be named is that there is another similar whitebeam called the Devon whitebeam, *Sorbus devoniensis*, which as the name suggests is found in Devon … with a few trees in Cornwall. And Somerset. And Ireland. It's a British and Irish endemic that could perhaps have been better named.

The no parking whitebeam, in contrast, *is* only found in Devon. Specifically, the Watersmeet–Lynmouth area in North Devon, where it's found in six adjoining 1km squares and nowhere else on the planet.

Despite not being named until this millennium, people have suspected for a long time that the trees here were something different, as they had leaves with sharper and deeper lobes than those of the more widespread Devon whitebeam. In the 1939 *Flora of Devon* a tree of this sort was specifically mentioned as growing by a car park at Watersmeet with a 'No Parking' sign nailed into the trunk.

This very tree was re-investigated in 2007 and formed the 'holotype' – the individual used to describe and define this new species. By this point the 'No Parking' sign had gone, but the name stuck. The scientific name of this species, *Sorbus admonitor*, comes from the same Latin origins as 'admonish'; this is the tree that tells you off (for parking violations).

As far as I knew, 15 years on, this original tree was still in existence; there's a picture of it in *BSBI Handbook 14: Whitebeams, Rowans and Service Trees of Britain and Ireland*. Whoever took the picture must have had a sense of humour as the angle they've chosen includes a sign off to one side that must be a spiritual successor to the original, which reads:

> The National Trust
> Staff Car Park
> Please do not park here

The tree and the location are still clearly closely attuned to each other.

The road down to the car park at Watersmeet is narrow and winding, halfway up a steep wooded valley. On Google Maps I could see that I was closing in on the pin that I thought marked the location of the tree. Then, there it was, on my left, next to a pull-in with enough space for three or four cars, surrounded by a drystone wall and with a steep drop-off beyond. In the corner stood a venerable-looking whitebeam. I parked my car off to one side in the shade – it was a blazing June day – and got out.

The tree in the corner looked different to the one in the book. Holding the relevant page in front of me, I walked until I was standing exactly where the photo had been taken. It was clear that the intervening years had exacted a heavy toll. Where the tree pictured in the book had two stout trunks, now only one remained, the left-hand trunk snapped and gone. The tree in the photo was verdant and leafy, whereas the one I was standing in front of had half its branches angled bare into the sky.

I got closer. There was a great hollow in the trunk at chest height, and at some point whoever was fixing the drystone wall had walled straight into this cavity; the tree, the wall, and the rocky hills all merging into one another. Craning, I could see a glimpse of clear, blue sky where this hollow breached the trunk, and ivy twined through its heart. The original no parking whitebeam was a tree in decline.

And yet, it was in leaf, and there were young branches springing up from near its base. This tree was fighting all the way down. Its leaves were beautiful. I don't know if it's this species or just the quality of light on that perfect day, but they were a truly mesmerising emerald green, shining with a gentle matt haze in the bright summer sun. They were also aggressively jagged, giving the no parking whitebeam a ferocious look to back up its assertive name.

Stepping back, I framed the shot, aiming for the same angle as in the book. As I did I noticed that the 'Staff Parking' sign from the book photo had gone. Great, I thought, I can park and explore the woods from here.

With one of the trunks of the tree gone there's a view out to the steep hills at the other side of the valley, a carpet of woodland broken up with grey patches of bare scree or sheer rocky slopes. These woodlands around Watersmeet are one of the most important sites for whitebeams in Britain, being home – according to the BSBI whitebeam book – to 108 of the 110 no parking whitebeams known, 270 of the slender whitebeams (out of an estimated global population of 300), and 28 of the bloody whitebeam (out of a global total of 70 trees). I wanted to find all three.

I followed a path that led steeply downhill from the corner of the car park by the no parking whitebeam. It was lined with the lilac flowers of thyme-leaved speedwell and the yellow trumpets of cow wheat, mixed with the occasional mini pom-pom flowerhead of sanicle. There was a lot of oak and ash in these woods, some with laddered fronds of polypody climbing over their branches. A green woodpecker laughed somewhere in the distance.

By a fallen oak trunk, I paused to refresh my memory on the two other whitebeam species I was searching for. The slender whitebeam, *Sorbus subcuneata*, also known as the 'Somerset whitebeam' — a curious name given that majority of the world population is in Devon — is best identified by its leaves. Unlike the no parking whitebeam's broader leaves, the slender whitebeam's are long and pinched, sharply lobed and forward-swept, nearly twice as long as they are wide.

The leaves of the bloody whitebeam, *Sorbus vexans*, according to the silhouettes in the book, totally lack the lobes (sharp or otherwise) shown by the no parking and slender whitebeams and are a simpler shape overall. In outline, they are almost an oval, but narrowed into an acute angle where they join the petiole (the leaf's 'stem').

According to the book the leaf is distinctly white below, as many whitebeams are. This is where the name 'whitebeam' comes from, most of them having leaves that are distinctly white below making the overall tree sometimes strikingly pale. 'Beam' is old English for tree; it's a 'white tree'.

As for its epithet of 'bloody', this refers to its blood-red fruits, distinctly unlike the greenish fruits of the no parking whitebeam or the orange-brown fruits of slender whitebeam. Its scientific name, *vexans*, means annoying (think 'vexing') and it was named this by Edmund Warburg in 1957 because of the awkward task he faced in separating it from other, similar species. This makes me wonder if 'bloody' *really does* refer to the fruits, or whether this is a joke from Warburg.

I carried on down into the valley. I passed gorse, smelling the distinctive coconut scent of its flowers, and sheets of great woodrush carpeting the steep woodland floor. A goldcrest sang its high, spiralling song in the trees above, and I heard the gentle hushing of the river in the base of the valley.

The path began to flatten out as it reached the riverside, but just before it did, I spotted a young no parking whitebeam sapling, its trunk only finger-thick and barely a metre tall, arcing towards the path, reaching out of the dappled shade towards the light above the river. This tree was presumably too young to be one of the 108 no parking whitebeams known from here 10 years ago. It was good to see that the population was reproducing and sustaining itself. The original tree, up the slope, may have been worse for wear, but down here a young tree was thriving.

I walked along the river, which gurgled merrily alongside me, and reached a hump-backed stone bridge with a plaque – Chiselcombe Bridge, as it was called, opened in 1957 to replace an 'ancient bridge' lost to flooding. Alongside it grew another no parking whitebeam, its branches entwined with the long, spiked leaves of wych elm. If you ever want to see a no parking whitebeam yourself, I recommend this one. Find the bridge and the tree is right next to it.

Across the bridge was a patch of scree with a twisted rowan and a tangle of wild strawberries. I took a few minutes to gather a palmful, warm from the sun, and savoured the brief tang of flavour of each one as I walked. The path rose above the river and for a short while I just enjoyed my foraged palmful of fruit and the greenish shade of the trees.

The *zit-zit* call of a dipper hooked my attention and as I craned through the trees to the river to spot it, I suddenly noticed that one of the trees I was trying to peer past was a whitebeam. Despite being rooted down the slope from me, it towered far above where I was standing so I swung my binoculars upwards to take a look. The leaves were jagged and toothed and *possibly* slender. But they were high above me and, despite fluttering only very gently in the breeze, I just couldn't be sure. But if there was one then there had to be more, right? I turned and scanned the slope above me. Hazel, oak, rowan ... a whitebeam!

The slope was so steep that I needed to grasp tree roots and dig my hands into the earth to haul myself up. After a few minutes of struggle, I reached my goal and propped myself up against the trunk of a supportive oak to stop me from tumbling back down the incline. I drank in the whitebeam. It was a five-trunked monster of a tree, all of similar girth and forging upward from a common set of roots. The majority of leaves were far distant above me in the shimmering green canopy, but a few lower branches were within grabbing range.

Bending a whippy branch down it was obvious to me that this was a slender whitebeam; the leaves were slim, tapered, forming an acute angle before joining the petiole. In the dappled sunshine these leaves were a bright lime green and delicately translucent; shadows from the foliage showing crisply through them, like the screen of a shadow theatre. They seemed thinner and softer than the leaves of the no parking whitebeam, but that could have been because this tree was growing in woodland shade rather than the full sun of the no parking whitebeams I'd seen so far.

After taking some photos, I trotted inelegantly back down the slope like a stumbling pony. Almost immediately around the next bend in the path was another slender whitebeam, right next to the path and easy to reach. Of course.

An hour or so slipped by as I wandered, catching sight of a grey wagtail on the river, discovering more slender whitebeams, and crossing another bridge. Beneath the crystal water, a whole tree stump lay submerged, draped in a faint fuzz of weed that gently undulated with the current. But as for the elusive bloody whitebeam? Nowhere to be seen.

Eventually, I meandered my way back to where I'd parked. That was when I saw it. Nailed to the fence on the other side of my car was a very obvious and quite new 'no parking' sign. I'd been so distracted by the tree I hadn't seen it. *Oops.* I sheepishly returned to my flagrantly parked car, nodding to the venerable no parking whitebeam in the corner. I have the feeling the trees won't hold it against me, though.

The rarest of the whitebeams I was looking for, the bloody whitebeam, had evaded me. With a world population of 70 trees and only 28 of them here, I was perhaps a bit ambitious to assume I could just turn up and hope to stumble across one. It was apparent that *Sorbus vexans* absolutely lives up to its name.

Though the Watersmeet whitebeams are rare, they are not actively threatened. Sure, by having a small population they could, theoretically, be more susceptible to awful one-off disasters – fire, landslips or other stochastic events – but they live in a protected area and their populations are steady. The same cannot be said for all of our whitebeams.

A few days after seeing the no parking whitebeam, and the day after meeting Andy and the York groundsel, I found myself in north Wales. I was heading for the Great Orme to see its endemic cotoneaster when an idea wormed its way into the back of my mind. There was another endemic whitebeam found along the shore of the Menai Strait, the narrow strip of sea separating Anglesey from the Welsh mainland.

This hadn't been part of my original itinerary because by this point I had foolishly imagined that I would have seen 'enough' whitebeams – I hadn't accounted for the sheer, seductive siren song of *Sorbus*. These trees of crags, gorges, cliffs and islands carve out their lives where other trees struggle, shaping themselves into endemic jigsaw pieces to slot into slivers of suitable habitat, niches so specialised that their global populations number only tens of individuals.

The night before my journey to Anglesey was thus spent sending hurried messages on social media and hoping for the best, and the best came through. Robbie Blackhall-Miles is a conservation horticulturist, owner of a very small, and accredited, 'backyard' botanic garden where he grows ancient lineages of plants from around the world, and the person leading on the conservation of the Menai Strait whitebeam, which he agreed to introduce me to the next day.

The following morning I got up and drove along the coast until I reached the Menai Bridge. Instead of crossing to Anglesey I carried on a few hundred metres further along the coast where I encountered some baffling roadworks, which sent me sailing straight past the meeting point clearly described to me by Robbie. More confused than frustrated, I swung the car round in the mouth of an empty junction and tried again. This time fortune was on my side; the lights were already green and I managed to nose my way down a nearly invisible track and along to a small parking area by some fenced-off football fields. *Phew*.

I expected Robbie to be waiting for me. Perhaps even waiting impatiently – after all, I'd organised this with him at the last minute and now here I was showing up late. Fortunately, the car park was empty, which silenced my catastrophising, and a few minutes later another car pulled in.

This was Robbie, and he looked every inch the botanist-adventurer: dressed in shades of green, long hair, a wooden oak-leaf pendant round his neck and sporting oil-slick sunglasses. He also had a dog with him.

'This is Rolo,' he said, once we'd introduced ourselves. 'He's not mine, I'm just looking after him for the moment.'

Rolo panted up at me welcomingly.

It was only a short walk from where we'd parked to get onto Nantporth Nature Reserve, a site managed by the North Wales Wildlife Trust. The reserve is a narrow sloping woodland, which stretches a kilometre along the shore of the Menai Strait. I followed Robbie through the winding and occasionally steep paths, passing common spotted orchids, luxuriant green fountains of hart's-tongue ferns and twining black bryony.

As we walked Robbie gave me the potted history of Cerddin Menai, the Menai Strait whitebeam. The earliest specimens traced in herbarium collections are from the 1870s, so botanists clearly recognised it as something subtly different to common whitebeam early on, but it wasn't formally named as a new species. In the 1950s the trees were mooted as being examples of the grey-leaved whitebeam, an identification that stood until the 1990s when they were shown to be more similar to both round-leaved whitebeam and Irish whitebeam. Further studies showed them to be closest to Irish whitebeam (which is endemic to Ireland) but they have different chromosome numbers. It was only in 2014, more than a century after being noticed as something different, that they were fully described as *Sorbus arvonicola*. Or, err, *Sorbus arvonensis* – both names seem to be used interchangeably. The BSBI uses *arvonicola* so I'll follow their lead. The scientific name *arvonicola* comes from the Welsh *Arfon*, which means 'facing Anglesey', with *icola* from the Latin meaning 'dweller'. It is the whitebeam that lives its life gazing across to Anglesey.

By this point in our walk, we had reached a set of steep mud steps that led out of the bottom of the woodland and onto a pebbly seashore dotted with clumps of weed, the tang of salt in the air. Ahead of us was the narrow sparkling band of sea separating mainland Wales from Anglesey, the latter's shore and few small islands only a few hundred metres away. To our left, in the distance, the Menai Strait Bridge arched across the water.

Robbie reached up to a tree next to the base of the steps we've just walked down and plucked a leaf. It was a whitebeam.

'Is this it?' I ask, eagerly.

'No', said Robbie, 'common whitebeam, but it'll be good for comparison when we do see one.'

He briefly ran through how this and the Menai Strait whitebeam differ. Both species have leaves that are toothed around the edges, but the common whitebeam's leaves are subtly lobed – the margin of the leaf sort of undulates in and out rather than tracing a neat line as the Menai Strait whitebeam does. It seems like a feature that might be hard to spot, but I took Robbie's word that it's not as tricky as it sounds.

With our comparison leaves in hand we walked along the top of the shore, following the crumbling concrete sea wall and accompanied by the occasioning piping calls of oystercatchers. We didn't have to walk far. Only 5m or so along from the steps was our first Menai Strait whitebeam. Based on my recent experiences, I had developed an impression that our endemic whitebeams were species of gorges, cliffs and steep slopes and I had assumed the Menai Strait whitebeam would have at least been on some ledge overlooking the water. Instead, it sat just behind the sea wall.

This Menai Strait whitebeam was a small example, not much taller than me, but its abundant foliage stretching over the wall presented a great opportunity to compare with the common whitebeam leaves Robbie had grabbed on the way past. It is a reasonably subtle species to identify, but by holding a common whitebeam leaf alongside it the differences leapt out to me. That gentle lobing seen on a common whitebeam leaf is totally absent from the Menai Strait whitebeam. Also, the teeth running along the edge of the common whitebeam leaf are rounded – if the leaf could bite you, it would do you no harm. The Menai Strait whitebeam has fierce, pointy teeth like a baby shark.

'There are fewer than 40 of them,' Robbie told me. 'There's about 30 along this shore here. Another four south-west along the shore that way.' He pointed behind us. 'There's one on an island in the strait, and one known in a woodland on the Anglesey shore. That's it. That's the global population.'

I nodded. A few weeks ago these numbers would have astounded me, but having seen rarer whitebeams in Andy Shaw's collection – the Ley's whitebeam has around 17 trees left in the wild – I felt almost numb to it. I mentioned Ley's whitebeam to Robbie and he shook his head.

'There may be fewer of those, and so technically rarer than this,' he said, touching a branch of the tree, 'but those trees aren't as actively threatened as these.'

We continued walking along the shore as Robbie told me more about the pressures facing the Menai Strait whitebeam, Rolo snuffling among the rocks and seaweed ahead of us. The seawall petered out and beyond that the beach stretched up to a short, undefended mud cliff around a metre tall. The tide had clearly nibbled away at this bank, exposing twisted tree roots to the air and seawater. An entire birch had tumbled away from this shallow cliff, its rootball in a muddy clump on the shore, the trunk lying dead and bone white on the shingle.

'The water is eroding the bank,' Robbie told me, gesturing at the fallen tree and the other exposed roots along the top of the shore, 'and the majority of the world population of the whitebeam is growing along here. They all risk falling into the sea.'

'Hasn't that always been a problem?' I asked. 'They've presumably always been here and not all washed away.'

Robbie told me that he had worked with students from Bangor University to better understand threats to the species. They quantified the erosion from winter storms and took into account predictions of sea-level rise. With these factors it doesn't look like the Menai Strait whitebeam has long left at Nantporth. It's assumed that, historically, a slower pace of erosion gave more time for new trees to seed further back from the shore but now the rate of erosion means trees are being lost much faster than they can replace themselves.

'This is a species directly threatened by sea-level rise,' Robbie said. 'If we don't do anything then this could be the first species Britain loses as a result of climate change. It is critically endangered.'

As the Menai Strait whitebeam is an endemic, if Britain loses it then the world loses it too. It often seems like climate change is portrayed in the media as something happening 'over there', news reports of harrowing stories of flood, famine and heatwaves elsewhere in the world. But the Menai Strait whitebeam is a tree on the cusp of extinction, a species quite literally on our own shores demonstrating the insidious and creeping nature of global heating.

A little further along the shore there was a whitebeam that had tumbled onto the beach; a few forlorn roots still anchored it in the sea-chewed bank of soil. Its lower branches were garlanded with seaweed, but the upper branches were still alive and flowering, though with leaves browning and curling at the edges. It was a common whitebeam.

'Common whitebeam seems to be less salt tolerant than the Menai Strait whitebeam,' said Robbie. 'When *arvonicola* fall onto the shore like this they look healthier doing it.'

Sure enough, we soon found a Menai Strait whitebeam that had slumped out of the bank and onto the beach. The lower branches that rested on the beach were skeletal, but the upper branches were full of bright healthy leaves. There must be a genetic component to their ability to cope with exposure to the sea, another piece of evidence showing how distinct this species is from other whitebeams, how attuned it is to this vanishing habitat.

A boat chugged through the strait behind us. A few moments later there was a rhythmic slapping as its wake reached the shore.

'That's another problem,' said Robbie. 'There's more boat activity down here than ever before. If it's already a high tide and the water level is at the bank, then the additional impact of the wavelets from boats just erodes the cliff further.'

I asked Robbie what can be done.

'Right here? Not much. But we are considering planting trees on some of the islands in the strait.'

He also told me that he'd spoken with a road agency who are currently removing trees affected by ash dieback. The road verge is close enough to the natural range of the Menai Strait whitebeam to make sense as a place to put them. There's also suitable habitat further afield, along the coast, but there are no historical records of the tree ever being found there. Was it lost before anyone ever recorded it, or was it just never there? Should we be considering introducing this species into new sites if its habitat is being lost here?

These are questions at the heart of the philosophy of conservation. But in my opinion, if anthropogenic climate change is the problem then we have a duty to safeguard the species, even if that involves finding new homes for it outside its current range.

We walked until we reached the biggest Menai Strait whitebeam of the day. It had at least seven sturdy trunks that stretched a good 10m into the sky. Robbie told me that this was a 'mother tree'.

'Of the 30 or so whitebeams we have left, only seven of them are mother trees – the big, mature, fruiting trees.' The rest of the trees are sort of 'adolescents' – younger trees that aren't at full size, don't fruit heavily and are not yet contributing to the population in the way the mother trees do.

She was undoubtedly a beautiful tree. Long trunks that curved out from the central base and then straightened out towards the sky; the bark a taupe-brown and gently mottled with pale grey-green patches of lichen. The leaves had the classic whitebeam glow about them; it must be something to do with the way that sunlight filters through their downy undersides, but the leaves are vibrant lime green and somehow 'soft' at the same time. The precisely toothed leaves give the Menai Strait whitebeam a certain sharp neatness compared to the more fuzzy and billowing foliage of a common whitebeam.

She was also perched on the ledge of the mud cliff only a metre or so above the pebbly strandline. Robbie told me that at least a cubic metre of soil had washed out from under her since last year. Some of her roots were now bare to the air. How long before she tumbles onto the shore? How long before the rest of the mother trees do the same?

Robbie checked his watch. He'd very generously squeezed this walk with me into his diary and he and Rolo needed to head off. I thanked him for his time and knowledge, and for his efforts to save this tree for all of us. He gave me a modest half-smile at that and told me that I shouldn't hang around too much longer anyway; the tide would turn soon.

With that and a wave, he left me. I wandered along the shore a little further in the hope of finding my own Menai Strait whitebeam and proving to myself that I could recognise them. I passed a broken lobster pot and a raft of seaweed, marvelling again at how radically different this habitat was to Watersmeet.

I found an oak that had collapsed out of the bank onto the shore, and just beyond it a small whitebeam grew at the edge of a perilously undercut chunk of cliff. I scrambled over to it and immediately recognised it as a Menai Strait whitebeam, those sweeping toothy oval leaves now distinctive to me.

When I finished admiring it and turned away I realised the tide was rapidly on the way back in. I hustled along the beach, back towards the fallen whitebeams I'd seen earlier. By the time I reached them the water was already lapping around their dead lower branches and I had to awkwardly duck under their trunks to keep going. When I reached the sea wall there was only a couple of feet of upper shore remaining and I scurried along it like a sandpiper until I ran out of beach. I was only a few dozen metres away from the steps Robbie and I had originally walked down but there was no more shore left. Instead, I clumsily hauled myself over the sea wall and threaded my way through the trees until I reached the steps. Looking back along the shore I could see that the beach was gone, the water now at the base of the sea wall and the bank beyond.

Another passing boat sent a series of wavelets through the water and I watched them slap at the bank, the tide still rising. I hadn't appreciated until this moment the relentless regularity of the sea; this wasn't an impact felt only at spring tides, this was a twice-daily gnawing by the water at this narrow fringe of habitat, undercutting the last few Menai Strait whitebeams on the planet.

I hoped Robbie could find somewhere safe for them to go.

CHAPTER 12

Berry Good: Great Orme Berry and South Stack Fleawort

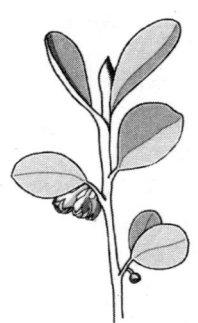

Because the tide had chased me away from the Menai Strait whitebeam so quickly, I still had hours to go before I needed to be on the Great Orme headland. This was fine with me, as it meant I could cross the Menai Strait and head to South Stack for a chance to find another bonus endemic.

There is something recursive about travelling to South Stack. You drive across Wales and head over the bridge onto Anglesey. You drive across Anglesey, reach the Cymyran Strait, and cross the bridge onto Holy Island. You drive across Holy Island, where a narrow channel of water separates you from South Stack and a bridge for foot traffic allows passage onto this final island.

I parked at RSPB South Stack. Despite the name, the reserve is on Holy Island and overlooks the rocky outcrop South Stack. The car park was busy, jam-packed with tourists here to enjoy the views, the weather and the birds. I triumphantly squeezed into the very last parking spot and then set out across the heathlands that carpet the clifftops.

These heaths were a riot of colour. The first light pink flowers of ling and the deep purples of bell heather were emerging, the white stars of heath bedstraw lined the edges of the paths, and yellow daubs of tormentil and blue puffs of sheep's-bit dotted the undulating ground. Despite the profusion of flowers, I was concerned. I'd mentioned to Robbie that if I had enough time, I might look for the South Stack fleawort and he ventured that mid-June might be too late to see it in flower. I hoped that perhaps a single one might be hanging on for me.

The South Stack fleawort is an endemic subspecies of the more widespread field fleawort. The field fleawort is found dotted across the chalky turf of southern England, 150 miles south-west of here, but the South Stack fleawort grows only on a few mildly acidic clifftops in north Wales. It also, despite the name, mostly grows on the cliffs of Holy Island *overlooking* South Stack, rather than on South Stack itself.

I followed the clifftop path, the sea a deep, glassy green below me, swelling around the rough spurs of rock rising above the water's surface. Here, out on the edge, grew cheerful tufts of thrift and low mounds of creamy-flowered sea campion. An unfamiliar wheezy cry caught my attention and I turned to see six black birds swoop past me in a loose flock. It took a moment – me being a creature of the east of Britain – for my brain to catch up. Chough!

Another seven birds materialised and soon the whole flock swept along the cliff-edge alongside me, showing off their long-fingered wings and curved, red beaks. I watched, spellbound by these magnificent crows, until the flock made their way along the cliffs and out of sight, their squeaky calls fading into the distance.

There was a boxy white building along the cliffs, crenellated like a castle with a stubby tower. This Victorian folly, Elin's Tower, is now an RSPB visitor centre and, passing by, I could see it was brimming with tourist families, some using the scopes at the window to view the little island of South Stack and its lighthouse a little way below us.

I was now definitely on those overlooking cliffs, and so I concentrated on my search. I'd seen field fleawort at a few sites in England before and so I had a sense of what I was looking for – a short erect stem that branches into a small number of yellow daisy-like flowerheads. I wandered back and forth, scouring the edge of the heath. Something yellow caught my eye and, hurrying over, I found that I had been deceived by a stem of goldenrod with a couple of flowers only just beginning to open. Maybe Robbie was right – maybe in the heat of May and June the flowers had finished earlier than I'd anticipated? But even then, the plants should still be here. They produce fluffy seedheads like a little dandelion, so surely they'd be visible. I broadened my search criteria and carried on. Nothing.

I spotted glittering emerald-green tiger beetles, purple-flowered mats of thyme, and the red succulent stems of English stonecrop bearing delicate white-pink flowers. Fleawort? No sign.

I had meandered back towards Elin's Tower in my vain, wandering search, and with my eyes to the ground I didn't spot the RSPB staff member sitting on a rock until I was almost right next to her. She was eating a sandwich and staring out to sea, but as I approached she met my eye and smiled.

'Looking for flowers?' she asked.

Clearly the RSPB have a fine-tuned sense of what their guests need. I told her that I was, and that I was specifically looking for the South Stack fleawort. She nodded, put the crust of her sandwich on the foil beside her, and pointed south down the cliffs, back the way I'd walked from originally, away from South Stack.

She told me she had seen a couple next to the path, right down towards the southern extent of the clifftop footpath. She added, 'They're dotted down the slopes of the cliffs too.'

Thanking her for her guidance, I made my way back from where I'd originally started and along a stretch of cliff that was new to me. Depending on the undulation of the path, South Stack was still occasionally visible behind me so I suppose these cliffs still technically 'overlook' it.

Then, there it was, right next to the path, just as described. It had finished flowering, as Robbie had foretold, but this was clearly what I was after. A rosette of surprisingly thick, fleshy leaves, dusted with a powdery, cobwebby substance. They were a fresh green, some tinged with purplish red around the edges. From the centre of the rosette grew a stout stem, 15cm tall, which forked neatly into three narrower stems, each topped with a fuzz of fluffy seeds like a little dandelion. I knelt down and took a photo of the plant, from an angle where South Stack could just about be seen as a blur in the distance with the sea stretching glassily to the horizon.

A thought occurred to me. When I visited Andy's plant nursery a couple of weeks ago, I mentioned that I was considering seeing the South Stack fleawort. Andy told me that he didn't have it in his collection but would like to. I hadn't considered it at the time – in my imagination I was going to see it in full, glorious flower – but now, face to face with a plant covered in seeds, an idea struck me: get a few seeds for Andy. I pulled a small glass tube from my pocket, gently plucked one seedhead's-worth of fluff and placed it inside.

Holding on to the hope that fleawort might still be flowering further along, I continued, the path crossing a short ditch where the vegetation was a little lusher. A hint of blue caught my eye, which revealed itself to be spring squill, a short, dusty-blue flower almost reminiscent of a tiny bluebell. Usually they flower in April and May, so seeing one in cheerful flower in mid-June was a treat – and perhaps a good omen. If a spring squill was still flowering, why not South Stack fleawort?

I peered down the sloping cliff-grasslands down from the ditch and was rewarded by the sight of another gone-over fleawort. Scanning with my binoculars, I spotted a couple more down the steep turf. Then, off to the left, a golden splash. I focused – a fleawort, in flower!

Moving quickly, I followed the path until I was directly above it. It was only a couple of metres off the path, but down a near 45-degree slope which terminated in a steep drop and – I peeked – a fall into rocks and foaming water. Hmmm. However, it *would* be sort of amusing to slide down a cliff and die whilst trying to get a good look at a rare flower, so on balance I decided it was worth attempting.

I sat on the side of the path and edged down the slope feet first, gripping my hands deep into the turf in case I slipped. I'll take this opportunity to say that I really don't recommend ever doing this. I am an idiot, you see. Shortly I got alongside the flower. As with the gone-over one I'd seen before, it had those thick, dusty, succulent-esque leaves and that stout, straight stem, terminating in a little trident-split with three flower-heads. One head was over, but the other two shone like little suns. Fleawort almost looks like the stereotypical child's drawing of a flower, an amber disk with a corona of a dozen crayon-yellow petals. The plant as a whole looked proud and sturdy, ready to brace itself against the brunt of maritime winds and clothed with that dusty fuzz to keep it warm.

It was also remarkable how different it looked to the field fleawort I'd seen on the chalk of Bedfordshire and Hertfordshire. I had half expected, given that it was *only* a subspecies of fleawort, that it might have only been so subtly different that I couldn't appreciate it. But to me, this plant looked surprisingly distinct: larger and stouter overall with thicker, fleshier leaves, and I don't recall seeing a fleawort on the chalk with such conspicuously downy leaves.

It was first discovered here in 1800, and in 1866 was formally described as something a bit different – as a 'variety' of field fleawort. It was only in 1974 that it was elevated to subspecies status, by none other than Arthur Chater, of Chater's bristletail fame. It was interesting to ponder why it isn't a full species in its own right – I've certainly seen different species that look more similar to each other than this and field fleawort, but it may be that the plants are shaped by the sea, climate and geology. Some species are 'plastic'; they can change how they look depending on where they're growing, influenced by environmental conditions. Or perhaps field fleawort and South Stack fleawort are simply two ends of a spectrum of variation?

In a sense, it's academic. The plants here, no matter their genetics, look and behave differently to the fleawort elsewhere. Species, subspecies, variety – it doesn't matter; we should be making sure to preserve the entire diversity and distinctiveness of populations of all species. This variation is where new species can emerge from; lose it, and we stymie the richness and future diversification of our fauna and flora.

I gently extracted my phone from my pocket and took some photos – bright, childish-yellow flowers against a bottle-green sea and an achingly blue sky – and managed not to slide off the edge of the cliff.

An hour later, driving down the North Wales Expressway, I spotted the limestone headland of the Great Orme projecting out into the sea like an enormous sea serpent. Don't take it from me, though; 'Orme' comes from the Viking word for serpent, snake or dragon.

This headland is a mile wide and a couple of miles long and its surface is dotted with limestone pavements and species-rich grasslands that boast mouth-watering natural history treats such as hoary rock-rose, spiked speedwell and goldilocks aster. Its cliffs are home to thriving, squawking colonies of kittiwakes, guillemots and razorbills, and it's one of only three sites in Britain for the exquisite silky wave moth. It is none of these delights that had drawn me here, though. Instead I was here to see one of the rarest species on the surface of the planet.

Despite my detour to South Stack, I was still too early to meet my expert. That wasn't a problem though, and I nosed my way through Llandudno and parked up as close as I could to the steep slopes of limestone grassland on the western side of the Orme where I could easily pass an hour or so amongst the flowers. It was another blazing day, and the shallow sea shone a pearly sapphire over the pale sands, the shadowed mountains of Eryri a backdrop across the bay.

As I got out of the car, I immediately found a dried-up slow worm at the side of the road. I don't see slow worms often enough – who does? – so even a dead one, especially one almost a foot long, is worth appreciating. In life slow worms have a very calm and stoic expression, but in death this one's mouth was drawn back, revealing a neat row of sharp, scimitar-curved teeth.

As I was crouching over the corpse, something caught the corner of my eye. A tiny jewel-blue butterfly flittered along the lane and landed on a flowering bramble. It struck me as unusual. Where I live, I only see two blue butterfly species regularly: the dusty-bluish holly blue and the shimmering-metallic common blue. This butterfly was noticeably smaller than either, but with the bluish intensity of a common blue. Could it just be a small one?

I got closer, being careful not to cast my shadow on it, but the butterfly either saw me or was fed up with the flower and shot off along the lane. I followed, walking past clumps of gravy-scented stinking iris, organ-purple flowers of hedge-woundwort and the delicate spikes of vervain. I saw several more tiny, enigmatic blues, but they were active and prolonged views were difficult. All I could determine was that the underside of the wings was *not* blue, eliminating holly blue. Instead, the underside had a grey-fawn ground colour, marked with scattered black spots and a smudgy crescent of orange blobs, like a common blue.

That's when it struck me, and I fumbled my phone out of my pocket to check. There is also the silver-studded blue, a species I've seen on heathlands in the south of England, but there was a faint memory of something else niggling in the dusty recesses of my mind.

Yes! A quick online search confirmed it. The Great Orme is home to a distinct population of silver-studded blues, *Plebejus argus*, that live on limestone grassland rather than heathland. They emerge a couple of weeks earlier than heathland ones, and they're much smaller, having wingspans in the range of 16–22mm, not overlapping at all with the 26–32mm of normal silver-studded blues. While elsewhere in the country silver-studded blues are strikingly sexually dimorphic, males being glittering blue and females chocolate brown, on the Great Orme the females have a distinctive scatter of metallic blue scales layered over warm brown. The butterfly found across most of Britain is represented by the subspecies *argus*, the same subspecies as found across Europe. On the Orme it's the same species, but of the endemic subspecies *caernensis* instead. Another bonus endemic!

I slipped my phone back into my pocket and walked uphill, working on the assumption that the scatter of blues I was seeing were wanderers from the sloping grassland above me.

Entering the grassland, I was confronted with a density of butterflies I have never experienced before. With each step I scattered a few from either side of the path, the crisply enamelled males and the midnight females darting away up the slope past the skeletal carline thistles and the purples of wild thyme.

It didn't take me long to find a few calmer examples resting on rock-rose, the foodplant of their caterpillars. Here a male and female sat with gleaming wings outstretched, and a third with wings closed hung from an arching grass stem. It was this butterfly that I focused on. The underwings were very like those of a common blue, black spots and orange splodges, but the silver-studded blue differs in that behind the orange dots are tiny patches – or 'studs' – of turquoise scales that glitter like crystals. This endemic was entirely restricted to the Great Orme until the 1940s when it was deliberately introduced to the Dulas Valley some eight miles away. Since then, it has slowly spread several miles along the valley and the total world population is now probably larger than at any point in the recorded history of the subspecies.

It was getting close to my meeting time, so I stood, scattering blues, and started descending the slope. I had almost reached the gate when another butterfly, far larger than the blues, swooped low and fast over the grassland. I carefully watched its movements and then, when it landed, scampered over to it. It was a grayling, doing its best to disguise itself against a small outcrop of limestone.

The grayling, *Hipparchia semele*, is a charismatic butterfly. It's typically the largest of our 'browns', larger even than the common and widespread meadow brown, with underwings mottled grey, brown and orange to perfectly blend into rocky or sandy habitats.

I've seen them before in the dunes of South Gare, North Yorkshire, where they proved masters of camouflage. They land and snap their wings shut, tilting them into the sun so that they don't even leave a shadow, appearing to vanish entirely. Even more excitingly, there's an endemic subspecies found only on the Great Orme, *Hipparchia semele* ssp. *thyone*.

In most of its populations, the grayling flies in July, August and into September. But here it can be seen as early as the first week of June. Like the silver-studded blue, it's a smaller subspecies. It's still a large butterfly, dwarfing the blues, but these Orme graylings can have wingspans up to a centimetre smaller than the typical widespread subspecies, *Hipparchia semele* ssp. *semele*.

As I watched, the grayling shyly lifted its upper wings, revealing their burnt-saffron undersides dotted with a single, staring eyespot. Then in a flash, it was gone, chasing across the rocky ridge after another grayling that dared stray too close to its territory.

I trotted back down to my car and set off towards the visitor centre on top of the Orme, delighted by my two bonus endemics. Both of these butterflies struck me with how markedly different they were from their 'mainland' forms. It's a shame that they're not more widely celebrated. Perhaps they need a snappy rebranding – instead of being dryly referred to as 'a subspecies of silver-studded blue endemic to the Great Orme' or a 'unique race of grayling found only here', they should become known as the 'Orme blue' and the 'Orme grayling'. Why is it that only 'full' species deserve their own vernacular names?

I made it up to the summit car park with five minutes to spare, and quickly rechecked my email from Sally. The warden of the Great Orme Country Park, Sally Pidcock had worked here for the past 26 years. There's probably no one that knows the Orme better, and almost certainly no one more intimately familiar with the exceptionally rare endemic found only on this headland. Her email read: *Come into the visitor centre, past the lantern, to the first unmarked yellow door.*

I walked around half the building, only now wondering what was meant by 'the lantern'. I was half expecting a wrought-iron Victorian-style lamp dangling from the edge of the building, but all I could see were a few cobwebby plastic security lights. I gave in and decided to head inside in search of further clues. Directly inside the doors of the visitor centre was a six-foot-tall lighthouse lantern on display. Ah.

I strolled past it and into the main visitor centre, spying a yellow door off to one side. I gave it a firm knock and the door was briskly opened by Sally. Behind the yellow door was an office with a couple of desks laden with paperwork. On one wall were stuck a few newspaper cuttings, at least one featuring the species I was here to see – the Great Orme berry.

Also known as the wild cotoneaster, *Cotoneaster cambricus*, the Great Orme berry is a species with a circuitous story towards recognition as a Welsh endemic. Sally sat behind her desk and enlightened me whilst I swivelled in her colleague's vacant chair.

The Great Orme berry was first discovered in 1783 by John Wynne Griffith of Garn, an eminent botanist – he discovered tufted saxifrage in Wales – and member of parliament between 1818 and 1826, a combination of abilities that seems almost unthinkable today. At the time it was considered to be the same species as the wild cotoneaster of Europe, with the Great Orme being its only site in Britain.

It became a must-see species for Victorian botanists, and unfortunately a must-have too. There are dozens of specimens that survive in herbarium collections, ranging from the 1820s through to the 1930s, and these depredations, combined with locals digging up plants wholesale to sell to tourists, led to the species becoming perilously rare.

'There are six wild plants,' Sally told me, 'and we keep the locations of all of them secret.'

She was very matter-of-fact, considering she was the warden responsible for these six individuals and thus one of the rarest species on the planet. She has been working at the Great Orme for nearly 30 years, though, so maybe you just get used to it. I asked her about it.

She rocked back in her chair slightly. 'Well, back in the seventies they thought there were only four wild plants left – a couple of others have been discovered since – so I suppose it's better than it was. And we've had the reintroduction work, pioneered by Maurice Morris.'

Back in the 1970s, local botanist Maurice Morris had been growing concerned about the deterioration of the last few plants of the wild cotoneaster on the Great Orme. At the time this was still thought to be the same species as one found in mainland Europe, *Cotoneaster integerrimus*, and so – despite this being the only site for it in Britain – it wasn't met with as much conservation attention as it deserved. Maurice took matters into his own hands and in 1970 carefully clipped three cuttings from the wild plants, took them home, and placed them in compost. They all died. The next year he took three more cuttings and gave them to a professional horticulturist, an expert, to get them to root. They all died.

At this point, with so few, and so aged, wild plants left, Maurice decided a different approach was required. He instead decided to 'air-layer' a twig. Choosing a long stem from the strongest wild plant, he wrapped a ball of moist sphagnum moss around it and secured it all with a bandage of black polythene. In his own account of his work, he wrote, 'This was done in August 1973 under very cramped conditions and with the knowledge that I was doing surgery on one of the national rarities.'

Fortunately, the operation was successful. Returning in spring the next year and unwrapping the plastic he found that the branch had produced some delicate roots part way along its length. Maurice was then able to snip the twig off and plant it at home. This one survived and became the first plant in cultivation. By 1976 he was able to take two more cuttings from this young shrub, and in 1979 the first seven cotoneasters were planted out on the Great Orme. Up until the 2000s, all reintroduced plants and all plants grown in botanic gardens were descendants of Maurice's original cutting.

'Then, in the early nineties', Sally told me, 'it was recognised that it was a subtly different species to the ones in mainland Europe and was renamed *Cotoneaster cambricus*.'

The Orme plants had already been noted as being somewhat different to European cotoneasters and had been described as a distinct 'variety' of *Cotoneaster integerrimus* in 1962, var. *'anglicus'*, which I imagine wasn't received very well by Welsh botanists. The change to *C. cambricus* was a much wiser choice.

Sally stood up. 'So, do you want to see one?'

Directly outside the visitor centre was a small rock garden with a couple of benches, some rocky outcrops and planted examples of some of the Great Orme's special species, including the Great Orme berry. We didn't dwell here, though, as Sally was going to show me some of the plants actually out in the wild.

'Remember that they're all in secret locations,' she told me. 'Make sure to keep your descriptions ...' she gently waved her hands as she searched for the word, '... ambiguous.'

With that in mind, Sally took me to a spot on the Orme. Maybe we walked, maybe we drove: it's ambiguous. We walked up a small hill (or did we?), past magenta patches of bloody cranesbill and frothy clouds of dropwort. We reached a small, fenced enclosure, which was almost completely filled by an enormous, bushy cotoneaster.

I am not usually a fan of cotoneasters. This is for three main reasons. Firstly, I don't think they are typically an exciting garden plant, usually small-leaved, dark and glossy, with mean little berries and unremarkable flowers. My grandma had one under her kitchen window and it never did anything other than sit there and look a bit plastic. Secondly, when they escape into the wild they are a devil to identify. The BSBI database lists no fewer than *ninety-nine* species or hybrids of non-native cotoneasters that have escaped into the wild. Even though they can be found in a variety of shapes and sizes, from little shrubs to medium-sized trees, every single one seems to have multiple confusion species making them impossible (for me at least) to name. But it's my third reason that's the most important: cotoneasters can be awfully invasive. Their berries can be eaten by birds and dispersed widely into the countryside where they can dominate wild areas, particularly in limestone areas like Portland in Dorset, or here on the Great Orme. Twelve species of non-native cotoneasters have been recorded from the couple of square miles that make up the headland, crowding out native vegetation and possibly taking the place of where the Great Orme berry once grew.

However, despite my general animosity towards cotoneasters, I was taken by this enormous, spreading plant. The leaves were large and rounded, like two-pence pieces, almost mint-green, and webbed with a delicate network of pale veins. Most strikingly, the leaves had distinct white edges, giving them a very crisp appearance. This white edging was a short, dense fuzz of cottony hairs, and turning the leaf over revealed the entire underside was exquisitely softly felted with them. Its young twigs were white with these same downy hairs, becoming reddish brown with age as the hairs fell away.

The cotoneaster flowers from April to at least June, and the twig I examined had both flowers and fruits. The blooms angled downwards, an inconspicuous white-pink flower clasped in a fleshy green-red cup.

The fruits were more interesting, like perfect miniature pears, green but blushing a warm red on the side facing the sun.

'In Welsh it's called the *creigafal y Gogarth*,' Sally told me, 'the rock-apple of Gogarth – Gogarth being the Welsh name for the Great Orme. Those fruits swell and look like little red apples later in the year.'

'It's stunning,' I said.

'It's probably the biggest one in the world,' said Sally, brushing her fingers through her fringe, 'and it's unique in that this is the only one that's been able to grow exactly how it likes. This isn't one of the wild plants – this was grown in the garden of a local botanist, Tom Parry. He started growing it in the early 1980s from one of Maurice's cuttings and with ample light, water and space it just became enormous. It was dug out with a mini-excavator in 2018 and planted out here, in the hope that some of the fruits it produces – many more than the wild plants – might lead to some seedlings appearing in the wild.'

'Have any seedlings been spotted?' I asked.

Sally shook her head. 'No one has found a seedling of one of these, ever. There's the six wild plants and a lot of reintroduced ones, but no new plants have been found yet.'

'Any theories as to why?'

Sally half shrugged. 'The six wild plants produce very few fruits, if any, and most of the reintroduced plants are still pretty small. There's probably not a lot of seed being produced overall every year, most of which – like with all seeds – probably ends up in the wrong place, or gets eaten, or ends up somewhere taken up with non-native cotoneasters which spread themselves a lot more readily.'

We walked over the brow of a low rise as Sally talked, coming across a group of 10 white, long-haired goats with curving horns. There has been a feral population of around 200 Kashmir goats on the Orme since the late Victorian era.

'Is goat grazing a problem?' I asked.

'Mmm, possibly,' said Sally, 'but they probably eat more non-native stuff because there is just vastly more of it, so at the moment they're probably doing us a service. Rabbit grazing is more of an issue, so we've taken to caging some of the reintroduced plants, like this.'

Sally gestured to a bowl-shaped cage, upturned next to a limestone outcrop surrounded by clumps of salad burnet. Growing through this miniature thunderdome-like structure was a small Great Orme berry, perhaps 25cm tall.

'We've found that it's best to grow the plants on until they're a few years old before planting them out,' Sally told me. 'Year-old plants don't have a very high survival rate. The cages help keep the rabbits off until they're tall enough to escape being nibbled down to the ground.'

'How many reintroduced plants are there?'

'That's a surprisingly hard question to answer because there is always some loss of the reintroduced plants over the first few years. We also have plants that we think we've lost that reappear – perhaps grazed off in a bad year and then popping up a year or so later when conditions are a bit better. But dozens, now, all in this area.'

Sally told me that this area was chosen for the reintroductions for two reasons: firstly, it was the most protected area, and secondly, it allowed for the study of the remaining wild plants in isolation. If reintroductions took place across the Orme and seedlings started appearing, it would be impossible to tell if it was wild plants or reintroduced plants that were reproducing.

'There is one of the wild plants just here,' said Sally, with a small smile, gesturing to me.

She took me to the edge of a limestone terrace, where the rock dropped away to a narrow ledge below, surrounded by a green dell of hazel woodland. Out of a vertical crack in the rock below grew a Great Orme berry, one of the six wild plants left on the planet.

'Feel free to hop down onto the ledge,' she told me. 'Just be careful about where you put your feet.'

I carefully jumped down onto the ledge, which was covered in moss, herb-robert and a tuft of wood-sage. Edging forward, I brushed back a curtain of cascading grasses to admire the plant. Tens of stems emerged from a narrow crack in the limestone, their leaves an even paler, purer green than the plants on the plain above us, perhaps because of the dappled light filtering through the hazels.

I spent a few moments admiring it, wondering how long this plant had been growing here. A century? Longer? It was entirely possible. I reached out and gently rubbed one of its felted leaves between my thumb and forefinger, an electric moment of contact with the rarest species I had ever seen – one of the rarest species on Earth.

I was struck by how, like the interrupted brome, the existence of this species hinged on a small group of people working together across the years. Without the foresight of Maurice Morris and his decade-long effort to propagate and reintroduce the Great Orme berry to the wild, where would we be today? Would efforts have only begun in earnest in 1994, when this species was finally recognised as endemic? This marvellous plant came within a hair's breadth of global annihilation, taken to the precipice of extinction by the passions and efforts of the botanists and collectors of the Victorian and Edwardian eras.

It's fitting that their modern and enlightened successors in conservation have worked so hard to rescue it.

CHAPTER 13

Mantle Peace: False-toothed Lady's Mantle

Back in winter when I'd been planning my year and scrolling through Tim Rich's list of endemic plants, I had noticed that it included two lady's-mantles. At the time my opinion of lady's-mantles – based on previous experiences of finding them, struggling with them, and giving up in despair – slightly put me off making them one of my target species. The problem was that there just wasn't much available guidance on how to identify them; my favourite wildflower guide only included two of the most distinctive species and my copy of Stace (Clive Stace's *New Flora of the British Isles*, the bible of botanists) made them seem complicated ('is the hypanthium tapered to a cuneate base?') so I mostly ended up sheepishly ignoring them.

But 2022 turned out to be a fortuitous year. A brand-new BSBI handbook on lady's-mantles was being published and I quickly ordered a copy. At the same time, I contacted its author, Mark Lynes, and asked if he'd be interested in showing me one of the endemic species. The two species on Tim Rich's list were the least lady's-mantle, *Alchemilla minima*, originally described as a species in 1949 by Max Walters, who supervised

Alan Leslie's PhD on goldilocks buttercups; and the Cairnwell lady's-mantle, *Alchemilla sciura*, described new to science in 2019 by Mark himself. As the least lady's-mantle is a Yorkshire endemic, and knowing that Mark was based nearby, I suggested that maybe that would be the easiest species to meet up and see.

Mark replied enthusiastically, though was quick to point out that in his research for his alchemilla handbook he had determined that the supposedly endemic least lady's-mantle was not actually a 'good' species; rather, it was a variety of the very widespread *Alchemilla filicaulis*, the 'hairy' or 'slender' lady's-mantle. An endemic that wasn't!

However, in the course of his research he had discovered two other brand-new endemic species of lady's-mantles in Yorkshire, and he said he'd be happy to show me one of those instead. We picked a date in June.

Do you ever visit a landscape and just feel at home? For me, that place is the Yorkshire Dales. Maybe it's partly because one of the first residential trips I went on, with my primary school, was to Malhamdale, or maybe it's some intrinsic quality of the landscape: the drystone walls, the fells, hunched churches and big skies, whole vistas straight from a Turner painting.

It was with great delight, then, that I arranged to meet Mark at Grass Wood, a Yorkshire Wildlife Trust reserve about 10 miles north of Skipton and close to the village of Grassington. As I drove past the sign for Stump Cross Caverns, about 10 minutes away from my destination, a red kite flew low over the road, twisting its forked tail. I'd never seen red kites in the Dales in my childhood. A better world is possible.

I pulled up in a tiny car park surrounded with hazel and bracken. There was another car alongside, but no one else around. I got out of the car, read a sign about ash die-back in the wood, another about ticks, and spotted a whitebeam among the hazels. It was as I was examining this – a common whitebeam, it turned out – that Mark appeared, crossing the road with a clump of uprooted lady's-mantle in his hand.

We greeted each other, and he swung open the boot of his car to deposit the earthy handful of vegetation inside.

'I'm guessing that's not the endemic one?' I asked.

He laughed. 'The complete opposite. That is the awful, invasive *Alchemilla mollis*, the garden lady's-mantle.'

All lady's-mantles share the same basic structure. Their most distinctive feature is their leaves. These are as wide as they are long, radiating from a near-central stalk, and are shaped like a chunky seven- or nine-pointed star. Or, if you're cool like me, they're shaped a bit like the Pokémon Starmie. The entire perimeter of the leaf is toothed, and the number of teeth and their individual shapes are key to differentiating the different species. These leaves, depending on species, can range from entirely hairless to distinctly fuzzy, and come in a variety of shades of green, from a slightly sickly yellow green to a glossy British racing green. They can also be flushed red or tipped with silver.

The flowers of lady's-mantles are not subtle, but they're not showy either. They range from a sort of cold lime green, like the colour of Romanesco broccoli, through to a pale golden yellow. The flowers have eight petals: four arranged in a cross shape and four others underneath, offset by 45 degrees, making it look like an eight-pointed star. (Technically speaking, they have no petals at all; what I am calling 'petals' are actually four sepals on top of four epicalyx segments). Each flower is small, about 0.5cm wide, but they come in clusters of dozens, giving an airy, foamy impression when seen in profusion.

The garden lady's-mantle, the one Mark plonked in his car boot, is a non-native species from south-east Europe and south-west Asia. First grown by Victorian gardeners, it escaped into the wild in the 1920s and its population has since exploded – it is now probably the most widespread and common lady's-mantle across Britain. Its key distinctive feature, which helps distinguish it from our native lady's-mantles, is that the whole plant is furred with gentle, soft hairs. The leaves, if rubbed between your fingers, feel almost like fine fleece. There is only one native lady's-mantle that approaches this level of hairiness, and that species is essentially restricted to Teesdale and feels more velvety than it does soft. Unsurprisingly, that species is called the velvet lady's-mantle, *Alchemilla monticola*.

'The garden lady's-mantle can totally take over a site,' said Mark, closing his boot with a thud. 'There's a reserve in Teesdale where there's so much of it that it's threatening the rare native lady's-mantles, so I pull up any clumps that I see appearing in this wood to stop it getting a foothold.'

We headed through a gate into the trees beyond: a mix of ash, hazel and the occasional bird-cherry, a couple still with a few late plumes of white flowers. The woodland floor had been a carpet of bluebells, now mostly over, the petals curling and dropping like damp confetti.

I was clutching my copy of Mark's book, *Alchemilla; Lady's-mantles of Britain and Ireland*, the 24th handbook published by the BSBI. I hadn't had it very long and hadn't had the chance to read up on the species we're looking for. All I really knew was its name, the false-toothed lady's-mantle, *Alchemilla falsadenta*, and that it was endemic not just to Britain, but to Yorkshire as well.

'Is Grass Wood the best place to see this species?' I asked, as we followed the dirt path lined with dog's mercury.

Mark chuckled. 'It's the *only* place that you can see it. There are two patches of it in Lower Grass Wood, on the opposite side of the road where we parked, and the rest of the world population is in here.' He spread an arm as he spoke, gesturing around us.

He told me the full story of its discovery and his interest in lady's-mantles. He'd once been a birder, a twitcher, who'd got into plants and then over a few years slowly found himself entranced by lady's-mantles. He began growing them in his garden to see the differences between species, and he started spending time with Margaret Bradshaw, the great botanist of Teesdale. In the 1940s and 1950s she had travelled across much of northern Britain collecting lady's-mantle specimens. In the process, she discovered *Alchemilla subcrenata*, the large-toothed lady's-mantle, new to Britain. Her PhD was awarded on the basis of her work on this group of species.

Margaret told him about an enigmatic lady's-mantle she had found in Grass Wood back in 1958. She was confident that this was something undescribed. Mark visited Grass Wood in 2010 and found it almost immediately, also recognising it as something 'different'.

'It took me a decade to get to grips with it and feel confident that I was ready to describe it as a new species,' he said. 'There is a similar species in Sweden, you see, and there was a time where I wondered if they were both the same thing.'

Mark examined herbarium specimens of the Swedish species but wasn't entirely convinced. Eventually he decided he needed to see it growing in the wild in Sweden and whilst there he also collected a piece to grow on in his garden. Eventually he was confident.

'It wasn't the same thing; this was something new. The Swedish species is called *oxyodonta*, which means 'sharp-toothed', so I named this one *falsadenta*, 'false-toothed', as a way of referencing how similar they are.'

Mark had just finished explaining when he let out an 'Ah!' followed by a more sombre 'Oh'. He had found a lady's-mantle by the path, but it clearly wasn't what we were looking for.

'This is *glabra*,' he said, crouching and touching a leaf.

This was the smooth lady's-mantle, *Alchemilla glabra*, one of the most widespread species of lady's-mantle in Britain. It had quite large leaves, approaching 15cm across, with seven triangular lobes. Imagine a heptagon, the shape of a 50p coin, but from each of those seven sides emerges an equilateral triangle: the lobes. *That* is about the right shape, though there is a gap at the back where the leaf-stem joins. Each of those lobes was neatly toothed and each tooth was wide and angled forward towards the top of the lobe, like the curving teeth on a buzzsaw blade. The key feature, though, was obvious when you touched it. Its leaf and stem, in contrast to the dense furriness of the garden lady's-mantle, were completely smooth to the touch.

'The trouble with *glabra* is that the leaves can be really variable in shape,' Mark told me. 'But a trick I have is …'

He bent the leaf over with his finger and thumb and rubbed the two surfaces together. They let out a surprisingly noticeable rubbery squeak.

'Does only this species squeak?' I asked, excited by the idea of such a bizarre identification feature.

Mark wrinkled his nose. 'A couple of other species with hairless leaf surfaces can do it too, but I think only *glabra* does it reliably.'

It's a useful identification pointer, then, and a great party trick otherwise.

Leaving the smooth lady's-mantle behind, we carried on walking. The path became a little rockier, the wood more open with sunny glades. There were carpets of wild garlic, a few stragglers of wood anemone holding on to their pink-streaked flowers, and a single late flowering stem of lily-of-the-valley with its cascade of immaculate white-bell flowers.

I felt like I was intently looking out for lady's-mantles, but it was Mark that spotted the next one. I suppose he had had over a decade's practice at this point.

'*Xanthochlora*,' he pronounced, dramatically. 'The pale lady's-mantle.'

Pale it is, the leaves almost a sort of sickly yellow-green, like a Golden Delicious apple. Distinctly different to the solid, healthy green of the smooth lady's-mantle we'd seen further back. I mentioned this to Mark.

'*Xantho* means yellow, *chloros* means green. That's exactly the feature it was named for. This is another one of our commonest species, found all over the north and west of Britain.'

Unfortunately, the colour isn't a completely reliable identification feature as other species can look a bit wan if they're unhealthy or growing in suboptimal conditions.

I bent and rubbed a leaf. It felt smooth and hairless to me.

'How do you tell it apart from the smooth lady's-mantle?' I asked. 'This feels hairless too.'

'Well, firstly, the leaf might not feel hairy but the stem clearly is.' He crouched and plucked a leaf, holding it up so I could see the obvious hairs on the stem. He then swivelled his cap backwards and lifted the hand lens, which hung around his neck on a blue lanyard, to his eye.

'Secondly ...' he started, scanning the bottom of the leaf, '... yeah, there you go, have a look at that. The top of the leaf is pretty much hairless, but the underside is hairy.'

He unlooped the lanyard from around his neck and handed his lens to me. I checked the leaf. The lower surface was covered with a fine scatter of regular hairs. Not the furry pelt of the garden lady's-mantle, but there were definitely hairs there.

'How is the false-toothed lady's-mantle different? Will I be able to tell the difference?' I asked.

Mark stood. 'Well, it would probably be easiest to explain the details when we've got one in front of us – there should be some just up here.'

We walked, a chiffchaff belting out its song overhead, whilst Mark gave me a run-down of the key features of *falsadenta*. Its leaves are dark green, unlikely to be confused with the chartreuse tones of the pale lady's-mantle. They're also largely hairless.

'But they feel different to the smooth lady's-mantle,' said Mark. 'That one feels sort of fleshy and squeaky, *falsadenta* feels more ... papery?'

They also do have hairs, but these are restricted towards the tips of the lobes.

'It's the teeth that really stand out,' said Mark. 'They're sort of silvery; they contrast with the rest of the leaf in a way that the teeth of other species don't.'

I spotted a lady's-mantle – this time before Mark did. It was not yellowish, and when I knelt to touch the leaf it felt almost rubbery. 'Smooth lady's-mantle?' I asked Mark, cautiously.

He nodded down at me benevolently. 'You've got it.'

I quietly celebrate but am cut short by Mark pointing down by his feet. 'And I've got *falsadenta*.'

I had been so taken with identifying my own lady's-mantle that I hadn't noticed our target species on the other side of the path.

It was exactly as Mark had described. Rich, dark forest-green leaves with contrastingly silvery teeth lining the edge of each lobe. I felt them. Hairless.

Mark handed me his lens again. 'Check towards the end of the lobes.'

Squinting through it I soon found a fine scatter of hairs.

I also noticed that the leaves seemed rounder than those of the previous species, the back two lobes bending so far back around the leaf-stem that they touched, or overlapped, giving the whole leaf a cupped shape like a shallow bowl. There were also distinct pleats between each lobe, presumably from the way that the leaf grows and unfolds, reminiscent of the creases left behind when a piece of origami is unfolded.

'The other good feature', said Mark, pointing at the tip of a lobe, 'is that the teeth at the end of a lobe are small, then behind them are a couple of distinctly larger teeth, then they get smaller again.'

This clump was growing right at the edge of the track through the wood.

'Do you worry it'll get trampled?' I asked.

'It likes getting trampled,' Mark replied. 'Well, not quite, but it doesn't do well in dense vegetation. It grows mostly on the edges of the paths where stray footfall keeps the rest of the vegetation at bay. If these paths were abandoned and closed up, a lot of it would disappear. The biggest threat to it would be mismanagement of the wood, but the Yorkshire Wildlife Trust knows all about it. Beyond that ... probably *Alchemilla mollis* invading the wood.'

'How does it feel to have named your own endemic?'

'It was really Margaret who spotted something different here, I just followed up on it,' he replied modestly, swivelling his cap back round.

I pressed him. 'But you described it. And some other endemics. And wrote the book!'

He seemed to squirm slightly at the praise. 'I've had to fight imposter syndrome the whole way,' he told me, in a confiding tone. 'I'm not a trained botanist! I'm a chartered legal executive by trade. I hadn't looked at plants since I was at school.'

I think a lot of us have probably felt like this at some point. That we can't possibly be the 'right' person to take up a challenge or make a difference, but Mark proves that no one is innately the 'right' person. He became a self-made expert through his decade of study, bringing order to a group of plants that had confused British botanists for over a century.

'There should be another good spot for *falsadenta* up here,' Mark said, diverting the conversation away from the possibility of further compliments.

We passed by an area of ash stricken with dieback, bare trunks of young trees with a few forlorn leaves flickering like tattered flags in the breeze. Between them, taking advantage of the light, sprung new trees, downy birch and sycamore. In the pathside vegetation there was a scramble of wild strawberries, and above them hung the heavy rhubarb-and-custard flowerheads of water avens.

Mark led us to a point where three paths joined, though rather than all coalescing at a single point they were all slightly offset, forming a triangular island of vegetation at the centre of this junction. This island was home to masses of lady's-mantles. Clearly the level of trampling here was just right: not so much that this triangle gets churned to bare earth, but enough stray footfall – perhaps in wet weather when the actual path turns to mud? – to suppress dense vegetation.

There was pale lady's-mantle here, its yellowish pallor now standing out to me, and another that was significantly darker and richer. And its teeth – were they silvery? Mark was watching me carefully as I considered. I looked closely at their shape at the top of a lobe.

'Is this *falsadenta*?' I asked.

'It is,' he said, beaming. 'You've got it.'

I'm not sure that's entirely true. It might just have been a lucky guess. But it did feel good to identify my own false-toothed lady's-mantle.

Mark knelt, parted some vegetation and summoned me over. Here, amongst the damp grasses, one lady's-mantle sparkled with dew. This is one of their special powers – they are highly water resistant and so rather than simply getting the leaves wet, the water sits as perfect beads on the surface. They also, through a process called 'guttation', excrete water through the tip of every single tooth, which then improbably balances there like a string of glassy marbles.

'Supposedly it was traditionally thought that the dew from lady's-mantles had magical powers, that it could turn substances to gold. That's where the name of the genus comes from, *Alchemilla*, from "alchemy". In Sweden they call it *daggkåpa*, "dew-cap"'.

We sat for a moment, admiring it, the scent of honeysuckle hanging in the air, its cream and yellow flowers scrambling through the tree above us.

When we got back to our cars, I asked Mark to sign my copy of his handbook. He was hesitant – 'I've not been asked to do this before ...' – but I convinced him.

As I drove away, I thought about how positive the story of the false-toothed lady's-mantle is. We have Mark, the autodidact botanist tracking down a mysterious alchemilla first seen 60 years earlier; we have a species confined to a single wood but whose future seems secure, whose population actually benefits from the presence of people and their incidental footsteps.

But then I drove by a small stone cottage in Grassington, its garden a riot of colour. Over a low stone wall bloomed a lime-green mass of flowering *Alchemilla mollis*, the dreaded invader, with one seedling growing heartily in a pavement crack below. How long can it be kept at bay?

Seeing this invasive lady's-mantle taking root so close to Grass Wood felt like an ominous sign, yet I couldn't help but feel positive. If it wasn't for Mark we wouldn't even know the false-toothed lady's mantle existed, let alone consider defending it against its alien cousin. It's a small victory, but knowing what's worth protecting is the most important place to start.

CHAPTER 14

Rooting For You: Elms

I have asked a number of non-naturalist friends what they know about elms and have identified that there are two 'facts' that everyone seems to know. The first is that elms are trees; the second is that they get Dutch elm disease.

If you speak to a general nature enthusiast you get two more 'facts': there are two (or three) types of elm, one being the wych elm; and Dutch elm disease killed most of the elms in Britain.

Leaving aside the accuracy of the statements above for the moment, here are some of my favourite elm facts. Elms were once amongst our tallest trees; the tallest native tree in Britain today is a 45m-tall beech but historically at least two elms have been measured at 46m. I grew up with books telling me how long animals were compared to double-decker buses so I will do the same for you – 46m is about two-and-a-half double-decker buses stacked end to end. These were the tallest native trees ever recorded in Britain.

Not every elm was a giant like these two, but the stout, stately trunks of elms were once a common and familiar feature of the English landscape. The work of John Constable often heavily features elms; there's a sketch of his from around 1802 of a proud stand of elms, a drawing from 1817 of a dignified copse in Old Hall Park, Suffolk, and a painted study of a mossy elm trunk from 1821. Even when they're not the sole focus of his work they're often a part of his landscape paintings, standing gracefully by the water in his painting *Dedham Lock and Mill*. I cannot overstate how prominent a part these trees once were of our heritage, the term 'elmscapes' having since been coined to describe the countryside of lowland Britain.

This all changed with Dutch elm disease. This mysterious pathogen had its first outbreak in Europe in the early 1900s. The fungus that caused it was isolated in the Netherlands in 1922, saddling it with the inaccurate nickname of 'Dutch elm disease' despite it not originating there. It was first noted in Britain in 1927, on an elm in Hertfordshire, and proceeded to flare up across southern England with isolated cases as far north as Fife in Scotland.

Many elms were killed by the disease, but many others recovered. By the 1940s the disease had died down and by the 1960s it was considered rare. In 1960 Dr Tom Peace of the Forestry Commission wrote a paper called 'The Status and Development of Elm Disease in Britain', which summarised this outbreak. He mentions that losses of elms were somewhere between 10 and 20 per cent and that only 'in a few localities has the disease materially altered the landscape' and that 'the disease has declined erratically, but continuously, since 1936–37, not only in the number of elms affected, but also more particularly in the severity of the damage caused.' He finished the paper with a paragraph that was presumably intended as optimistic but now reads as darkly prophetic:

The disease may long continue as a minor nuisance, but unless it completely changes its present trend of behaviour it will never bring about the disaster once considered imminent. Indeed, in order to wipe out most of the elms in Britain it would have to achieve an even higher level of virulence than it did in its worst years in the nineteen-thirties.

By the end of the 1960s this was exactly what had happened. A new strain of Dutch elm disease, caused by a different but very closely related fungi, spread throughout Britain on the backs of elm bark beetles and killed off around 30 million elms. A 2010 paper by Isobel Tomlinson and Clive Potter described it as 'one of the most dramatic environmental events to affect the British countryside in living memory'. We now live in a country missing these former elmscapes, where there is a sharp divide between the people who remember them and those – like me – for whom our denuded elmless countryside is the new normal.

It came as something of a surprise, then, when I met up with Brian Eversham, proclaimed elm enthusiast, CEO of the Bedfordshire, Cambridgeshire and Northamptonshire Wildlife Trust (whose photo collection of goldilocks buttercups I'd referenced extensively earlier in the year), and learnt that this isn't *quite* true.

It was August, six weeks after meeting Mark and his lady's-mantles in the Dales. Since then, Britain had seen its hottest day ever and most vegetation seemed a bit crisped, browned and unhappy. Fortunately, our elms seemed unaffected.

'Death is rarely fatal for elms,' Brian told me. We were walking down the path in Oak Wood, Cambourne, not far from the local Wildlife Trust headquarters.

He explained. The disease usually leads to the death of the main trunk of the elm, what we recognise as 'the tree', but that doesn't kill the actual organism. Elms are enthusiastic, vigorous suckerers – fresh new growth sprouts liberally from the base of the tree. If the main trunk dies off, within a few years there is a hearty thicket of bushy new elm growth at the base. And if left to its own devices, this growth will send up new sapling-like trunks.

'However', said Brian, as we walked, 'within a few years they get big and thick enough to become a suitable host for the bark beetle that carries Dutch elm disease, and they die off again.'

As he spoke, we walked into a small meadowy area surrounded by exactly this sort of growth – a veritable hedge of bushy young elm growth with the occasional wrist-thick trunk stretching upwards, their neat rows of leaves on opposite sides of the branches silhouetted ladder-like against the sky. There were a few taller, thicker trunks too – bleached, skeletal and dead. These had got large enough to host the beetle and had been killed off by the disease.

'But the organism isn't dead. In fact, all of this', he said, sweeping a hand around the clearing, 'is probably, genetically, all one individual. I've visited lots of sites where the elms were recorded as "dying" of Dutch elm disease 40 years ago and more than 90 per cent of them are still there today, sending up new trunks and looking pretty healthy.'

Elms may be the tree best adapted to deal with a disease like this. Their boundless ability to regenerate and perpetually exist in a shrubby form makes them uniquely resilient; elms aren't victims – they're born survivors!

Ahead of us, Francesca, a student from Cambridge, was fighting her way through the brambles with an enormous pair of industrial loppers. She paused to catch her breath and smiled back at us.

'I'm studying the invertebrates that feed on elm,' she explained, adjusting her grip on the loppers. 'We're trying to understand whether these invertebrates actually recognise different types of elm. Are they adapted to feed on specific species? Or do they treat all elms the same? If the insects are selective, it could tell us a lot about how distinct some of these types really are.'

As she lopped some side branches from the tops of the tallest trunks, Brian gave me a run-down of the history of elm classification. He pulled a few books from his bag to show me. The standard plant identification guide from 1952, the first edition *Flora of the British Isles*, included seven species of elms, as well as two subspecies, three varieties and three hybrids. By the time of the third edition in 1987 this had shrunk to just two species, reflecting the different opinions of the two great 'elm men' of the twentieth century, Ronald Melville and Richard Richens.

Melville was of the opinion that the diversity of elms in Britain represented a number of different species and the various hybrids between them, and the 1952 *Flora* reflects this. Richens, however, considered that there were only two elm species in Britain as well as a single hybrid between them. Everything else, the forms that Melville had ascribed to species and hybrids, Richens considered to simply be varieties – but not natural varieties. He thought them to be 'cultivars' – human-selected and propagated forms of elms – brought to Britain by successive waves of human migration and then persisting here in the wild.

The current standard plant guide, Stace's *New Flora*, is perhaps more indebted to Melville, as it includes seven species, five subspecies and seven hybrids. However, the current BSBI elm referee, Dr Max Coleman, is closer to the Richens school, recognising two species and one hybrid between them.

I mention all of this context for a couple of reasons. Firstly, to set the stage that elms are a subject of continued debate. Secondly, to make the dramatic reveal that Sell & Murrell's 2018 *Flora of Great Britain and Ireland* splits our elms into no fewer than 62 *species*, 40 of them named new to science in this book. Of these 62 species, 50 of them are British endemics and Brian has dedicated several years of free time to tracking them down, gathering herbarium material, and trying to write usable keys so that more botanists can begin to record the true diversity of elms.

Francesa had succeeded in lopping a few high branches and triumphantly carried them through the thicket of brambles.

'Why the top branches?' I asked, given that there was plenty of low, shrubby growth nearby.

'The mantra for identifying elms is that you have to work with short shoots in full sun – the sucking growth from the base isn't typical, neither is shaded material,' said Brian, taking one of the branches and showing it to me. 'This is *Ulmus procera*, the English elm.'

The leaves were dark, glossy green with short, jagged teeth around the edge, heavily pock-marked with galls caused by the elm mite, *Aceria campestricola*. Brian ran through the features that make this the English elm: broadly rounded leaves that aren't much longer than wide, with their broadest point in the middle; also, the sheer number of mite galls.

'This is why this study on the preferences of invertebrates is so important,' said Brian. 'This elm mite is usually incredibly abundant on English elm, but almost absent on some other elms. It's evidence that these forms named by Sell and Murrell could be "good" species; we can recognise them, and so can the species that feed on them.'

Back in the wood, as we walked along a shady path, Brian pointed out another elm gently sweeping out over the path like a parasol. He pulled down a branch and we huddled to inspect the leaves. Even to my untrained eyes, these looked significantly different from those of the English elm we had just seen. Each leaf was at least twice as long as wide, rather than short and stubby, and the asymmetrical base of the leaf – a general feature of elms where one side of the leaf base is lower than the other – looked to be even more asymmetrical. It was also, notably, free of mite galls.

'*Ulmus cuneiformis*,' pronounced Brian, 'the wedge-leaved elm. Do you see how it sort of fans out over the path? I often see it growing like this, over paths and streams. Maybe it was originally a stream-side species.'

He released the branch and it bounced back up above us. 'Oh,' he said, almost as an afterthought as the bough swayed above us, 'that's one of the endemics.'

We all stood for a moment, taking in the elm's graceful sweep over the path. I couldn't help but feel a quiet thrill – a new species! I always find it deeply satisfying to encounter something I've never seen before, but there was something particularly special about this one. Elms, with their nascent Sell & Murrell taxonomy, are species I would never have confidently identified without Brian's expertise. What's more, it was my first endemic elm. Before I embarked on tracking down endemics, I had assumed that they would all either be rare, remote or challenging to find, yet – much like I found with Goldilocks buttercups – this elm was growing in plain sight, right above a well-trodden path. How often must we pass by unique species without a second glance?

Having now seen a grand total of two elm species and finding them clearly distinct from each other, I wondered why the subject of elm taxonomy was so fraught. I put the question to Brian.

'I think a large part of it is that their reproductive strategy is unlike anything else in Britain,' he said, and proceeded to outline it to me.

We all know what normal sexual reproduction is, and by now, thanks to goldilocks buttercups, you hopefully have a handle on apomixis, where plants clone themselves through their own seeds. Elms, theoretically, are sexually reproducing species – in fact the wych elm still is. But the bulk of these newly described species – despite having flowers, producing pollen, and having all the paraphernalia that suggests they should reproduce like a normal plant – don't reproduce this way. Our spring weather is too cold for the regular development of viable seed. These elms probably haven't regularly reproduced in Britain since – deep breath – the warmth of the Bronze Age.

I literally stopped in my tracks as Brian told me this. 'Bronze Age ...' I mumbled, trying to calculate, 'so that's...'

'Around 3,000 thousand years or so,' offered Brian.

That means that for three millennia, or thereabouts, elms have resorted to reproduction-by-suckering. The natural lifestyle of elms in Britain has been partly like a normal tree – growing a trunk, standing gracefully over the landscape – but then, when eventually it succumbs to wind or time, the suckers take over and grow into the next stately trunk. Many trunks, hundreds of years, but one individual. This must have happened countless times over the past few thousand years. However, now, with Dutch elm disease, the stout trunks are largely gone and most elms survive as perpetual bushes, any eager branches that reach to the sky knocked back by disease as soon as they're big enough to draw the attention of beetles. Have you ever seen an entire hedgerow of elm? That may all be one genetically unvarying individual, cloning itself across the landscape.

This is partly why Sell and Murrell's elm taxonomy is so controversial. British botanists are happy with sexually reproducing and apomictic species, but splitting species that propogate themselves purely through vegetative reproduction seems to be a bridge too far. I can understand the reasoning behind this; a species is approximately defined as a group of interbreeding individuals who have barriers to breeding outside this group, those barriers being reduced fertility, courtship strategies, physical differences, seasonality etc.

However, these elms can't sexually reproduce at all due to our climate. Maybe if we had warmer spring weather, we'd find that they'd all crossbreed freely. Could the 62 species we see today instead reflect thousands-of-years-old clones of a single, variable ancestor, preserved by their inability to outbreed? I put these questions to Brian.

'Maybe they aren't species,' he replied, 'maybe they are subspecies, or varieties, or some combination of all three. All I can say is that they are recognisable entities, with very few intermediates between them – and you'd expect to see more intermediates if you were looking at hybrids or individual variation. More work is needed before we can be confident. For now, we've got Sell and Murrell's descriptions of them as "species" as a starting point.'

We rounded a trunk lying on the path and Brian continued. 'And if we know that invertebrates have preferences for these different species – or forms, or whatever we decide to call them – then that's valuable information. Around here we have the white-spotted pinion, a moth that was once found across most of southern England. It's an elm-feeder and after Dutch elm disease took hold, its range retracted to Cambridgeshire and nearby counties. If that moth does better living on certain types of elms, then it's important we know that for its future conservation. If the moth can tell the difference, we should pay attention.'

Our walk led us back to the Wildlife Trust headquarters, where the three of us stopped for lunch and Brian laid out his herbarium sheets of elm specimens. He had, so far, tracked down 61 of the 62 species described by Sell and Murrell. The variation is staggering. We munched our sandwiches as we inspected this crisp array of neatly mounted specimens.

At one end of the spectrum there is the Cornish elm, *Ulmus cornubiensis*. This has exquisitely neat and minute leaves, the largest being barely 4cm long; the edges are bluntly toothed and the leaf bases have only the smallest of asymmetries. A few pages later there is the Assington elm, *Ulmus serrata*, whose smallest leaves are 4cm long and largest are 7cm long; these are edged in remarkable curving jagged teeth like pairs of devil horns. The rhombic-leaved elm, *Ulmus rhombifolia*, is yet again larger, with leaves reaching 9cm long, but its most significant feature is the leaves' rhombic or diamond shape, different from the gentle curves of other species. Also, this species has small, gentle teeth in the lower half of the leaf and aggressive, curving fang-like teeth in the upper half.

This is when I spot Chater's elm, *Ulmus chaterorum*. This is our second endemic named after Arthur Chater, the first being Chater's bristletail, and he was also the first to split off the South Stack fleawort as an endemic subspecies. His elm was a bit more generic than the ones I've described so far – a little asymmetrical, slightly toothy, but with an elegant elongated narrow tip to the leaf.

Did I think *all* of the 61 specimens looked sharply distinct? No, not all of them, not to my untrained eye – but that's true for a lot of species, including the dandelions and goldilocks buttercups on which there is general agreement on their species diversity. However, seeing them fanned out on the table it was hard to reconcile their diversity with these simply being two or three species.

After lunch, and after spotting the arrowhead form of a hummingbird hawkmoth roosting above the cupboards in the Wildlife Trust kitchen, Brian drove Francesca and I out to Hayley Wood. As we wove down the minor roads through the sun-browned countryside, Brian told us about how East Anglia and Cambridgeshire are hotspots of elm diversity.

'We have about half of the 62 Sell and Murrell species in East Anglia,' he said, as we rounded a corner, 'but there's less diversity as you go west, with only around six species in Cornwall. It's the same when you head north. I think this could reflect the history of how these species arrived in Britain after the Ice Age.'

He outlined four colonisation routes. There are six elms that are pretty much restricted to Cornwall and the South West, which might reflect colonisation from the west of Europe. There are species of the south coast that may have made it across to Britain before the Channel formed. Essex has about 10 elm species that may have found their way there along the valley of the River Rhine and up the Thames which, at the time, was a tributary of the Rhine. Finally, the rest of the species might have made their way across the lost landmass of Doggerland.

These final three routes essentially converge on central England. It was warmer then, too, and these ancestral elms may have all hybridised and formed new elms different to those left behind in mainland Europe.

'Richens spent years studying elms in France,' Brian said (Richens being the twentieth-century elm specialist who thought most elms were cultivars), 'and found only a few elms there that were the same as ours. Fifty of the 62 Sell and Murrell species are thought to be endemic. Buff Wood [a woodland managed by the Wildlife Trust on the boulder clay of Cambridgeshire] has more species of elm than the *entirety* of France.'

'How many is that?' I asked.

'I've found 29 species in Buff Wood compared to eight or nine for France as a whole,' he replied.

With that bombshell, we pulled up at Hayley Wood. I've visited Hayley Wood several times before, but always in April. In spring, this is simply one of the most glorious woods I've ever been to. Carpets of bluebells, bright patches of primrose and, most magical of all, the nodding heads of oxlips. In August, and this August in particular, the wood seemed parched. The path beneath us was cracked like a dry lakebed and the usual drifts of dog's mercury were limp and drooping.

Thankfully, though, the elms were looking good. Brian led us through a maze of paths until we reached a point where the wood bordered a field. Even though we were here expressly looking for elms, I didn't spot it at first, but here, amongst the bushy growth at the edge of the wood, stood a low spreading tree. Because of its elongated, glossy green leaves I think I had mentally interpreted it as some other species entirely, and I said as much to Brian.

'I think the leaves look a bit like a white willow,' he replied, 'but a bit broader.'

He was spot on. These leaves were elongated, tapering at the tip, verging on almost three times as long as they were broad – a million miles from the nearly round leaves of the English elm we'd seen earlier. This was the Hatley elm, *Ulmus sylvatica*, a species currently known from three sites in Cambridgeshire and nowhere else.

Francesca approached with those industrial loppers and confidently placed the jaws around a twig – a short shoot in full sun – and tugged on the line that nipped the blades closed. A leafy branch twirled to the ground. Francesca picked it up and we gathered around it. I was struck by how smooth the leaf was – I think of elms as characteristically rough species – and how remarkably asymmetric it was, one side of the leaf extending nearly a full centimetre further than the other down the petiole. The elongated tip of the leaf had a subtle curve to it, almost as though the shorter side of the leaf had shrunk and tugged the leaf-tip over to one side. In all, it was a striking species.

Brian had one more elm he wanted Francesca to sample. Leaving this hot, sunlit edge behind we went deep into the wood, off the paths and into the cooler, darker understory of the trees. The vegetation was thinner here in the greenish gloom, and we followed Brian as he navigated a route despite the lack of obvious landmarks. A jay squawked at our presence.

I had just stopped to admire a midland hawthorn – one of my favourite trees and a species that can thrive in the low sylvan light of woodlands – when Brian told us we had arrived. He patted a trunk, and I followed it skywards. This elm was a *tree*. This wasn't a bushy, scrubby, Dutch-elm-disease-fighting, scrappy survivor, no. This was an *actual tree*, as tall and significant as any other tree in the wood. This was the Hayley elm, *Ulmus crenata*, named for the wood we were standing in.

'They seem to be resistant to the disease,' said Brian, looking up at the tree almost proudly, 'which is another piece of evidence that these elms could be distinct species.'

I patted the trunk myself. This was the first time I had ever seen an elm getting a chance to be a proper tree. It was about 30cm thick and towered metres overhead, the crown lost in the canopy of jumbled leaves above.

'There are about 100 of them,' said Brian, 'all in this wood'.

I stared up into the branches. I wondered if we once had more types of elm; if perhaps there were other woodlands and hedgerows that were grubbed out, cut down and lost in the last few centuries that had held their own endemic elms. Our countryside is now so significantly altered that it's hard to imagine that we have managed to preserve the entire diversity of elms that existed 3,000 years ago when they declined to reproduce like normal plants.

'Do you want to cut a twig off this one?' asked Francesca, thrusting that industrial lopper in my direction.

With those mechanical jaws gently wavering from side to side, I raised the device as high as I could to a small shady side branch. The positioning was awkward, small movements in my arms translating to significant wobbles high above, but eventually I had those sharp blades where I wanted them. With a few sharp tugs on the line, I nipped the loppers shut and sent a few twigs twirling down towards us.

'It's not an ideal specimen,' said Brian, sweeping it up, 'as it wasn't growing in full sun and so isn't entirely typical, but you can get an idea of it.'

The leaves were large, as long as my palm, and wide with it – much stouter than the relatively slender leaves of the Hatley elm. Some had stubby leaf-tips, others slightly more elongated and curving to one side. The base was asymmetrical, but not dramatically so. In fact, some of the leaves were almost shaped like a parallelogram, like a normal leaf had been squashed slightly off-kilter.

As we made our way back to the cracked and droughted path out of the wood, Brian offered me a leafy twig from the Hayley Elm, which I eagerly accepted. I'd press it and keep it, maybe frame it.

I thought about how elms are so often framed as victims of Dutch elm disease, their story one of decline and loss. But being here, seeing these remarkable trees and learning their stories, made me realise they're so much more than that. They're survivors, endlessly enduring.

Brian's work to clarify elm taxonomy is crucial in understanding this story. Without efforts like his, the significance of our native elms might go unnoticed and uncelebrated.

Though the elmscapes of history have been lost, the elms themselves are still there. We just need to look harder and appreciate the diversity of what remains.

CHAPTER 15

By a Single River: Baker's Hawkweed

From the stoic resilience of our endemic elms, my attention turned to a species on the absolute brink. While elms have endured Dutch elm disease and centuries of habitat change, hawkweeds battle obscurity, their diversity often overlooked and their taxonomy incompletely deciphered. This time, my journey took me from the welcoming woods of Cambridgeshire to the rugged landscapes of Teesdale.

On a bright but drizzly September morning I set off from my parents' house in east Yorkshire on a drive northwards. The drizzle cleared as I passed Pontefract and in the fresh blue skies between Wetherby and Boroughbridge I saw a few red kites, which I considered a good omen for the day. I pulled off the main roads as I got to Barnard Castle and enjoyed the country roads that lead into the wilds of Teesdale.

I love Teesdale. This scenic dale between North Yorkshire and County Durham is home to an almost implausible array of fantastic wildlife. Short-eared owls, merlin, ring ouzels; I've even seen black grouse lekking here at dawn before and heard their bubbling calls roll around the low hills. Botanically speaking, there's the 'Teesdale assemblage', sometimes romantically referred to as the 'ice flowers', a collection of arctic-alpine plants that occur at their southern limit in Britain. The most astounding of them, in my opinion, is the spring gentian, a flower so breathtakingly, intensely cobalt blue that in photographs it looks simply unreal and when seen in the flesh it almost feels as though your eyes are malfunctioning. The spring gentian is not endemic, though, and I was at completely the wrong end of the year to see them anyway. The flower I was looking for was much less overtly showy, a lot more enigmatic, and vanishingly rare.

I pulled into the car park at the Bowlees visitor centre and was delighted to find that there was no fixed price – the machine accepted donations of any amount and provided parking for the day regardless. This egalitarian payment system warmed my heart and I happily forked over a few quid for a ticket.

As I stood by the boot of my car and got into my walking boots I realised that I had once again made the same mistake that I always do on these trips. How would I identify Linda, my expert? I looked around the car park on the off chance that someone was standing under the gently dripping wych elms looking faintly botanical. This was not the case. I looked at my phone. No signal, of course. I looked in the boot of my car and spotted a branch covered in crinkly leaves, left over from a failed solo-attempt to identify an elm after meeting Brian a couple of weeks earlier. I considered whether holding it would be useful, a sort of botanical flag, then dismissed the idea. Instead I pulled out Mark Lynes' book on lady's-mantles. I wasn't here to look for lady's-mantles, but it's a strong marker of 'this person is interested in plants' and would hopefully allow Linda to spot me.

'Hello! James, is it?'

I jumped briefly out of my skin, too focused on my internal debate about my ability to be recognised to notice that I had, indeed, been recognised.

We shook hands, introduced ourselves, and Linda led the way out of the car park and down a lane lined with drystone walls and a verdant swathe of one of our best-named plants: good-king-henry. Good-king-henry, which looks like a bit like a giant, perennial cousin of the common fat-hen, isn't native to Britain but has been here since at least Roman times, originally imported from the mountains of central Europe for use as a vegetable, its young stems eaten like asparagus and its leaves cooked like spinach. It's now out of fashion as a foodstuff but clings on in the wild, growing around abandoned houses, roadsides and around farm buildings. It's not a species I see very often so I gleefully took a few pictures.

We carried on down the lane, across a field and towards the River Tees. Linda Robinson is the BSBI plant recorder for north-west Yorkshire (Yorkshire being so large that it is subdivided into five smaller areas for recording purposes), and as we walked she confided in me that she doesn't usually pay much attention to this side of the river, this being the County Durham side. Her recording only starts in earnest when she crosses the bridge over the river to 'her' county.

We walked through a narrow wooded area to the bridge. This is Wynch Bridge (or Winch Bridge, they're used interchangeably). The first bridge on this spot was built in 1741 and, apparently, was the first ever suspension bridge built in England. The current bridge dates from 1830 and seemed simultaneously over-engineered and fragile. Stout metal posts painted midnight blue anchored the bridge on each side of the river, and a spray of thick cables spanned them, holding up the walkway. The walkway, in contrast, was made of wooden boards and the path itself was less than two feet wide. A sign above the bridge ominously read 'This bridge is to carry ordinary foot traffic only and should only be used by one person at a time.'

There was currently a small, white dog unhurriedly crossing the bridge towards us. Its owner waited patiently on our bank of the river. 'If I walk too far ahead', he explained, nodding to his dog still plodding at its own pace across the bridge, 'he just ends up following the nearest person wherever they're going. Still, means I get to stop for a breather.'

The dog made it to our shore and Linda bent to give him a stroke before crossing. I watched her reach the other side – mindful of the sign – before stepping onto the bridge. A few metres below me the peaty water of the River Tees frothed over submerged rocks. At the other side of the bridge Linda was closely examining a raised bank of vegetation. As I reached her side she said, 'I planted one out here in July.'

The bank was a rich tangle of herbs with purple pom-poms of devil's-bit scabious vying with the sickly green-cream flowers of wood sage. I didn't see the yellow, dandelion-esque flower I was expecting.

If you are a birder then you are probably very familiar with the phrase 'little brown jobs', often abbreviated to 'LBJs', an informal term used to describe those songbirds that – to the untrained and uncultured eye – all look like generic brownish sparrowy-type things.

With plants, the equivalent term I've heard is 'DYC', 'damned yellow composite', referring to the profusion of confusing, yellow, dandelion-type species, which beginner botanists soon learn to deliberately overlook in favour of something easier.

How many birds might count as LBJs? A few dozen, perhaps, if we include unusual vagrants. With DYCs the challenge is an order of magnitude larger. We have 230+ species of dandelions, around 10 hawk's-beards, a trio of hawkbits, and then, deep breath, more than 340 species of hawkweeds. (And whose disturbed mind came up with the idea to put 'hawk' in the names of three similar looking groups of flowers?)

Hawkweeds are a notoriously difficult group. This is partly because there are an awful lot of them, partly because the features that separate them are often very subtle, and partly because even the experts are yet to figure them out. New species keep being discovered and there is no comprehensive guide to their identification. And those 340+ species I mentioned? Of that total, *at least* 330 of them are endemic to Britain and Ireland.

Once you've got your eye in, hawkweeds are actually not that difficult to tell apart from other yellow-flowered members of the daisy family. Telling them apart from each other is the tricky bit, and this is something that very few people have the skills to do. It all comes down to a complex mix of characters – the shape and toothing (if any) of the leaf, the hairiness of the leaf and how that hair is distributed, the colour of the leaf (some are mottled purple), the size of the flower, subtlety in the shades of yellow of the flower, etc. This is all far beyond me, so I was relying totally on Linda's expertise.

The species Linda was hoping to show me was Baker's hawkweed, *Hieracium bakeranum*. This flower was first collected here, by Wynch Bridge, in the 1840s, and it has never been found anywhere else outside Upper Teesdale. It was recorded semi-regularly from its discovery through to 1900 – though at the time it was thought to be *Hieracium crocatum*, a species that is now known not to occur in Britain. There was then a gap of about 30 years before it was recorded again by Pugsley (the same Pugsley who you may recall seemed so incredulous about

Lundy cabbage). Pugsley was something of a hawkweed enthusiast and in 1948 he published a paper recognising that this hawkweed by the Tees was something unique, naming it after the botanist John Gilbert Baker, who was one of the first to collect it.

It then dropped off the radar until the 1960s, when it was recorded by J. N. Mills and P. D. Sell (yes, that Sell, of the Sell and Murrell endemic elms fame) and then wasn't recorded for *another* 30 years until Vincent Jones, the late great Yorkshire hawkweed expert (not the footballer-turned TV hardman), re-found it in 1996. He could only find six plants.

Baker's hawkweed seemed to be dwindling away. In 2011 Vincent searched the banks of the Tees thoroughly and found just five plants in three locations along the river. By 2017 the botany report for north-west Yorkshire detailed only three remaining plants. This was around the time Linda got involved.

'There it is,' said Linda, pointing, 'or what's left of it.'

Baker's hawkweed should be a tall, straight-stemmed plant with narrow, lanceolate leaves like green spearheads and a small forking cluster of bright yellow flowers. Instead, the one in front of us had been nipped off a few inches above the ground. Only a short section of stem and a few of those hairy willow-like leaves remained.

'It was flowering well when I planted it out,' said Linda optimistically, 'so there's a good chance that it set some seed before it was decapitated.'

Back in 2018, seed was gathered by Tim Rich, hawkweed expert and author of the endemic plant checklist, from the last trio of plants. Unfortunately, the streak of bad luck for the species continued. The seed was mildewed – some fungal thing perhaps brought on by damp weather – and only a single seed sprouted, growing into a sickly plant that died before flowering.

In 2019 Linda tried again. By this point one of the last three plants had died off and disappeared and so she dutifully gathered seed from the last two lonely plants on the planet. She sowed it immediately into pots of compost and left them outside over winter to face the elements, as they would in their Teesdale home. In the spring they sprouted – dozens of them.

'I ended up with more than 30 of the dratted things,' she told me, with all the affection a mother might have for an errant child.

Of course, 2020 was the year of Covid-19. Rather than returning some plants to the banks of the Tees and bolstering the wild population, Linda ended up nurturing a garden full of Baker's hawkweed for two years. There's something to be said for being responsible for nearly the entire world population of a species through two years of a global pandemic.

'Oh they're not hard to look after,' she said, with a dismissive flapping gesture in my direction when I mentioned this.

It was only in 2022 that Linda was able to return and start bolstering the wild population. She gave a number of them to Natural England, which they've planted out on an island in the Tees, and she planted out half a dozen pots in suitable spots along the riverbank a couple of months ago. This headless specimen was one of hers.

The plan was to check in on these reintroduced hawkweeds and – I hoped – visit the last remaining wild plants. For me, even though the reintroduced plants are the same species, there is a world of difference between the last wild plants on Earth and these new hopefuls that haven't yet been in the ground two months. I don't want to be misconstrued here, I think Linda's reintroduction work is amazing, vital and uplifting, but for me there is a unique thrill in seeing wild plants, growing where they chose to grow, the last in an unbroken chain extending back to the dawn of the species.

We set off walking west along the river. Linda sighed at a fence that bordered the path, separating the river, riverbank and any walkers like us from the fields with their grazing sheep.

'The powers that be put the fence in, oh, six or seven years ago. The sheep used to graze down to the edge of the river but now –' she gestured to the thigh-high vegetation '– it's all gone rank. Without the grazing, the thuggish species take over and you lose the special stuff.'

She told me about the rock lady's-mantle, *Alchemilla wichurae*, which, in England, is only found in the Yorkshire Dales, the Lake District and here in Teesdale. It's not an endemic, but it is a localised species of special habitats: limestone and moist soils near rivers and waterfalls. There used to be a patch of it along the path where we were now walking. Linda used to dutifully garden around it, trimming back the rising tide of rank vegetation, but she couldn't get here during the two pandemic years. This year it was gone.

'I used to work at Moor House National Nature Reserve and my old boss, Michael Rawes, and his assistant David Welch, published research which showed that when you exclude grazing from grassland there is an eight per cent reduction in biodiversity in the first ten years.'

She gazed at the spot where the lady's-mantle used to be.

'That's what's happening here,' she told me, sadly, 'no one seems to care.'

It's the purpose of the fence that's the most frustrating thing. The fence is here because people cannot be trusted to do one simple, responsible thing: keep their dogs on leads. Historically, some people would let their dogs off the lead, and some of these dogs would chase and harm the sheep. The solution? Build a fence and keep the sheep and dog-walkers separate. The downside is the inexorable loss of species richness from this botanical hotspot.

I asked if the lack of grazing had anything to do with the decline of Baker's hawkweed and Linda wrinkled her nose in thought before telling me that it was starting to disappear before the fence was installed. 'We don't know why the hawkweed is disappearing,' she said, 'but I doubt that the lack of grazing helps.'

There was an island in the river, its shingly shore fringed with a waist-high shrub covered in buttercup-like flowers. This was something I had hoped to see – shrubby cinquefoil, *Dasiphora fruticosa*, another of Teesdale's special species. For whatever reason, this flower is only found in two sites in Britain, and the River Tees is the best place for it. I jumped from the path down onto the rocky platform by the water's edge to get a better view of the island, then spotted a single plant growing on a bank of shingle on my side of the river. It was a gorgeous plant, blanketed with deep, lemon-yellow flowers and with neatly divided leaves giving it an almost 'fluffy' appearance.

'It's almost too nice, isn't it?' said Linda, catching up with me. 'I expect most people walking along here must think it's something escaped from a garden – it seems too showy just to be growing here naturally.'

She was right. There was something almost exuberantly excessive about the profuse yellow flowers. I took some pictures before walking back across the rocks and jumping up to the path. Linda eyed the route I'd taken suspiciously and selected a different approach. 'I've had my hips replaced,' she said, finding a shallower incline to ascend the bank. 'I've got no spring left.'

Around the next bend in the river we looked for another of Linda's planted-out hawkweeds. She consulted a hand-drawn map and walked back and forth along a few metres of riverbank. 'Here's me thinking I'd remember where they all are. What a prat!' she muttered to herself.

I joined the hunt, searching amongst the tangle of northern bedstraw and knapweed. I found a patch of slightly disturbed ground but couldn't see anything that looked like a hawkweed. Linda, still patrolling the bank, stopped by my side, and clapped me on the shoulder. 'Oh, you found it!'

I'd found the spot but missed the plant. Right in the middle of the disturbed patch was the hawkweed we were looking for. Like the first one, it was decapitated, which I used as an excuse as to why I'd overlooked it. Two headless plants in a row wasn't very encouraging, but as Linda was quick to point out, hawkweeds are perennials. Even if they got nibbled down this year, as long as they adjusted from their pampered garden life to the harsh realities of the riverbank then they should pop up next year.

Playing devil's advocate, I asked Linda why, when there are hundreds of very similar hawkweeds, it was worth saving this one. She fixed me with a steely gaze. 'Hell's teeth! Why not? When I realised how rare it is, and that it's only found in my recording area, I knew I had to!'

I hurriedly reassured her that this wasn't *my* opinion and she visibly softened. 'Oh, I know,' she said, 'otherwise you wouldn't be here. It worries me that people might think that, though.'

There were more of Linda's reintroduced hawkweeds to look for but, before we reached them, we would go past the spot where, in 2019, the last two wild plants on the planet were growing. Linda consulted her sketch maps again as we walked.

'We should go through a gate in a wall,' she said, scrutinising the fine pencil lines on her paper, 'and past a hazel on our right …'

It wasn't long before we got to the wall and the gate, but the hazel evaded us. Could it have fallen and been washed away in the last two years? It seemed unlikely that it could happen without leaving a trace. Much walking up and down the river ensued, until eventually Linda recognised a group of trees and realised that the hazel was much further away from the gate than she had remembered.

She clambered down the grassy bank, gesturing for me to follow, and rounded a small group of trees.

'They were somewhere here,' she said, gesturing with both hands at the couple of square metres of herbage in front of us. There was no sign of any dandelion-like yellow flowers.

'They will probably have finished flowering by now,' said Linda, 'or have had their heads nipped off by deer or something like the others.'

We searched. Without flowers I resorted to combing through the plants and looking at leaves, hoping to spot something that matched the lance-like leaves I'd seen on the headless plants earlier. A couple of times I got excited and thought I'd found something but on both occasions I had found headless black knapweed – abundant along the river – whose leaves, at a glance, could be mistaken for Baker's hawkweed by an amateur like me.

The atmosphere, bright and cheerful up until now, took on an air of tension. Could it be that the last wild plants were gone? We searched through the patch once and then started again at the beginning, combing through the jumble of stems one at a time.

'Here it is,' said Linda with a satisfied sigh, 'at last.'

She was on her knees and holding a leafy hawkweed stem. At the base of the stem were those large, spearhead leaves, and this time I noticed that these had three minute teeth on each side. Every inch up the stem was another leaf, decreasing markedly in size, the smallest one at the top as fine as a scalpel blade. It wasn't flowering, but this plant had its head intact; a neat grey disk with spoked edges was perched at the top of the stem where the flower had once been.

Linda gave it a gentle tap. 'Look, it's flowered and set seed; that's encouraging. Though it's a lot shorter than usual – normally it's big, buxom stuff.'

Pugsley's original 1948 description said it ranged from 50cm to 90cm tall. The plant in front of us was barely cresting 40cm. 'Maybe it was the drought this year?' I suggested.

'Aye, maybe,' she replied, combing through the grass with her other hand. 'Look, here's another stem!'

We concentrated our search, finding five stems in total and painstakingly followed them through the herbage to where they all joined up. It was all one plant, and as far as we could tell – me, the amateur, Linda the expert – this was the last remaining wild plant on Earth.

Linda sat back with a sigh. 'At least it looks to have set a good bit of seed this year,' she said. One of the spent flowerheads had a few resolute seeds clinging on. Linda plucked them off and, after a moment's consideration, handed them to me. 'See if you have any luck with it. You might not – they could be infected with the same mould as back in 2018.'

I very carefully put the seeds in a tube with a twist of tissue, and tucked it in my pocket.

We scrambled back up the bank and carried on along the river. We came across an area of riverbank fenced off with lurid orange netting strung between neon yellow posts. The vegetation was strimmed flat inside.

Linda was irritated. 'It's just not the same as grazing; it's not widespread enough ... ah, I'm turning into a grumpy old woman!'

It's understandable, though. It must be hard seeing a site you know well being slowly stripped of its botanical richness through the thoughtless inactions and ineffectual efforts of others.

I found the parlous situation of Baker's hawkweed hard to rationalise – how can this situation get so dire without multiple organisations stepping in to help? – and I was astounded by Linda's dedication and near-solo effort to not let this species slip away. If it wasn't for Linda, and people like her, the world would be a much darker and sadder place.

We reached Holwick Head bridge, an altogether sturdier looking structure than Wynch Bridge, and began our search for another of Linda's planted hawkweeds. I spotted it this time – a hearty, spreading plant with five stems terminating in five spent flowerheads, the dozens of seeds long since scattered along the rocky river by the wind. Linda crouched by me, quietly pleased to see that not all of her reintroductions had ended in decapitation; that some seed definitely *had* made its way back into the wild.

Hopefully some of those seeds will end up in just the right spots to become the next generation of truly wild Baker's hawkweed, making that last native wild plant just a little less lonely.

I decided to post the seeds that Linda gave me to Andy Shaw and his plant nursery in Wales. In August 2023, he emailed me to let me know that he had *massive plants with literally hundreds of flowers*. I'm delighted to have played a *very tiny* part in securing the future of this species in cultivation, forming a link between the dedicated efforts of two amazing individuals.

CHAPTER 16

Down to Earth: British Earthstar

A month had passed since my trip to Teesdale to see Baker's hawkweed and it was now definitively autumn. By now, I'd seen a diverse array of plants, a vibrant assortment of invertebrates, and a red grouse, but I wanted to branch out further and track down a species from an entirely different taxonomic group – fungi. My research and emails to experts had yielded only a single species considered unique to this island, and so I had travelled down to Norfolk to see what might be Britain's only endemic fungus.

I pulled into the car park of Lynford Arboretum on a wet October morning. Autumn is the best time of year for finding fungi because the cooler, damper weather encourages them to produce their fruiting bodies and the species I wanted to see today was no exception.

I kept my eyes peeled for a black car, which Jonathan, my expert for the day, had told me to look out for. As I swung into a parking bay I saw two men in the patch of grass in the middle of the car park, clearly looking at something growing out of the turf. This is classic naturalist behaviour and so I felt reasonably confident that one of these men must be Jonathan. Not only that, but also one of these men just looked like the sort of person who'd know a lot about fungi. Honestly, close your eyes and picture a man who spends his time out and about looking at mushrooms. Did you picture a man with a big white beard, green jumper and a gnarled walking stick? That was this guy.

I got out of my car and walked across the grass towards them. The other guy, the one who didn't look like a grandfatherly woodsman, stuck out his hand. 'James?' he enquired.

This was Jonathan. With his neat, greying beard, glasses and pink-grey fleece he looked more like a businessman on a day off. We shook hands, and he introduced his friend as Chris. Chris and I shook hands too, and as we did, he said, 'My name is easy to remember, just think of Chris-tmas,' whilst gesturing at his snowy beard. It was a good line.

This is probably a good point for me to make a confession – I am hopeless at identifying fungi. I am decent at plants and if I get stuck, I can work my way through a key; I know my invertebrates pretty well; I can tell the difference between a robin and a blue tit. But I know *embarrassingly* little about fungi. The biggest problem, I find, is lack of decent field guides. It's very easy to buy a generic pocket-sized book called something like *The Field Guide to Mushrooms and Toadstools* that covers about 200 species with a bias towards the most colourful and dramatic-sounding, while ignoring a lot of other similar species. But my online research tells me that the UK has around 15,000 species of fungi, so *a lot* is being ignored. Of course, how can a book cover 15,000 species? It can't – that would be like wanting a comprehensive book on 'insects'. When I've asked fungi-folk to recommend the best texts on mushroom ID I usually find one of three obstacles: the book either costs as much as a kidney; has been out of print for two decades; or it's a text that covers all of northern Europe and is written in German.

This was why it was so exciting to meet Jonathan Revett, a man who not only knew his mushrooms but had discovered an entirely new one – the so-called British earthstar, *Geastrum britannicum*, a fungus seemingly endemic to Britain.

I almost immediately confessed my fungal naivety to Jonathan, who suggested we kick off the day with a brief foray around the arboretum before piling into his car and heading off to the site where he had discovered the British earthstar new to science. I eagerly agreed.

Our first find was the shaggy ink-cap, growing in a cluster a metre from where we stood. This mushroom starts out as a white cylinder with a 'fluffy' texture of curling scales, hence its other name of 'lawyer's wig' of which it makes a fairly reasonable impression. As the mushroom matures it shapeshifts into a more traditional umbrella-like shape, but as it does so the edges of the cap begin to digest themselves into a dripping, black liquid – the 'ink-cap' – which not only *resembles* ink but can actually be used to *make* ink.

At the mouth of the car park Jonathan plucked a small white mushroom and, removing a chunk of the cap, handed it to me. 'Stinking baby parasol,' he said, gesturing for me to sniff it, 'smells like burning rubber.'

Close up the mushroom wasn't simply white. The cap had a raised bump in the centre, like a boss on a shield; in mushroom circles this is known as the 'umbo', which is just a fun word to read and say. The umbo was a deep brown, as though the mushroom had been lightly toasted like a baked Alaska. I leant in and sniffed the raw edge of the cap. It really did smell like burnt rubber, or like something was very wrong with the clutch in a car.

'Is that "stinking-baby" parasol as in a … smelly infant?' I asked, 'Or a "stinking" baby-parasol as in … there are lots of baby-parasols and this one smells?'

Jonathan wrinkled his brow for a moment as he mentally parsed the question. 'The latter.'

I nodded, as though this had been an important question in the first place.

Across the road there was a scatter of club-like fungi with slightly lumpy heads. Jonathan swiftly identified them as a honey fungus, which surprised me as I had seen honey fungus before and they looked like proper mushrooms, not these odd knobbly clubs, but apparently that's just the way honey fungus grow and mature.

'Oh, and they can glow in the dark,' added Jonathan, casually, as though that wasn't one of the single most exciting things I've ever heard. I demanded more information. It turns out that it's not the mushroom itself that glows, but the black, bootlace-like 'rhizomorphs' – essentially fungal 'roots' – that snake under the bark of dead and dying trees. You need a moonless night and plenty of time for your eyes to adjust to the darkness to be in with a chance of seeing a honey fungus bioluminesce.

A few steps further on I spotted an intense violet-pink mushroom, a lurid, feverish colour. This was a wood blewit. Next was the bleach bonnetcap, a species that, when a section of the cap was peeled back, released a pungent, nostril-wrinkling hit of ammonia.

Then there came the mild milkcap, a stubby brown mushroom with a proportionally stout 'stipe' and a cap that flares up at the edges revealing the frilly gills below. (A 'stipe' is the mycological name for the 'stem' or 'umbrella handle' part of the mushroom. You could call it a stem and everyone would understand you, but there would always be one purist who would be mentally shaking their head at you.)

'The group is called milkcaps,' said Jonathan, breaking the cap in two, 'because they produce a milky liquid when broken.' He proffered a chunk, white droplets of liquid already beading along the broken edge, reminiscent of the milky latex you see when you break the stem of a poppy or greater celandine.

'Milkcaps can look very similar to each other, so the taste of the milk can be a useful clue.' Jonathan dabbed his finger in the milk and licked it. He paused. 'See, that milk is quite drying, so this is the mild milkcap.'

'Can I taste it?' I asked.

'Go ahead, if you want.'

I dabbed my finger in the liquid. This is probably a good time for me to say DON'T EAT FUNGI YOU FIND OUTSIDE, even if you feel confident in what you've found. It's just not worth the risk. There were only two reasons I was happy to taste anything; firstly, I trusted Jonathan's knowledge and years of experience; secondly, it would be sort of hilarious if I died from mushroom poisoning whilst trying to learn about fungi.

I licked the milk from the tip of my finger. It tasted entirely neutral. I waited a moment or so and felt a hint of astringency, the dryness, on my tongue. I then waited a few moments more to see if I would keel over. I didn't. Jonathan clearly knew his stuff.

Chris was a few paces away from us, prodding something at the base of a tree stump with the tip of his walking stick. 'Witch's egg,' he called over to us.

The witch's egg is a strange, sack-like organ that grows just below ground level and barely crests the surface. If left to its own devices it matures into a 'stinkhorn'; a fleshy stipe emerges (or 'hatches' I suppose) and thrusts skywards, producing a strong aroma that falls somewhere between sewage and carcass.

Jonathan knelt and dug around the tip of the egg, excavating an off-white, pulpy sack. It reminded me of a reptile egg in the way that the surface wrinkled and dented. He poked around in the nearby soil and found four or five others nearby.

'As there are a few I'll show you what one looks like inside,' he said, pulling out a pocket knife. Unfurling the curved blade he cut the egg in two, and gently pulled the two hemispheres apart. Have you ever seen those cross-section diagrams of Earth? The ones that show the planet with a section missing and all the different layers – the crust, mantle and core? The egg was built in pretty much the same way. The 'crust' was the surprisingly thick rubbery outer skin of the egg, the 'mantle' was a centimetre-or-so thick layer of a clear jelly-like substance, and the 'core' (though off-centre, down at the bottom of the egg) was a dense clean-white mass with a – perhaps unsurprisingly – mushroom-like texture.

'That middle part is edible,' said Jonathan, tapping the white core with the tip of his knife. 'I was leading a foray in Germany once and we cut one open like this and someone tried it; apparently it tastes like chestnut.'

'Can I try it?'

'Feel free,' he said, passing me a half.

As I didn't have a knife I tried to peel the edible section out with my fingers. It was a lot tougher than I expected, though, and I accidently grasped the egg too hard and squeezed the layer of frogspawny jelly over my palm and fingers. It was stickier than I imagined and, defeated, I discarded the crumpled egg without enjoying so much as a nibble and spent a few moments scraping the gunk from my palm onto a nearby tree trunk.

By the time I caught up with Chris and Jonathan they'd already found something else to show me, a small cluster of peach-grey, funnel-shaped mushrooms. They

even had a deep depression in the cap, adding to the funnel-like impression.
Jonathan held one in his hand. 'Sniff,' he instructed.
I did. I took a few deep nosefuls. It was familiar, annoyingly familiar. Not a beautiful smell, but not awful either. A sort of damp aroma – for some reason I was thinking of wet seeds. I shrugged and gave in.
'It's called the chicken-run funnel,' said Jonathan, 'because it supposedly smells like wet feathers.'
It did smell like wet feathers! I recognised the smell now from my childhood, collecting eggs from the chicken hut on a rainy morning. A bizarrely specific smell, astutely recognised by whoever named it.
Jonathan and Chris carried on finding and naming species: cauliflower fungus, red cracking boletus, shaggy parasol, funeral bells, false chanterelle, sulphur tuft, wood woolly-foot, pinecone cap.
We reached a small area planted with conifers. Beneath the trees the earth was mostly bare and scattered with pine needles. Jonathan told me that this is the sort of habitat that a lot of earthstar species like – conifer needle litter, bare-ish ground with little competition.
'We usually find crowned earthstar here … Ah!' He pointed. Emerging from the drift of old needles a few feet from us was the off-white manikin figure of an earthstar. We knelt and admired it.
If you've never seen an earthstar before then the first thing to know is that they are utterly unlike a traditional mushroom. There's no stipe, no cap, no gills. Instead, improbably, they look like a white-grey ball resting neatly in the centre of a star-shaped piece of mushroom-textured flesh. This bizarre appearance makes more sense once you understand how the earthstar grows. A simple ball-shaped growth emerges from the earth. This then starts to split at the top and down the sides, separating

into triangular sections, which peel backwards to rest on the ground, revealing a new, smaller ball inside. This smaller ball is filled with spores, which puff out of a small hole at the top of the ball. Some species have a simple hole, which can be raised into a sort of small volcano shape (these earthstars are described 'beaked'). The ball has a very thin skin, which dents and crumples easily. When raindrops land on the surface of the ball it forces out a puff of spores. The internet is filled with artful photographs of earthstars captured with a plume of smoke-like spores curling from them. We have 19 species in Britain, many of which are widespread, others of which are incredibly rare. The crowned earthstar is one of the widespread ones.

Jonathan gently extricated it from the pine-needle debris. 'This is one of last year's,' he told me. Some earthstars – perhaps helped by their sheltered, dryish positions under conifers – can dry up and remain recognisable for months or years after growing. He handed it to me. It was crispy and dry, but otherwise completely intact. The star-shaped base had eight rays – crowned earthstar can have anything from five to 14 rays – and they were thin and stiff; a fresh earthstar would have plump, fleshy rays. It was about 10cm across, point to point, and sat about 5cm tall. The central puffball was dry and crumpled. I gave it a prod to see if anything happened but any spores must have long since dispersed. I felt I now had my eye in, ready to search for the endemic.

We whizzed through the Norfolk countryside in the back of Jonathan's car. Chris was sitting in the front passenger seat and I was sitting directly behind Jonathan, firing questions at the back of his head. How had he discovered the British earthstar?

Twenty-two years earlier he ran a fungi event at the Wildfowl and Wetlands Trust (WWT) centre in Welney and had encouraged participants to bring along any fungi they wanted identifying. He remembers that one couple turned out a basket of mushrooms of all shapes and sizes. He worked through them: parasols, boletes, etc. Then, jumbled amongst the commoner species, he spotted it. An earthstar – and not just any earthstar. This earthstar had rays that arched so far back that it lifted itself off the ground, almost like someone doing the crab pose in yoga. Or like when alien spacecraft are shown landing in cartoons and they extend legs to hold the saucer aloft. In the majority of earthstar species found in Britain the 'star' lies pretty much flat. Only two species (or so it was thought at the time) hoisted themselves off the ground and stood on tiptoe like this. As it was small, only a few centimetres tall, Jonathan thought it must be the uncommon rayed earthstar, *Geastrum quadrifidium*.

Jonathan interrogated the couple as to where they'd found it. It turned out they had been driving along an unassuming road near Cockley Cley in Norfolk and had spotted a big clump of parasol mushrooms from the car. They pulled into a nearby field entrance to pick one to take to the fungi event, and whilst they were there also picked up a few other mushrooms, including the earthstar. Jonathan managed to pinpoint the spot from their description and was able to visit within a few days, where he found the earthstar in some abundance.

Jonathan was telling me this as we wound our way through country lanes, occasionally meeting my eye in the rear-view mirror as he regaled me with the story of the earthstar's discovery. He suddenly gestured to the left. 'This is the verge, just a bit further down here.'

It was a totally typical verge. Planted with twisted Scots pines and fringing an arable field, it looked like a hundred other Breckland roadsides. We carried on down the road for 100m or so before pulling up at the side of a wide field entrance.

Getting out of the car, Jonathan pointed back down the verge. 'It was just along there where I first found them. I propped a discarded lager can in a tree branch so that there was a marker for Chris to come have a look too.'

As well as pines, the verge held thickets of bramble. I skirted these as I followed Jonathan. Chris took the simpler route of walking along the margin of the field. The search method was straightforward – look in the bare-ish, needley patches beneath the pines – but the surrounding overgrown vegetation made this harder than it sounded. That said, we were barely out of the car two minutes before Jonathan found an earthstar.

'This isn't it,' he said, as I made it to his side. He was brushing soil off an old-looking earthstar, clearly one from the previous year. 'See how the legs arch down to lift it off the ground? Only three species do that – *Geastrum fornicatum, quadrifidium*, and the one we're looking for, *britannicum*.' He handed the specimen to me. It was about 8cm tall, its rays sharply reflexed back to give it such height. 'This is *fornicatum*, the arched earthstar. It's much bigger than the other two that stand up on tiptoe. The one we're looking for will be half the size.'

I perched it in my hand to take a photo; it rested like a little spaceship on my palm. I'd barely managed to snap a decent picture before Jonathan called me over. He'd found one.

It was much smaller than the arched earthstar, almost like a perfect version in miniature. Jonathan stood it on his hand on the tips of its five neat-rayed legs, its 'head' brownish with a faint greyish bloom, slightly crumpled from a year of wear and tear. The British earthstar.

'I came here in October 2000, expecting to find the rayed earthstar, *quadrifidium*, but I soon realised that none of the earthstars here fit the description. The rayed earthstar – also called the "four-footed earthstar" – usually has four rays or "legs". None of the earthstars here had four legs. It didn't match anything in the literature; it didn't match anything online – not that there was a lot online back then.'

Jonathan collected a few specimens, wrote up a note explaining why he thought they were different and sent it off to Kew. I generally think of Kew as being plant-focused, but they also do a lot of work with fungi. In fact, they are home to the world's largest 'fungarium', which has over a million dried specimens; it's basically the fungal equivalent of a herbarium. Kew received Jonathan's specimens and, after what one assumes must have been a cursory examination, wrote back saying that they were simply unusual examples of the rayed earthstar.

Jonathan wasn't sure they were right, but who was he to argue with the experts? So he and Chris kept visiting year after year, exploring the extent of the colony, counting them and identifying other fungi along the verge.

'Here's another one,' called Chris, pointing under some arching bramble stems with his stick. It looked like a shiny acorn nestled in the litter. I knelt to reach gingerly through the thorns to pick it up, noticing as I did that Chris's cane was tipped with a thimble.

'It's so I can give things a little tap and hear whether they're a pebble or something more interesting,' he told me. 'I can't be bending down for stones doing an impression of interesting little mushrooms all the time.'

The British earthstar I picked up was absolutely perfect. Five neatly reflexed legs and a plump shining ball perched neatly on top. I thought it must be freshly emerged, but when I showed it to Chris he pointed out that the legs were paper thin rather than the fleshy legs of a fresh earthstar. It was just very well preserved, and probably rehydrated by the recent damp weather.

'Do you see all this bramble, bracken, rank grass?' asked Jonathan. 'This didn't used to be here. When we were first surveying the colony 20 years ago it was mostly short grass and bare patches under the pines – perfect for earthstars, and other things.'

He went on to tell me that in the early years of checking in on the mystery earthstars that no one else seemed to appreciate, he and Chris found another rare fungi, the sandy stiltball. The name is very apt; it likes sandy places and it looks like a fuzzy brown ball on top of a stick. It's also very rare, perhaps only ever recorded from a couple of dozen sites in the UK, several of which are now lost. Because of this the verge was made a roadside nature reserve in the early 2000s. Perversely, the designation of the site to protect the species found here had exactly the opposite effect. The council stopped mowing the verge – because, as we all know, suddenly changing the management of a site for no reason is the best course of action. Despite Jonathan's attempts to inform the council, the management was never reinstated and the verge became overgrown with brambles and bracken. The sandy stiltballs now haven't been seen in years and the number of British earthstars has declined.

'I might start coming and cutting it myself,' said Jonathan as we picked our way through the bracken. 'It's probably easier than getting anyone at the council to take notice.'

He continued telling me the story of the British earthstar. After a few years of checking in on the population, and still convinced it was something different to the rayed earthstars he saw elsewhere, he tried again. This time, instead of Kew, he sent specimens to a Dutch expert who had recently undertaken work on the genus. The result? The same as with Kew – they look like a variant of rayed earthstar.

Even more years passed. Jonathan had basically given up hope of getting them recognised. Until one day in 2015, out of the blue, he heard that some Spanish mycologists had been working on earthstars, undertaking DNA testing on specimens from across Europe. Included amongst their samples were some of the specimens that Jonathan had sent to Kew. They ended up discovering seven previously unknown earthstars from across Europe, with one of them being Jonathan's. They named it *britannicum* as Britain was – and remains – the only place that this species has ever been found.

I was now desperate to find one of my own and I had my eye in on the right sort of habitat – bare pine needle litter under Scots pines, often under fallen branches or light thickets of bramble that served to keep the ground partially clear. Having seen the previous couple that Chris and Jonathan had found I knew that they were often part-buried in the needle mulch, usually only the puffball on top being obvious. I scanned likely patches with no luck.

Jonathan found another, and then another very close to it. I dejectedly scrambled over to see them, wishing I could find my own. These two were also very well preserved, peeking cheerily out of the loam a foot apart from each other, separated by an empty cider can and a discarded pasty packet. There were a lot of empty cans along the verge.

'You know how some fungi grow with certain trees?' asked Chris, a twinkle in his eye. 'Some growing alongside conifers, or beech trees, or oaks? Well, British earthstar seems to like to grow alongside old cans of cider.'

Jonathan chuckled. 'Yeah, there's a mycorrhizal association with them.'

Mushroom jokes, eh? What a fun guy.

It was then that I spotted my own; a third British earthstar in this little cluster. I'd been staring at the litter trying to think of my own joke to add when it jumped out at me. I teased it out of the litter and sat it on my palm, its round 'head' plump with a greyish bloom, almost blueberry-like.

'Take one home with you,' said Jonathan. 'It'll last forever if you keep it dry.'

I gently placed it in a tube and put it in my pocket.

One of the strangest things about the British earthstar is how widespread it is. By the time it was described in 2015 there were already rumblings amongst British mycologists about this possible new earthstar, and by the end of that year a paper was published that listed its discovery in 10 British vice-counties – a number that has only grown in the years since.

So is it a widespread species that has simply been overlooked? Well, that's where the story gets a little stranger. Digging through all the specimens in Kew's fungarium, many of which date to the Victorian era, *did* reveal specimens of the British earthstar that had been overlooked and misidentified as something else, but the earliest one was collected in 1994, only six years before Jonathan discovered it in Norfolk. How can a species that we now know to be so widespread have avoided being collected until 30 years ago? I put this to Jonathan.

'It could be an alien,' he replied, 'perhaps an undescribed earthstar species from somewhere else in the world that reached here maybe 50 years ago and spread. By the time I found it, it had already spread to most of Britain. That would explain why there aren't any earlier records than 1994 – it either wasn't here yet or wasn't common enough yet to be found. That said, it's still not been found anywhere outside Britain.'

It's a plausible idea; that rather than being a 'true' endemic it could possibly be another example of a false endemic, this one so ambiguous that it's hard to tell either way.

I countered this to Jonathan with my own theory. Could the British earthstar be an endemic species, one that was formerly rare, hence not being in historic collections, but then had benefited from a warming or wetter climate to spread across Britain in recent years?

'Could be,' said Jonathan, 'though you're clearly biased towards wanting it to be endemic.'

Jonathan was right. As we got into his car and headed back to the arboretum I mulled it over. As far as we currently know, the British earthstar is a unique, British species. However, if we did suddenly discover that its 'real' home was halfway across the world, that wouldn't stop it being a fascinating fungus with an unrivalled story behind it.

I still hope that my theory is right, though.

CHAPTER 17

Between a Rock and a Wet Place: Derbyshire Feathermoss

The British earthstar turned out to be my last endemic of 2022. Originally, it wasn't meant to be. I had planned a trip to Plymouth in December to seek out our only endemic spider, but stormy, wet, and unsettled weather forced me to postpone. That adventure would have to wait until the end of 2023.

As the cold winter months settled in, life took a different turn. I left the RSPB after a decade and began a new chapter with the BSBI. While adjusting to the change, I also started refining my targets for the year ahead. One gap stood out: I had yet to see an endemic mammal. This spurred plans for an expedition to the far north to find the intriguing Orkney vole. Around the same time, I saw a series of posts on social media with photographs of the endemic whitebeams of Arran and, now hopelessly addicted to *Sorbus*, I couldn't help but organise a pilgrimage to see them. Finally, aware of the gaping hole in my taxonomic reach, I began researching endemic bryophytes.

Trying to work out how many endemic bryophytes – the mosses and liverworts – we have was not an easy task. Unfortunately, there is no handy report detailing all of our unique species, and so I spent several hours searching online for 'endemic moss Britain' and 'liverwort, endemic Britain', collating my finds into a list and double-checking with every moss book I could get my hands on. I can't claim that this list is 100 per cent accurate, but it's probably pretty close.

I think that we have a single definite British endemic liverwort, *Herbertus borealis*, the delightfully named northern prongwort, found only in two adjacent 10km squares in Wester Ross in Scotland.

We also have a liverwort that is very likely another example of a false endemic. In Brookwood Cemetery, near Guildford in Surrey, there is a strange leafy liverwort. First spotted in 2004, it is clearly in the genus *Lophocolea* but doesn't match any of the five species known from Britain. It was suspected to be a species accidentally introduced from elsewhere, but it matches none of the hundreds of *Lophocolea* species known from anywhere else in the world. Is this an endemic species with a fondness for this single unassuming cemetery? Or is it possible that it's hitched a lift from somewhere else where it remains undiscovered? The latter seems more likely, especially as two of the five *Lophocolea* species in Britain are introduced from elsewhere. It has been scientifically named as *Lophocolea brookwoodiana* in honour of its only known site.

There are also two near-endemic liverworts: Fitzgerald's notchwort, *Leiocolea fitzgeraldiae*, which is found in Wales, Scotland and Ireland, and greater copperwort, *Cephaloziella nicholsonii*, which has been recorded from Britain and Ireland, with unconfirmed records from Germany and Spain.

We have a couple of near-endemics on the moss side of things too: the Cornish path moss and Skye bog-moss, both of which were discovered in Britain and subsequently found in Ireland.

Scotland does well with endemic mosses, having three utterly unique species: Dixon's thread-moss, *Bryum dixonii*; Scottish thread-moss, *Pohlia scotica*; and Scottish beardmoss, *Bryoerythrophyllum caledonicum*. Two other mosses were once considered as Scottish endemics: Arisaig crisp-moss, *Tortella limosella*, which was found only once, on a sandy seashore in west Scotland and is now considered an aberrant form of the very widespread yellow crisp-moss; and *Bryum lawersianum*, a moss discovered on Ben Lawers and last seen there in 1924 but now considered just a form of the widespread Arctic thread-moss.

In Wales there is the mysterious *Orthotrichum cambrense*, a distinctive moss discovered in 2011 on trees around the car park at Dryslwyn Castle. Is this a rare native that has spread from an unknown site onto these recently planted trees? Or could it have been introduced from abroad with them? No one knows, and so this is either an endemic or another false endemic.

Finally, in England, we have the two endemic feather-mosses. There is the Yorkshire feather-moss, *Thamnobryum cataractarum*, discovered in 1992 and known only from a single gorge in the Yorkshire Dales, and then there is its even rarer relative, the Derbyshire feather-moss, the species I had chosen as a target because of the sheer secrecy that shrouds it.

In 1998, to celebrate the 25th anniversary of the founding of the Derbyshire Dales National Nature Reserve, a group of journalists were invited to see a species that was not only the rarest one on the reserve, but one of the rarest species on the planet. They gathered at the predetermined meeting point where they met with the reserve manager who blindfolded them all, carefully guided them into his vehicle, and drove them a winding route through the twisting valleys of the dales so that any hope of identifying the exact location of the exquisitely rare Derbyshire feather-moss, whose global population grows on a single riverside rock, was impossible.

Twenty-five years later, on a cool April day, I drove into Derbyshire with my own ambition of seeing this species. I hoped that Joe Alsop, the current senior reserve manager, wasn't intending to subject me to the same blindfold treatment.

Driving to my meeting point from North Lincolnshire allowed an appreciation of the stark contrasts in the underlying geology of Derbyshire. To get to my meeting point in the limestone of the White Peak I first drove through the Dark Peak, a horseshoe-shaped band of millstone grit, which lends a darker, acid quality to the soils. The land here seems colder, bleaker; carpeted with heather, studded with gloomy rocky crags and thickets of birch. Then, suddenly, the landscape changes entirely. The heather is gone, the birch retreats, and you find yourself on a dome of limestone where the rock outcrops are pale and the drystone walls and villages are quaint and cheerful.

I pulled up at the spot that Joe had sent me directions for, finding him already waiting for me in a green Land Rover. After a quick exchange of greetings, Joe informed me that we would be travelling to a second location. I braced myself for the blindfold but, apparently, I was judged trustworthy enough to simply follow Joe's car for a few minutes along winding, shady roads until we reached a short, muddy roadside pull-in beneath a valley-side canopy of trees only just beginning to unfurl their leaves.

Joe walked round to my car door as I pulled on my wellies. He had very clearly specified in his messages to me that I'd need them. As I booted up, I asked him about just how private they kept the site. Could I, for example, when writing this up, mention the village we had met up in before driving here?

'I'd prefer you didn't,' said Joe. 'We try and keep the exact site secret.'

Curious, I asked Joe if he received many requests to visit the moss.

Joe paused for a moment. I assumed he was mentally totting up the torrent of moss-related inquiries he must deal with on a daily basis. 'Well, you're the first since I took on this job.'

'When did you get the job?'

'2016.'

Perhaps the secrecy around Derbyshire feather-moss is so great that people aren't even aware enough of its existence to ask? Or maybe moss just isn't as big a draw as, say, orchids?

Footwear sorted, Joe and I hopped over the wall bordering the pull-in onto the top of a steep slope carpeted with swathes of wild garlic and dog's mercury. A narrow mud track, more a badger-path than a human trail, zig-zagged its way down the valley. As we tramped along the path Joe told me more about the nature reserve. It's home to the largest extent of ravine woodland in Britain and they're currently doing what they can to mitigate the impact of ash dieback. Ash is the dominant tree in these woodlands at the moment, but this wasn't the case historically so they're taking this opportunity to diversify the tree species to a more natural mix that would have once been characteristic of the area, planting small- and large-leaved limes, wych elm, and to a lesser extent yew and field maple. I asked him what his favourite species on the NNR is. 'It's the woodlands for me,' he said, 'the lime trees.'

Patches of pink-blushed wood anemone dotted the slope, their nodding heads turned coyly to the sky. A few leaves of garlic at the edges of the path were bruised as we walked and the heavy scent of garlic mingled with the rich organic scent of damp leaf litter. The sound of the stream at the bottom of the valley got louder and the ground levelled out to a shining carpet of opposite-leaved golden saxifrage, which hugged the muddy edge of the watercourse.

We stood at the side of the stream, the rushing water shallow and gin-clear. On the opposite side to us towered a limestone cliff studded with moist, shiny green clumps of hart's-tongue ferns and sporting rocky ledges crowded with woodland flowers like hanging gardens. Towards the base of the cliff, only slightly higher than our head-height, was a long horizontal cleft in the cliff, easily tall enough for a person to stand in. To the left of this cleft there was the shadowy, oval mouth of a cave leading darkly into the rock. To the right there was a small waterfall, the cascade about two metres wide and a metre tall, the clear water frothing as it fell, so white as to be almost tinged blue.

There wasn't a huge amount of information about the Derbyshire feather-moss available online. I'd read that it was originally discovered in 1883, at this very site, by George Alfred Holt, a pharmacist from Manchester. From what I'd read I'd gained the impression that the moss was found on a single rock in a river – in my imagination this had become a boulder emerging from a stream like a whale's back, carpeted with a fine baize fuzz of this exceedingly scarce moss – hence the wellies that Joe had told me to wear.

Joe stepped into the stream and I followed, feeling the bright coldness of the water through my boots. The water was only mid-calf deep but the streambed was made up of smooth, rounded cobbles that threatened to turn an ankle if you weren't careful. We waded until we stood a metre in front of the waterfall, the top of the cascade at chest height.

Joe pointed at the waterfall. 'Here it is,' he said, his voice raised to counteract the rumble of the fall. I stared at the water.

'In the waterfall?' I asked.

'Yes,' Joe replied, 'but the waterfall isn't always here – in fact the stream we're standing in isn't always here. A few weeks back when we organised to meet the waterfall wasn't flowing.'

I was edging closer to the waterfall as he spoke. Sure enough, there were areas where the water wasn't being churned into froth and instead was flowing glassily over a tangled green mat of moss. I reached out and touched it through the icy flow, the water churning into spray over my hand. The moss was rougher than I expected, not a gentle soft turf but wiry strands tough enough to withstand the torrent.

I stepped back. Joe had magically pulled some papers out of thin air and was leafing through them. 'These are some notes from the last survey back in 2005. Ah! And here's a sketch map.'

On the paper was an unmistakable drawing of the waterfall in front of us with different patches shaded and circled, annotated with the names of mosses. Two very similar species live on the surface of the rock: the fox-tail feather-moss, *Thamnobryum alopecurum*, a common and widespread moss that is found in almost every square kilometre in Britain, and my target species, *Thamnobryum angustifolium*, the endemic Derbyshire feather-moss.

It had once been questioned whether the Derbyshire feather-moss was even a species at all, or whether it was just an environmentally induced form of the fox-tail feather-moss, adapted to growing submerged in fast-flowing water. A rather neat experiment answered this question by growing it in cultivation and demonstrating that the Derbyshire feather-moss still looked like Derbyshire feather-moss even when grown out of water under the same conditions as fox-tail feather-moss, showing that the differences must be genetic in nature.

The diagram showed that the left-hand side of the waterwall face was dominated by the fox-tail whereas the right-hand side was the domain of the Derbyshire feather-moss. 'They move around, though,' said Joe. 'Each survey shows the two species in different proportions and in slightly different places. It probably depends on wetter seasons vs drier seasons but no one knows.'

I poked my finger into the chill torrent and ever-so-gently extended a frond of moss out from the surface of the waterfall. Moisture beaded between its minute leaves and stem, softening its form and giving it a translucent, gleaming-emerald appearance. I gently blew on it, scattering droplets, revealing its true structure. A long, trailing stem from which grew many radiating narrow leaves (its scientific name, *angustifolium*, means 'narrow leaves') giving it the look of a tiny conifer; like a single branch of a Christmas tree. I gently slid it off my finger and the force of the water laid it back flat against the rock.

'One single rock face on Earth just feels so … vulnerable,' I said. 'How safe is it here?'

Joe listed off some threats. Firstly, the risk of bryologists collecting it. This wasn't really a modern issue, but many species of moss had in the past been collected rampantly by Victorians. That said, it wouldn't take many modern amateur bryologists to 'just take a small specimen' for the population to become depleted. Secondly, accidental damage during recreation. The cave nearby was a draw for people – who doesn't want to clamber up the rocks to peer into the dark stony heart of the Earth? – and if people were climbing the face of the waterfall when the water was dry, then they could easily and accidentally scrape the face of the rock with their boots, gouging out precious chunks of moss.

'What's the cave called?' I asked. Joe told me. I made a note.

'But obviously that would give the site away,' he added.

I tried to surreptitiously scribble out the note. 'Oh yeah, obviously,' I lied.

The final issue Joe told me about was pollution. The moss spends about half its time submerged in the waterfall, so if the water quality deteriorated or if a spill of some evil chemical got into the watercourse, that could spell disaster. 'That's the big one,' said Joe. 'I don't know if you know much about limestone hydrology but water acts very strangely flowing through it. We've had a national specialist trying to trace the source of the water for five years now – doing dye tracing and so on – and we still have no idea where the water comes from.'

I looked at the waterfall in front of us, which, though unchanged, now took on a mysterious air. Gallons of water were thundering over it from a completely unknown source. Limestone slowly dissolves in water and over centuries this weaves unseen passages through the rock. This water could be travelling miles, spending days or weeks underground before emerging here, its origin and path totally obscure. All that the nature reserve can do is keep working on finding the source and hope that no disasters occur in the meantime.

A dipper skipped across the rocks behind Joe before swooping up to its mossy nest under a rocky crag. This is a species highly sensitive to changes in water quality and its presence within earshot of the waterfall shows that, for now at least, all is well.

We sloshed out of the stream and began the trudge up the side of the valley. There were no guarantees that the moss I had seen and touched was the species I had been looking for, though I had at least been looking in the right spot according to an 18-year-old survey. Usually I would have been frustrated by this lack of certainty, by not being able to pinpoint exactly what I'd seen, but in this case I was happy to leave it enigmatic. Despite my efforts to gain access to this secret site, the moss had, in the end, kept its exact location a secret from me.

Joe casually mentioned to me as we were walking up the valley that he'd heard that there was a possibility that a second population had been found in Cumbria a few years ago but that he'd heard no more about it. When I got home I set to researching this – I had to know whether the Derbyshire feather-moss was obscenely rare or merely critically rare – and I ended up down a rabbit hole.

I found a reference online to Derbyshire feather-moss being discovered in Cumbria in 2008. I couldn't find out much more but I also couldn't stop pulling threads and so I ordered a niche and marvellous book called *England's Rare Mosses and Liverworts – Their History,*

Ecology, and Conservation by Ron D. Porley. This book turned out to be delightfully readable and as soon as it arrived in the post I found myself eagerly searching through it for the Derbyshire feather-moss account. There, in black and white, was my answer.

In 2008 there was a period of particularly low water levels on Cumbria's River Eden. Mark Lawley, expert bryologist, was exploring this rarely revealed habitat when he discovered an intriguing moss from rocks that would usually be submerged and inaccessible. This moss turned out to be the Derbyshire feather-moss, newly discovered at its second site on Earth, and seemingly more abundant on the Eden than in its original location.

It was an odd feeling reading this. By any measure this was fantastic news but for a brief moment I felt a slight sense of loss – as though a modicum of glamour had been eroded from my experience of seeing Derbyshire feather-moss 'at its only site on Earth'. It was interesting to confront this sensation. As a conservationist I don't want species to be perilously confined to single sites, and yet clearly some part of me relished seeing a species so rare and restricted.

I wonder how widespread this fetishisation of rarity is? I remember once talking to an older birder who told me that seeing red kites had been 'spoilt' by how many there were now; surely the most negative possible framing of an unbelievable conservation success story.

A few months later, as if to make the writing of this chapter even more complicated, a paper was published in the Journal of Bryology by a team of five authors announcing *another* discovery of Derbyshire feather-moss, this time from the Italian Alps. This would be the third population in the world and the first outside Britain, stripping it of its endemic status but making it much more secure from a conservation perspective and implying that additional populations may be found in this new search area.

However, the paper also mentions minor differences in the appearance of the moss in all three locations (the Derbyshire population being more distinct, the Cumbrian and Italian populations being more similar to each other) and casually mentions that, genetically speaking, all three populations seem to be the same as the common and widespread fox-tail feather-moss. It appears that each of the three populations, rather than representing the geographical spread of a single species, may actually represent three independent instances of the fox-tail feather-moss evolving towards the same appearance when exposed to similar semi-aquatic conditions, perhaps too early in the process for any significant genetic differences to accumulate. Should they then even count as a species? And if so, would this make them all the same species or three different ones?

The paper states:

It could be argued, therefore, that it is inappropriate to include them all under the umbrella of a single species. However, pending further studies on their molecular relationships, and because of their close morphological similarity, we refrain from describing them as separate taxa at the present time.

Is there a future with an Italian feather-moss, a Cumbrian feather-moss, and with a Derbyshire feather-moss once again relegated to a single rock face? I have no answer to this, but it's clear that endemic species provide a valuable perspective on the dynamic and ongoing nature of evolution and the delineation of different taxa.

In any case, this story of evolution in action had set me up perfectly for my next target; a vole on a path of divergence from its nearest relatives and a trip that would take me further north than I'd ever been.

CHAPTER 18

Orcadian Adventures: Scottish Primrose and Orkney Vole

Britain has no endemic mammal species. We were scoured too recently by the last Ice Age for any of our mammals to split off entirely from their mainland Europe counterparts. However, a few of them have started to diverge into unique subspecies.

A few of the more distinct and well-known include the Skomer vole, *Myodes glareolus skomerensis*, a subspecies of bank vole which is distinctly larger than its cousin on the British mainland and is endemic to the Welsh island of Skomer off the coast of Pembrokeshire. There's also the St Kilda field mouse, *Apodemus sylvaticus hirtensis*, a subspecies of the wood mouse found only on the Scottish island of St Kilda and which can be up to twice as large as mainland wood mice. St Kilda was also once home to the endemic St Kilda house mouse, which was also larger than typical house mice. Unfortunately, this unique subspecies went extinct in the 1930s when the entire human population left the island. The mouse, utterly dependent on people, disappeared soon afterwards.

Slightly less well known, and possibly more dubiously distinct, are the supposed subspecies of bank vole found on Mull and Raasay, known as *Myodes glareolus alstoni* and *Myodes glareolus erica* respectively, and the subspecies of wood mouse found on Fair Isle, *Apodemus sylvaticus fridariensis*.

I'll take this opportunity to point out that our native and incredibly rare wildcat is often described as being the endemic subspecies *Felis silvestris 'grampia'* but in 2017 the Cat Specialist Group included it within the nominate subspecies, *Felis silvestris silvestris*, meaning that wildcats in Britian belong to the same subspecies as those found across the rest of Europe. Our wildcat is also often unhelpfully described as the 'Scottish wildcat' despite wildcats once being widespread across Britain. If we cement its identity as purely Scottish then we risk making its current restricted range seem natural, rather than a human-induced fragment of a once-widespread species.

The endemic subspecies that captured my imagination, the one with the best story, was the Orkney vole, *Microtus arvalis orcadensis*, which is found only on eight islands of the Orkney archipelago.

As the ferry passed Hoy, the rockiest and most craggy of the Orkney islands, I went out onto the open deck to see the Old Man of Hoy. This towering rock pillar, with the vague silhouette of a man standing to attention, stared out across the steely-blue sea and ignored the seabirds swirling past him.

I wasn't going to Hoy, though; instead, our ferry skirted its coast and carried on towards Mainland, the largest of the islands that make up Orkney. A great skua (also known as a bonxie), thick-billed and barrel-chested, powered past the deck, and as we docked at Stromness the calm water in the harbour was dotted with black guillemots in immaculate plumage. I watched as they dived, flashing their wax-red feet as they disappeared under the surface.

Robert had joined me, equally ensnared as me by the possibility of seeing the utterly unique Orkney vole as well as anything else unusual we might find on these northern islands. It had been a little over a year since our last trip together in search of the northern February red and Scottish crossbill and the highs and lows of success and failure still lingered between us.

As we drove from the harbour, I realised that my mental image of Mainland had been entirely wrong. Never having visited before, I'd imagined Orkney as rocky, craggy, towering and stark, but it's not like that at all. It's lush green, gently undulating and cheerful, as if the Yorkshire Dales were an island. Despite it being the end of May, a month after my trip to see the Derbyshire feather-moss, we still spotted roadside verges covered with flowering daffodils and hybrid bluebells and, oddly enough, occasional hearty clumps of rhubarb.

We stayed at Abune-the-hill in the north of the island, in a single-storey pale grey building with a graphite-grey slate roof. Three other cottages clustered nearby and a few other houses dotted the horizon, but otherwise, it was just green sheep pasture, a grey sliver of sea, and the low rise of Costa Hill in the distance. Inside, the cottage was cheerful, with stone floors, wooden furniture, and cosy fittings, and we got to unpacking. First, I carefully unwrapped essential pieces of equipment I had brought with me: Longworth mammal traps.

The Longworth is *the* classic live-mammal trap. Designed in the 1940s, it is still the mammal trap of choice amongst ecologists and researchers. It comes in two parts: a short aluminium corridor, square in cross-section, which interlocks with a larger rectangular box. At the open end of the corridor is a hinged door which is linked to a bar. When a small mammal walks over the bar the trap door swings shut and catches the animal inside. The large rectangular box is provisioned with dry hay and food so that the captive can eat and stay warm and dry until released.

They also cost about as much as your own private island – well, around £50. Ideally you want to run more than one trap. If I ran a single trap each night I was on Orkney, I would have five chances. If I had two traps, I'd get ten chances. I had three traps with me. One of these Robert and I had clubbed together and bought, rationalising that we'd both enjoy seeing an Orkney vole and that there might be other small mammals we'd want to see in future. The other two traps were a slog to locate. I contacted a whole host of organisations asking if they had any I could borrow – no response. I asked friends at the RSPB, but they didn't have any. I emailed someone who lived on Orkney who'd blogged about using a Longworth to catch an Orkney vole – no response. In the end it was my caving companion Heather who came to the rescue; her dad had two that he used to catch mice in his garden office and he was willing to let me borrow them. Three traps, five nights and 15 chances to catch an Orkney vole.

I carefully filled the boxes with hay, a scatter of seeds, some chunks of carrot, and a few mealworms in case a shrew wandered in. Then, once I'd pulled Robert away from his unpacking, we went outside and set them up on the verges near our cottage. Brushing through the long grass by the stone walls lining the field we found evidence of vole runs, rounded tunnels formed by voles scampering through the base of the grasses. We placed our traps nearby, being careful to remember exactly where we'd put them. One was by the base of a Japanese rose, the others marked by distinctive stones in the wall. Task complete, and tired from a day of travel, we went to bed.

There was nothing in the traps the next morning. We got up early and eagerly wandered down the road to check, peering at the dark mouth of each trap in the hope of seeing the doors sprung. Empty. We rationalised that the voles might need time to get used to these new objects and smells in their habitat before being enticed by the delicacies within, so we left the traps in place.

There was nothing more we could do in our search for Orkney voles, other than wait, so instead I went searching for another endemic, the Scottish primrose, *Primula scotica*. This beautiful flower – a relative of the more familiar and widespread cowslip and primrose – is only found, in the entire world, on the northernmost coast of Scotland and in the Orkney archipelago.

From what I'd researched, the best site to see it on Orkney was at Yesnaby on the west coast of Mainland, but before I went I decided to check with John Crossley, the BSBI recorder for Orkney. Before I could even mention my plan, John told me that *everyone* goes and sees Scottish primrose at Yesnaby and it would be much more valuable if people looked for it in places where it hadn't been recently recorded – like out on the northwest coast of Rousay, the island just to the north of Mainland.

The ferry crossing to Rousay only took 20 minutes, and it was a strange feeling to spend that time in a car, on a boat, watching stiff-winged fulmars swoop by only metres away. Rousay – a low, humped island, grass green around the edges and fading to a sombre heather-brown on the shallow hills – grew slowly on the horizon like the back of a great serpent as we approached.

When the low-slung boat gently thunked onto the jetty, the ramp unfolded with a whir of hydraulics. Tourists carefully reversed their cars off, while islanders zipped away with practised ease. We disembarked, passing the Rousay Heritage Centre and a few dozen houses with gardens filled with fuchsia and clumps of early pampas grass, before joining the single, circular road that laps the island. This road neatly bisects the terrain: below it, fields roll toward the sea, while above, the landscape darkens, stretching up to the cluster of hills that dominate Rousay's centre.

Robert drove me round to the north-west of the island and dropped me off near the Loch of Wasbister, a small body of water with a neat crannog (a Neolithic artificial island) set amongst green fields. Swallows chattered over it as I got out of the car. The ferry times only gave us a few hours on the island, and Robert wanted to explore rather than spend his time looking for a flower that we might not even find. We arranged to meet up in a couple of hours, and he sped off on his own island adventures.

I made my way up a track, heading for the coastal clifftops where Scottish primrose had last been recorded around a decade before. I passed through a farmyard, through a gate, and out onto a wide expanse of tussocky clifftop. The weather, greyish so far, added in a blustery wind and I soon found myself adding a second jumper, gloves and scarf to ward off the late-May chill.

Wandering, head down, concentrating on the turf around my feet, I kept my attention focused for any hint of the magenta flowers of Scottish primrose. Instead, I spotted the dusty blue of spring squill, the pale lilac of cuckooflower and, out towards the cliffs, the bright Barbie-pink pom-poms of thrift. It began to rain.

I kept my head tilted down to try and keep the rain off my glasses, but it rained so hard and at such an angle that the water dripped off my eyebrows and ran down the lenses. I took them off, hooking them into the neck of my waterproof, and squinted at the turf instead.

Daisies, some marsh marigolds, and even – when crouching – the tiny subtle Christmas tree-like fronds of crowberry. I started to wonder if perhaps I was simply too late in the year, or too early. The Scottish primrose flowers twice a year: in May and then again in July. It was the 29th of May – had I come just too late and missed it? But if that was the case, I should have been able to find gone-over flowers and their grey-green rosettes of leaves.

Half an hour of walking along the clifftops in the driving rain revealed nothing. Then, suddenly and dramatically, the rain stopped and the sky cleared to a blinding blue. It went from winter to summer in the space of five minutes. I was soon too hot, and shed my scarf, gloves and two layers of clothing.

I wandered closer to the cliff, which dropped 20m down to foaming blue-white churn below. The ledges of the cliffs were dotted with the white-and-ash figures of fulmars, which croaked and cackled and watched my progress with their smudged-eyeliner gaze. Amongst them were more proud pink tufts of thrift, like tiny balcony gardens decorating their nests.

By this point I was out on Sacquoy Head, a wide promontory that is the most northerly point on Rousay. I suddenly realised that I was the furthest north I'd ever been, delighted that a tiny flower – though one that I couldn't find – had brought me on such an adventure. The Scottish primrose grows even further north, and across the sea ahead of me I could see Westray where it's also found. Beyond that, out of my view, was Papa Westray, which is the most northerly site for this little primula.

But where was it? I redoubled my efforts. I walked zigzags across the headland, trying to cover as much ground as possible. One of these erratic paths took me further south, and it was as I crouched, debating over another tuft of leaves, that something whistled past my head. I spun around, almost losing my balance, and saw that a bonxie had just given me a warning pass. It was now far ahead of me, small above the horizon but, like a pendulum reaching the end of its parabola, it turned and swung back in my direction. I knew that bonxies would dive-bomb people that came near their nests, but would it actually hit me? Or was it just to warn me off?

It felt like it was accelerating towards me, those dark eyes staring me down out of its chocolate-coloured head. I decided to stare back, gambling that this was more a warning than a direct attack. We both flinched at the same time, the bonxie wheeling off in one direction, flapping its dark wings, as I stumbled back in the other.

Keeping one eye on the wheeling pirate, I looked around. Could I have got this close to a nest without realising it? There – further down the slope, maybe 30m away, I spied three more bonxies standing on the turf. I guessed that's where they must be nesting, and set off in the opposite direction, back the way I came.

The original bird had been joined by another, and as I scampered away they zipped past me, one after the other, like fighter jets on a mission. They didn't seem to want to hit me; it was more like they were escorting me off the premises. After a couple more increasingly languid dives they seemed to decide that they'd done all they needed to. They wheeled around once more, flashing the white patches on their wings, and disappeared off low over the turf.

By this point I was close to the farm again and, on checking the time, found it wasn't long before I needed to meet Robert. I forlornly made my way back down the track to the road, a pair of hooded crows letting out laughing caws as I passed.

I only had to wait a moment before Robert pulled up. 'Find your flower?' he asked.

'No,' I replied, downcast, and told him about my encounter with the bonxies.

He listened closely as I spoke, and then shook his head when I finished. 'I'm really jealous,' he said, starting the engine. 'I'd love to be hit in the head by a bonxie.'

We checked the Longworth traps when we got back to the cottage in case any voles had wandered in during the day. No luck. Maybe in the morning.

There was nothing in the traps in the morning. Robert and I swept our hands through the dewy grass, located the traps hidden snugly on the verge, and realised with disappointment that they hadn't been sprung. Two of our five nights gone, six of our 15 'trap-nights'.

To add to the sense of mild despondency, it was a grey, windy day. I had considered trying to see Scottish primrose at the Yesnaby 'tourists' spot', but the weather wasn't particularly enticing. Instead, I decided to go to Skara Brae.

I drove down the coast and parked up by the visitor centre. There was a blackboard with recent wildlife sightings: arctic tern, raven, great northern diver, but also 'yeti (far away)' and 'a ginger cat'. I got my ticket and followed a grassy path along the top of a pale sandy beach, accompanied by the sound of piping oystercatchers.

Skara Brae is sometimes referred to as 'Scotland's Pompeii' and is often described as being older than Stonehenge or the pyramids. The truth is that the site does not *visually* live up to these lofty comparisons. As you approach it looks like a series of low, Teletubby-like hummocks, until the path rises and you find yourself looking down on turf covered drystone walls, dark tunnels, and bare sandy openings.

It's only as you walk around and read the signs that you realise what you are seeing. This is the most complete Neolithic village in Europe, a cluster of houses over 5,000 years old, built sunken into the ground to protect the inhabitants from the elements. What's more, they are complete with furniture.

Peering down into the small rooms I saw stone-sided cots for sleeping, rectangular hearths in the middle of each house, strange deep boxes made of thin slabs set into the floor and, most impressively, a set of stone shelves in each room. I needed to keep reminding myself that all this was older than the pyramids. I could see why the comparison is made now – it's not for its grandeur and scale, it's for an intimate and intact snapshot of an ancient home.

Skara Brae is also, in a sense, a giant midden – a heap of refuse left by generations of people. When I said the houses were sunk into the ground that isn't strictly true; they were sunk into a mound of rubbish. Pot sherds, ashes, limpet shells, all the various materials that build up around a community over time. And, amongst it all, the bones of Orkney voles.

There is a mystery that surrounds the Orkney vole. It is an endemic subspecies of a vole that *does not occur* in the rest of Britain. Mainland Britain has three species of voles: the bank vole, *Myodes glareolus*; the field vole, *Microtus agrestis*; and the water vole, *Arvicola amphibius*. The Orkney vole is something else entirely; it is a unique subspecies of the common vole, *Microtus arvalis*. The common vole is widespread across Europe, absent from Britain, but somehow, mysteriously, present on Orkney.

An early theory to explain this was that the common vole colonised Britain after the last Ice Age, spreading north and reaching Orkney by some sort of land bridge. It was followed by the rest of the voles, which outcompeted it and led to its extinction in mainland Britain. This theoretical land bridge to Orkney had disappeared by this point, leaving common voles safe from their rivals in their island home. There is, however, absolutely no evidence for this idea. No common vole bones have ever been found in Britain, and the common vole is typically found *less* far north than the other species, which makes it an unlikely vole to colonise Britain first. This theory has been scrapped.

It now seems almost certain that the common vole was brought to Orkney by people. It's arguably our oldest non-native species, introduced so long ago that it has diversified from its cousins in Europe – being significantly larger and around twice as heavy – and is now classed as an endemic subspecies. It is the oddest of creatures – a non-native *and* an endemic.

Radiocarbon dating of voles' bones from various sites, including Skara Brae, has found that the earliest date back to around 5,100 years ago. This is unlikely to represent the very first voles on the island, but they probably didn't arrive much earlier than that. Genetic work has shown that the closest relatives of the voles today live in northern France and Belgium. It seems likely that between 5,000–6,000 years ago some Neolithic people brought voles – either accidentally or intentionally – from mainland Europe to Orkney.

You can imagine it, can't you? Neolithic sailors setting off on an ocean voyage, perhaps some domestic animals with them and bales of hay for feed. And nestling in that hay? A few stray voles ready to start a population on Orkney. But this cosy image probably isn't right either. Orkney voles have a healthy amount of genetic diversity; they don't seem like they are descended from a small bottlenecked number of accidental founders.

More clues come from Skara Brae. A number of the vole bones found in the middens are charred. It is entirely possible that the voles were deliberately brought to Orkney as a food source before being released or escaping into the wild. Over the intervening 5,000 years they diverged from their ancestors, becoming big, bulky, northern voles utterly unique to this island group.

I walked around the rest of the small site, peering into these cosy ancient homes, picturing ancient lives and imagining the countless bones of voles buried in the midden beneath my feet. Then, feeling raindrops begin to blatter against my cheek, I left and drove back to the cottage.

There was nothing in the traps.

There was nothing in the traps the next morning either. Three nights down, two to go.

'This isn't working,' I said to Robert, picking up one of the traps from out of the grassy verge. 'I think we need to try somewhere else.' The problem was that this was the best-looking site within easy walking distance of the cottage. The fields nearby didn't look suitable, being full of close-cropped grass.

We took the traps inside and I looked up Orkney voles for the dozenth time. But something stood out to me which hadn't before. One website said that Orkney voles could be found around ruined buildings. When I first read that I had dismissed it – I mean, how often do you see a ruined building? – but here on Orkney we passed by several abandoned houses every time we went out. There was one only a short drive away. The first time we saw it I thought it was a war memorial, built out in the middle of nowhere, but as we passed it I realised it was a chimney, all that remained of a building that had crumbled around it.

We put fresh carrot in the Longworths and drove out to the ruined house. There wasn't much of it to see. The chimney, a few low piles of stone and a contorted dwarf mountain pine, presumably the remnant of the garden. We began searching for the best places to put the traps. I found the remnant of an old rockery, still covered in bright green shiny clumps of London pride and producing a froth of airy pink-and-white flowers. Alongside grew a thick succulent carpet of roseroot, its leaves glaucous green and its flowers acid yellow.

As we stepped across the yielding ground we could feel the rubble under our feet, covered now by a blanket of moss, grass and garden flowers run riot. Robert flipped over a board and peered underneath, gesturing me over and pointing at snug hollows in the dry grass beneath.

'There's poo too,' he said. There was. It was too big for a shrew and too small for anything else, so it must be a small rodent. There were only three contenders: our target, the Orkney vole; the wood mouse; and the house mouse. House mice don't seem to easily survive in the absence of people (hence the extinction of the endemic St Kilda subspecies) so I wouldn't expect to find them in a ruined house in the middle of nowhere.

'It's a 50–50 chance then,' said Robert.

We put one trap by the rockery and one by the chimney. Robert placed the third near the board he had turned over, replaced exactly as it was before. There were a lot of mammal signs here. My hopes began to rise. We resolved to come back and check the traps in a few hours.

Though windy, it was a bright, sunny day, and so we carried on to Yesnaby. This is arguably the most westerly point of Mainland, but as the west coast is pretty much straight it's something of a moot point. A single lane track with occasional passing places led through the fields until suddenly the Atlantic opened up in front of us, today a bright blue tossed white with frothing waves.

We parked up by a concrete platform and a few small derelict brick buildings, all that remained of a wartime gun battery. As we got out of the car the wind hit us like a slap. Despite the sun, it was scarf weather again.

Around the remains of the gunnery was tight, coastal turf, pruned short by the wind and dusted with salt from spray in stormy gales. There were swathes of spring squill, patches of crowberry with red-green berries like tiny apples, and splashes of yellow from clustered pea-flowers of kidney vetch.

A wheatear appeared on the turf in front of us, then flicked away, flashing his dramatic black-and-white tail. We walked inland from the cliff-edge, rationalising that there may be more flowers further from the brunt of the wind. I found a patch of sea milkwort flowering happily, the pale white-pink petals darkening to a deep flesh colour in the throat of the flower.

And then, finally, at last, Scottish primrose. It was shockingly small. I *knew* it was a tiny flower, but it still caught me by surprise. I dropped to the ground, laying flat on my front to admire it. The plant I had found was a little past its best, a single, perfect flower remaining. It was smaller than my little fingernail.

Imagine the primrose you're familiar with, the butter-coloured flower of spring. Shrink that flower down so it's a quarter of the size of a 5p coin and make it a deep, vibrant magenta, with five notched petals like hearts surrounding a lemon-yellow centre. This sits on a short, sturdy stem, which emerges from the middle of a tiny rosette of dusty-green, oval leaves. The whole plant was barely 2cm tall, exquisitely miniature, and I think our most beautiful endemic flower. I shouldn't have favourites, but I do.

I called Robert over and he knelt to photograph it. As he did, I wandered nearby, watching a meadow pipit let out a trill from its parachuting display flight. Refocusing on the ground, I immediately spotted another primrose. This one was in immaculate condition, five perfect flowers jostling for space at the top of the stem. By now I was getting my eye in for their basal leaves and realised that there were more plants around us that had already finished flowering, the short, proud stems terminating in a cluster of gone-over flowers draped with wilted grey-purple petals like streamers after a party.

We started seeing more and more flowers, studding the maritime grassland like fragments of amethyst. We lay on the sun-warmed turf, sheltered from the wind so close to the ground, and took picture after picture, a skylark serenading us from above.

Eventually, sated, we returned to the car, and stopped off to check the traps on the way home. Still nothing.

Hours later, as the long Orkney evening dwindled its way to twilight, we decided to check the traps again. We didn't want anything that we were lucky enough to catch to be stuck in the traps for longer than necessary, so we decided to check now, as it was getting dark, and again early in the morning.

We drove the short distance to the ruined house in silence. We were both aware that finding this vole was the reason for our Orcadian voyage. As delighted as I'd been to see the Scottish Primrose, we could have seen it on the northern coast of Scotland. Finding the vole was our purpose for travelling out to these islands, and I didn't want to miss out on the single mammal I wanted to tell the story of.

We pulled up by the side of the road, the chimney of the ruined house silhouetted black against the very last light of sunset. I checked my phone. It was just after 10 p.m. Summer days are incredibly long on Orkney. A curlew whistled across the fields.

We turned on our phone torches and went to check the traps. I went for the rockery trap whilst Robert went for the chimney one. I bent and parted the grasses and saw that the trap was, as usual, untriggered. I let out a sigh as I straightened up, just as Robert said in a low voice, 'This one is closed.'

Could this be it? Robert gently picked the trap up and scrunched his face. 'It doesn't feel any heavier. Maybe it accidentally closed.'

Still, better to be prepared. I scrambled over the rockery and back to the car to grab the large transparent plastic bag that we'd been carrying around with us. When I got back to Robert he had checked the third trap by the board – nothing.

I shook open the bag, placing the bottom on the ground and holding the mouth wide. Robert carefully lowered in the trap and unclipped the nest-box. Then, holding it just above the bottom of the bag, he gently tipped it. At first all that came out was a shower of seeds and some carrot chunks but, as the angle increased, the ball of hay slid out – and with it came a stout, grey-brown creature. An Orkney vole.

After righting itself from its unceremonious eviction it sat calmly in the bottom of the bag, a perfect ball of sleek fur, looking at us with eyes like jet beads. It was close to a field vole in appearance, but with an even shorter tail and smaller ears. It was also bulkier; the largest Orkney voles reach around 70g compared to field vole's 40g. It rubbed its paws across its whiskers as we drank it in, spotlit in the light from our phones.

The word 'vole' comes from Orkney originally, descended from the extinct Norn language that was spoken here up until a couple of centuries ago. I'm not a linguist, but as far as I can tell this is the only word from this language that has made it big and is in widespread, everyday usage. Before this word was borrowed from Orkney all small mammals were bundled together as 'shrewmice', but with the adoption of 'vole' we saw the division that endures to this day: shrews, mice and voles. There's a feeling of great significance in seeing this creature that's endemic to Orkney, the first animal to ever be called 'a vole', after which all voles around the world get their name.

After a few moments and a couple of pictures, we folded down the edge of the bag and let the vole scurry out, watching it quickly vanish amongst the mossy rubble.

The drive back to our cottage was silently triumphant, the tension of the past days now dissolved in satisfaction. Finding this elusive rodent had been at the core of our trip and, despite the uncertainty and suspense it caused, having now succeeded I wouldn't have changed a single moment of it. Our encounter with Orkney's most storied endemic mammal felt profound, a hard-won glimpse of a creature rooted in the language and landscapes of these islands. It was a memory that would linger.

This wouldn't be my last trip to a Scottish island though. Already my sights were set on Arran, an island that's home to a contender for one of the rarest species on the planet.

CHAPTER 19

The Rarest Tree on Earth: Catacol Whitebeam

What comes to mind when you picture the rarest tree on Earth? I think that, had I been asked to imagine such a thing before knowing the answer, I would have envisaged a rocky plateau in a tropical rainforest somewhere, harbouring a small cluster of trees found nowhere else. It's a romantic image, and not particularly accurate.

There are a few claimants to the dubious honour of 'rarest tree on Earth'. There is *Hyophorbe amaricaulis*, the 'loneliest palm', with a single tree growing in the Curepipe Botanic Gardens in Mauritius. There's the bastard gumwood, *Commidendrum rotundifolium*, of St Helena, with only one wild tree left. And, although not exactly a tree, there is Wood's cycad, which is extinct in the wild and all the trees that exist in botanic gardens across the world are clones of a single individual. Then there is the Catacol whitebeam, a single tree found in Catacol Glen on Scotland's Isle of Arran.

When first described as a new species in 2006 there were only two Catacol whitebeams known. There once was a third tree, a sapling, but this had disappeared by the time the species was named. Of the two remaining trees known in 2006, one had gone by 2016 and in that year it was assessed by IUCN as Critically Endangered. This leaves just one lonely wild individual left – a contender for world's rarest tree.

Or, at least, that's what I read when I was first researching whitebeams, back last winter, but when I met Robbie Blackhall-Miles last year to look for the Menai Strait whitebeam he'd told me that what was thought to be the last remaining Catacol whitebeam possibly wasn't totally alone. In 2020, Robbie had visited Arran. Whilst exploring further up the river from the single known tree he found one short, unhealthy-looking, heavily deer-browsed sapling, which appeared to be another Catacol whitebeam. The experts looked at his photos and agreed, and the known wild population was doubled. Since then, however, no one has seen this extra tree again. Has it been nibbled to nothing by the deer? Has it been washed away by the river? Or is it hanging on, lonely and unacknowledged?

Scotland was calling to me again. I needed to go to Arran. My aims there would be twofold. First, find the three species of endemic whitebeams on Arran – as well as the Catacol whitebeam there are two other unique trees known solely from that island – and then my second mission was try to and confirm the continued existence of Robbie's extra tree.

A couple of months after my trip to Orkney, I found myself in the car park at Lochranza, in the north of the Isle of Arran. This late-August day felt almost like the first day of autumn, the morning air cold and the leaves on the trees around the car park showing the first hints of colour. The feeling was enhanced by the mournful whistle of siskins as they fluttered between the branches above.

Jack Plumb, a good friend of mine and former colleague from the Back from the Brink days, was accompanying me on this trip. He and I had adventured together before, searching out large coneheads in Kent and moon carrot near Cambridge, and I knew that he'd easily get his eye in for Arran's endemic whitebeams.

As we changed into our walking boots, I pointed out the route to Jack.

'We basically just follow the river, Abhainn Mòr,' I said, tracing the OS map with my finger, 'and we should see two of the whitebeams pretty easily. The third one is the tricky one.'

I had also made a map on my phone with the route laid out and pins to help me locate the rarest tree, but, as with most of the island, I wasn't getting any signal.

'Do you know where the rarest one is without the map on your phone?' asked Jack, lacing his boots.

I had spent the past week researching as much as I could about the Catacol whitebeam and the sinuous curves of the river were now as familiar to me as a loved one's face.

'I've got a good idea of where the well-known tree is. See this m-like curve?' I said, poking the map, 'and this second one further south? It's in that 200m gap between that second "m" and that waterfall to the east.'

This was uncharacteristically confident map-reading for me, but this tree had captivated me for the past month. I had read everything I could read; I had emailed people for advice; I'd scrutinised the photographs in the BSBI whitebeam handbook for clues as to where the tree was growing – I'd even made a document on my phone with diagrams of the leaves of every whitebeam species found on Arran. There was no way I was going to fail to find this tree.

'What about the extra tree? The one Robbie found?'

'That's ... hazier,' I replied, 'it's somewhere further up the river, but we'll worry about that after we've found the original tree.'

Shouldering our bags, we crossed the bridge over the river and started following its course up the glen. Before we could get very far, we saw a beautifully illustrated information board devoted to the three endemic whitebeams of Arran and laying out their evolutionary history. Originally Arran had two *Sorbus* species: the rock whitebeam, *Sorbus rupicola*, which has elongated oval leaves with teeth at the end, the whole leaf often dished like the bowl of a spoon; and the rowan, *Sorbus aucuparia*, which has seven or eight pairs of leaflets ('pinnate' leaves, like an ash) with a single central leaflet at the end. You have probably seen rowans planted in urban car parks, where they are understandably popular due to being a compact and beautiful tree with distinctive red berries that are irresistible to waxwings.

At some point in the past these two very distinctive and different-looking trees hybridised and produced offspring, which then continued to reproduce themselves independently of both their parents, becoming a new species, similar to the York groundsel I'd seen last year. This new species, the first endemic tree to emerge on this island, was the Arran whitebeam, *Sorbus arranensis*. It must have arisen as a species some time ago as there are now more than 400 of them across much of the island.

The second endemic species to emerge was the Arran service-tree, *Sorbus pseudofennica*. This originally arose as a hybrid between the Arran whitebeam and rowan, which means it has rowan in its ancestry twice (I love how bizarre and convoluted whitebeam evolution is). As Arran whitebeam is one of its parent species, it must have evolved even later, but it has still had enough time to have reached a population of nearly 500 across the north of the island.

The third endemic tree, my holy grail, is the Catacol whitebeam. This species emerged most recently, as a hybrid between the Arran service-tree and – once again – rowan.

We set off up the river. At first there was a thicket of trees along the path; grey willows, oaks and blackthorn, and I peered amongst them looking for something more unusual with no luck. It didn't take long for us to leave the trees behind us, however, and soon we were walking in open country, surrounded by the varied purples of three species of heathers, following the river up the sloping glen between two domed treeless ridges. In fact, considering we were looking for trees, the entire landscape was surprisingly bare. The flanks of the mountains were grey with scree, brown and purple with heather, but the trees we saw were few and far between, dotted here and there on distant crags or hugging the steep channels of waterways trickling down from distant outcrops. Looking ahead at our path there didn't appear to be any obvious trees at all. We soldiered on.

Because of where I grew up, I'm used to rivers in heathery places like the North Yorkshire Moors being tea-coloured and peaty. I see heather, I think brown water. Not in Catacol Glen though; here the water was so clear as to be almost blue, the granite river bed and loose boulders close to pearly white, the course of the river a shining white thread ribboning through the u-shaped valley beyond us.

And then, suddenly, a whitebeam. Celebration! It was no wonder we hadn't spotted it on the horizon sooner; despite being a couple of metres tall it was only just level with the path because it was growing below us, sprouting up from the steep bank cut by the river. Hunched double

I inelegantly shuffled down the bank, grasping woody handfuls of prickly heather to prevent myself slipping into the rock and water below. Ungainly as it was, I was soon close enough to get a proper view of the deeply jagged-lobed leaves. This was the Arran whitebeam, the first of our three target endemics. I called the ID up the bank to Jack, who had sensibly decided not to risk his life.

In contrast to the subtle Menai Strait whitebeam, Arran's special trees are gloriously, plainly distinct. The Arran whitebeam has leaves that look very much like their ancestry would suggest – a tree trying to reconcile one parent with simple, oval leaves and another with many pairs of leaflets. These dark green leaves, with their swept-forward, toothy projections, give the tree a deeply textured, almost crinkly appearance. I photographed the leaves as best I could, hyper aware of either dropping my phone down the slope or sliding down myself, and then scrambled my way back up to the path.

Of course, literally round the next bend there was another, much-easier-to-see Arran whitebeam, taller, healthier looking and with a flush of cheerful red berries. This one was also growing out of the steep rocky sides of the river and it was becoming clear that these craggy banks were a refuge for whitebeams. Looking around us, at the bare mountainsides and the nearly treeless glen, it was painfully clear that this landscape was overgrazed. Why else would the only trees in the landscape be clinging to slopes and ledges away from the hungry mouths of deer or sheep? Grazing pressure is a delicate balancing act; too little, as Linda told me when we searched for Baker's hawkweed last year, can reduce biodiversity, but too much can be just as damaging.

Up the glen we climbed. Sometimes the path was an easy dirt track through mounds of heather, sometimes it led through a scattered drift of granite boulders and Jack and I needed to carefully step from rock to rock, mindful of twisting ankles. Least pleasant of all was when the path turned to wet seeps and we were forced to hop from tussock to tussock in an attempt to keep our feet dry, the only solace being that these boggy spots were home to the tiny, glistening rosettes of the carnivorous round-leaved sundew.

As we climbed, we talked. There had recently been a story in the news about a mountaineer accused of leaving a fallen porter to die in the snow in their attempt to summit a mountain. Our trek up the glen didn't really compare, but we agreed that people can do terrible things for the sake of their obsessions.

Eventually we spied a fence. It ran across the glen, the path, and even crossed the river. What it was keeping in or out was a mystery to us; the landscape on either side was identical. What it did do, however, was make a narrow area of the riverbank inaccessible to grazers. The river at this point was cutting deep into the rock and was flowing a few metres below us at the base of a near-vertical rocky cliff. At the top of this steep drop was a thin strip of land bounded by the fence, which was thronged with whitebeams. Picking our footing carefully through the soft, springy heather, we made our way around the edge of the fence and to the nearest tree.

'That's the other one, isn't it?' asked Jack, watching me inspect a branch. 'The service-tree?'

He was right. From a distance I think it would be possible to confuse the Arran whitebeam and the Arran service-tree, but up close they were unmistakable. The leaves of the Arran service-tree clearly show the mixed-up parentage of this species. Half the leaf, from the tip to the middle, is broadly oval with deep, jagged lobes, much like the Arran whitebeam. However, immediately below this the leaf splits into two paired leaflets, clearly betraying its rowan forebears. There's something pleasingly intermediate about this species, blatantly displaying its twin ancestry.

'Why is it called a service-tree, anyway?' Jack asked me.

I had no idea. Well, I had half an answer. The Arran service-tree was named after the Swedish service-tree because they look similar – so similar that they were once thought to be the same species, *Sorbus fennica,* a theory for a time being that the seeds were brought to Arran from Scandinavia by the Vikings. When this was disproved, and it was recognised that the trees on Arran were something unique and different, they were named *Sorbus pseudofennica* – the 'fake' *Sorbus fennica.* But why 'service-tree' in the first place?

I've looked it up now, as I'm writing this. Several species of whitebeams are known as service-trees and apparently it comes from the Latin word *cerevisia* meaning 'beer' as, supposedly, the Romans would brew an alcoholic beverage from the fruits of *Sorbus* trees. The 'service' in 'service-tree' is thus nothing to do with the actual word 'service'; it presumably originated as a mondegreen, people mishearing an unfamiliar word as a known one – *cerevisia* for 'service'.

Working our way along this narrow walkway at the top of the squat gorge we found more trees than we'd seen in the past hour – multiple Arran whitebeams, several Arran service-trees, the occasional rowan with its neat, even-sized paired leaflets, even a small clump of aspen. This thin strip of land ended where the path crossed the river, and below us a waterfall surged over the milky rock and plunged into a bluish pool. Blocked from walking along the end, we backtracked round the fence and went through the gate.

We now had one endemic tree left to find – the Catacol whitebeam. This was going to be the hard one. Finding an Arran whitebeam or Arran service-tree hadn't proved too tricky – there may be fewer of them in the wild than tigers (about 1,000 Arran whitebeam and service-trees combined, vs around 4,000 tigers) but the trees are condensed into a relatively limited area of a smallish island. But with the Catacol there was only one well-known tree, plus Robbie's mysterious extra sapling. Ideally we'd find them both.

'Do you know where it is from here?' asked Jack, as we shouldered our backpacks after a quick stop for a drink.

I consulted the map. 'It should be growing on our side of the river, and if we reach a waterfall and a stream coming down from the east then we've walked too far.'

Almost immediately after I said this, we encountered the stream coming down the hillside from the east.

'Ah,' I said.

This eastern stream was once home to a Catacol whitebeam that had disappeared about 10 years earlier, killed off by deer or swept away in a flood. Re-examining the map as we retraced our steps, it seemed impossible we would have missed the well-known tree. A chill ran through me. Could it have gone? Imagine being the person to discover that a species had vanished – that is, unless Robbie's sapling was still hanging on.

We got back to the fence. Upon a closer reading of the map, it seemed the Catacol whitebeam should be along the edge of the river that we had explored not long ago. My heart sank. We'd looked at every tree growing out from the gorge, hadn't we?

I voiced a theory to Jack. 'Maybe one of the trees I called a rowan was actually a Catacol whitebeam? Maybe I didn't look closely enough?'

'Maybe!' said Jack, with forced pep in his tone, which suggested he knew full well we'd checked them all properly the first time.

Still, it was an easy theory to test. We passed back through the gate and inched our way along the edge of the gorge. I checked a rowan – it was indeed a rowan. I checked the next rowan. It was still a rowan. The Catacol whitebeam is most similar to a rowan, but it shouldn't take such close examination to be sure. I knew I was grasping at straws.

We reached the clump of aspen and something caught my eye. Edging to the very brink of the steep riverbank, I looked down. Below us, hugging the vertical rock face, was a tree. A tree that looked, from a distance, like a rowan. I got my binoculars out and, leaning as much over the drop as I dared, I peered straight down.

'That's it!' I shouted.

'Really?' replied Jack, 'How do we get to it?'

We needed to backtrack down the river until the path was level with the water. Then it required hopping from gleaming white rock to shiny white boulder, using them like stepping stones to travel up the river without falling in. Eventually, after several minutes of careful jumping and scrambling, we reached the narrow ledge just above the surface of the river where the Catacol whitebeam was growing, only a few meters from the waterfall. The ledge it grew on was spongy with assorted herbs – goldenrod, devil's-bit scabious, cross-leaved heath – and the ledges of the rock face behind were wet and slick with ferns and dripping vegetation.

The tree itself was magnificent – bigger than every other whitebeam or rowan we'd seen so far. It had 12 trunks of varying thickness rising from the same base, some a little narrower than a wrist, a few almost thigh-thick. There was a 13th trunk, which at a glance looked to be part of the same tree, but it had lighter green leaves and was the only one with fruit. On closer inspection, it was a rowan growing snug amongst the stems of Catacol.

The two species together made for a great comparison. Rowan has its six to eight paired leaflets with a single leaflet the same size at the tip. Catacol has four or five paired leaflets with one much larger lobed leaflet at the tip.

Nor was this the only parent hovering nearby. On the direct opposite bank there was an Arran service-tree, and closer to the waterfall was an Arran whitebeam. It was possible to turn around on the spot and see all three endemics and one of their parents – the rowan – from the same vantage point.

As we stood comparing leaves and congratulating ourselves on our luck – loudly, over the dull rumble of the waterfall behind us – a common hawker buzzed around us and landed on one of the lower branches of the Catacol whitebeam.

I forget now whether it was Jack or I that moved in to get a better view, but the dragonfly took flight and – quite bizarrely for an elegant and acrobatic flyer – caught its wing against a twig and tumbled, falling into the river below. We watched in horror as the water swept it over the rocks and out of view. It was an ill omen.

With all three endemics seen there was one mission left for us – to find Robbie's 'other' Catacol. As far as we knew, no one had seen it since Robbie's original discovery, and in the photos he'd shown me, it looked pretty weedy and unhealthy, suffering from the depredations of sheep and deer. We hoped to confirm it was still there and still alive, that the world population stood at a dizzying two trees.

Hopping from rock to rock we made our way downriver and out of the mini gorge. We had almost made it back to where the slope was gentle enough to scramble up when Jack slipped and his foot plunged into the river. Obviously, this was a disaster, as having one wet foot and several miles to walk is one of the most horrendous fates imaginable. But it was worse than I thought. As we completed our scramble back up to the path Jack massaged his leg with a grimace. He'd been hit by a car whilst cycling years before and, since then, if overstretched, his leg would stiffen up and become agonisingly painful. He was concerned that his slip might set it off.

'We can start heading back?' I offered.

'No, bud,' he replied, gamely. 'We've got that other tree to find.'

'We don't have to – we've seen all three species, we can leave the other Catacol a mystery.'

'Nah, if we take it slow, I'm sure it'll be fine. How far is it?'

From this point my research was a little hazier. Robbie hadn't been able to supply me with an exact dot on a map but had described it to me as being further upriver than the known tree and before reaching Loch Tanna. He'd found it whilst walking from the loch to the river, and said it was the first tree he came across. The edge of the loch was about 600m away from where Jack and I were standing.

'I can do that if I take it easy,' said Jack, as I explained. 'Let's just take it slow.'

We made it about 15m before Jack's leg really became a problem. He sat on a boulder by the path and kneaded it with gritted teeth. 'Actually, it's pretty bad.'

'Bad as in we should start heading back?' I asked. 'Or bad as in rescue services?'

'Bad as in I should sit on this rock a bit,' said Jack.

We sat for a bit and ate some Skittles whilst a raven cronked over the bare hills ahead of us.

'How about', started Jack, thoughtfully, 'how about you carry on and look for the other tree whilst I sit and rest my leg? It's a few hundred metres, so it'll take you what, half an hour? Forty minutes?'

'I can't leave you here in pain!' I said.

'It's fine whilst I'm sitting down.' he replied.

'Shouldn't we start on the slow, careful walk back down if it's bad?'

Jack looked down the valley, the pale ribbon of the path stretching far off into the distance and seemed to wince at the thought. 'I think a rest beforehand is a good idea.'

There was a part of me that *knew* I should insist we head back and get Jack back to civilisation as soon as possible, but another part of me *really* wanted to find that other tree.

'OK,' I said, slowly, 'I'll be half an hour. Take the last of the focaccia.' I thrust a foil-wrapped slab of rosemary focaccia that I'd baked for the trip into his hands. 'And the Skittles.' I stood up. 'You sure this is okay?'

'No problem, bud.' he replied.

I carried on up the path.

I went at a brisk pace. Half an hour was my target. The loch was 600m away. I did some mental maths – if normal walking pace is four miles an hour then that's a mile per 15 minutes, and a mile is, what? 1.5km? So that's 3km in half an hour, but I'm on rough terrain so ... halve it? That's still plenty of time.

Behind the calculations there was another voice in my head, pointing out the irony of mine and Jack's earlier conversation about the mountain climber. I'd been quick to condemn, but wasn't I doing the same thing in miniature? Abandoning a friend (albeit briefly!) to reach my own goal of finding the second Catacol whitebeam? Admittedly, I was going to go back, and soon, and the August weather wasn't in any way life-threatening, but still, it didn't feel good.

I'd decided on my search strategy. Rather than investigate trees on the way up, I'd power up the slope, get to the loch, turn back, and then look out for the 'first tree', as Robbie had described it. Beside me, as I marched, the river meandered and narrowed, becoming more of a stream, then a runnel, then a trickle, and then it vanished. The valley flattened out into a boggy plain that stretched out to the edge of the loch, which shone dully, merging with the sky at the horizon. The path vanished, and each step became a mushy hop from tussock to tussock with dampness seeping into my boots with each stride.

I stopped and scanned with my binoculars. There were absolutely no trees to be seen between me and the loch, no hidden river gully for them to be tucked in out of sight. There was no need, then, to even tackle this swampy ground and reach the edge of the loch. I swivelled and started making my way back the way I came, now acutely on the hunt for whitebeams.

Robbie said it was the first tree he saw. The first tree I saw on the way back looked to be entirely dead; it was only when the river reappeared on my descent that I spotted it, growing out of the opposite rocky bank. The main trunk was horizontal, a metre or so long, with a few bleak leafless branches that had once striven upwards. If this was the second Catacol whitebeam, it was dead and gone.

I didn't think this was the right tree, though. Surely Robbie would have said if it had been on the opposite side of the river? Maybe he didn't see this dead tree, or if he did, he didn't even count this dry lifeless bough as a tree. I carried on.

The next tree, beyond a small waterfall, was on my side of the bank. In fact, as I got closer, it turned out to be two small trees growing side by side, their leaves, from a distance, clearly pinnate like those of a rowan or a Catacol. I gingerly slid down the bank a small distance to get close enough to pull a branch back towards me. It was a rowan, and so was the smaller tree next to it. I felt deflated. Either I'd missed Robbie's tree – which felt impossible – or it was gone, and the Catacol whitebeam was once again relegated to one lonely individual. I vainly looked back up the river but no trees suddenly appeared behind me.

I found two more trees before I got back to Jack and his boulder. The first was a stunted, heavily browsed rowan sapling surrounded by hard-fern and heather. It had barely any leaves, and those it did have were twisted and unhealthy. The next rowan had once been a bigger tree whose trunk had snapped off a metre above the ground and fresh, verdant sprays of leaves were springing from a new branch snaking up from the base. That was it; all I gained from abandoning Jack were four rowans, a dead tree, and a heavy sense of sadness that I might have been the one to discover that the Catacol whitebeam is once again a contender for the world's rarest tree.

I reached Jack, shared the sad news, and over the next few hours we slowly and carefully picked our way down the glen and back to the car.

Our bad luck wasn't over yet though; on returning to our campsite we found the field where we had pitched our tents otherwise empty. The proprietor collared us as we parked up and told us a storm was forecast and we needed to move our tents as the nearby stream would probably burst its banks. In a rising wind Jack and I dismantled our tents and carried them to another field, Jack gritting his teeth in pain all the while.

Overnight, the storm blew so fiercely that all my tent's guy-ropes snapped and I was woken by the ceiling of my tent slapping me in my face as it bowed in the brunt of the wind.

The next day my car broke down, threatening to strand us on the island. By some glimmer of fortune, it was easily fixed by an island mechanic, and we were able to leave.

A week later, back at home, I was sorting through all my photos from Arran on my phone whilst reading through Robbie's blog post about his discovery of the second Catacol whitebeam on my laptop.

I couldn't believe it. Robbie's Catacol whitebeam was a stunted, unhealthy-looking sapling, but in the background there was a distinctive grey boulder lying in the middle of a dry section of white river rocks. I flipped back a few photos in my gallery. There was a stunted tree with the *exact same boulder in the background!* I scrolled through my images further. Here were pictures of the few stunted, curled leaves. I had written it off as a very unhappy rowan, but as this was the same as Robbie's tree, and Robbie's tree had been confirmed by the experts, then this must be a very unhappy Catacol whitebeam. Still, it was alive!

I sent a picture of the tree and the leaves to Jack, whose leg had recovered after a bit of rest. A message pinged back:

Oooo yeah, for most of those leaves I'd say Catacol, nice one Jimmy!

Nice one indeed. Though our trip to Arran had been beset by trials and tribulations, we had managed to confirm that the rarest tree on Earth was at least a *tiny* bit less rare.

CHAPTER 20

Small Wonders: Horrid Ground-weaver and British False Flat-backed Millipede

Plymouth – 'Britain's Ocean City' – in December was far milder than I'd expected. I had casually donned a scarf as well as a jumper before leaving my accommodation for the weekend, but found myself too warm by the time I arrived at Plymouth station. Whilst waiting in the short-stay car park I pulled the scarf from around my neck and tossed it into the back of the car. My phone said it was 12°C with patchy sunshine. I hoped these were good conditions to look for my final invertebrate target, one of the world's rarest spiders – but as the horrid ground-weaver is a winter-active species, maybe they prefer it colder? As last December's unreliable weather had forced me to postpone this trip by an entire year, I was sensitive to any possibility of climate-induced failure.

My phone chimed with a message *just arrived* and a minute later I spied two people radiating ecological energy walking across the car park. I opened the door.

'Finley, Louis?' I asked.

Finley Hutchinson and Louis Parkerson are conservation biology and ecology students at Exeter

University, based out of Penryn Campus in Cornwall. They'd travelled up to show me the horrid ground-weaver and take in the other natural-history delights of Plymouth. Like me, they were both pan-species listers, that new breed of natural historian with an interest that stretches across the entire spectrum of nature. Finley had spotted the horrid ground-weaver in Plymouth the year before and had offered to show me – and Louis – the spot where he'd seen it. After a brisk greeting they hopped in the car and we set off.

In 1989 an unknown species of spider was found in a disused limestone quarry in Plymouth. Two years later, in 1991, a second individual was found in the same spot, spurring efforts to find more and describe it. Despite further searches, no further individuals of this enigmatic species were found in 1992 or 1993, and in early 1994 it was discovered that the quarry was going to be developed later that year. An invertebrate survey was commissioned and four more spiders were found, and in 1995 they were described as an entirely new species of spider – *Nothophantes horridus*, the horrid ground-weaver. Not only was this a new species, it was also in an entirely new genus, showing just how distinct this spider is. To date, it's still the only spider in the world in the genus *Nothophantes*.

And why *horridus*? What's so 'horrid' about this little spider? Well, *horridus* is the Latin for rough, bristly or shaggy and this spider is covered in fine hairs. It's perhaps an unfortunate name for such a rare species, not one to easily endear people to it. In fact, when I first messaged Finley about seeing the horrid ground-weaver he responded with *Do you mean* Nothophantes? *I don't really like the common name.* I can see why – this tiny spider needs all the support it can get and spiders have it hard enough without being 'horrid' to boot.

After the spider was described as a completely new species, known only from this single disused quarry in Plymouth, it was abundantly clear to the developers of the site that they couldn't in good conscience threaten the existence of the species by progressing with building work. The site was set aside as a nature reserve and …

…No, sorry, I'm *totally* joking. The site was developed anyway. Please take a moment to reflect on that. Without knowing if this species would *continue to exist*, development that could have easily rendered an entire species extinct went ahead anyway. The 1990s truly were a cruel and unusual time. It's hard to imagine the same decision taking place today. Fortunately, in 1997 two more horrid ground-weavers were found in another disused quarry only 200m away from the first. These two were males, the first males ever seen. This site, then, could be a safe haven for this species.

No, sorry, I'm *totally* joking. In 2014 a planning application was submitted to develop that quarry too, and it was only through a concerted public campaign spearheaded by Buglife that the application was turned down. The 2010s truly were a cruel and unusual time, but at least this time sense prevailed.

Other locations have come to light in recent years, but in total the horrid ground-weaver has only ever been known from four sites within a tiny slice of Plymouth, one of which – the original site – has been so extensively developed that the spider has been lost.

We parked up on a polished street of brick new-builds and Finley, Louis and I walked to the start of the search area: a humble, 200m stretch of footpath on the edge of a housing estate near Billacombe.

'Not quite what you imagined?' asked Finley.

It wasn't. I hadn't been sure until I met Finley which site he was taking me to, so I was half expecting a disused quarry floor full of bare ground, rocks and patches of scrub. Instead, we were walking down a stretch of neatly surfaced footpath, fringed with a narrow belt of woodland on the left and bordered with a row of hazels and garden walls on the right. This area was another disused quarry 10 years ago and is now several hundred homes. However, in this case the developers worked with the expert advice of Buglife and a population of horrid ground-weavers has persisted despite the modification of the path and the landscape around it.

Finley pointed to a heap of suspiciously organised stones on the left. They weren't neatly stacked but they looked somehow deliberate.

'John Walters has left these piles of stones here for the spiders,' he told me.

John Walters is an artist and ecologist. His website and social media feeds are a marvellous blend of his wildlife watercolours and his photographs of some of our most obscure species. I first met John when I was working on Back from the Brink where he was studying the narrow-headed ant – another Devon speciality – but the horrid ground-weaver is clearly a particular passion of his.

'We're just going to turn the stones over and see if we can spot any.' He crouched and flipped one over. 'And we need to look out for the punk harvestman too,' he added.

The punk harvestman, or the hedgehog harvestman as I know it, *Centetostoma bacilliferum*, is another Plymouth speciality, though unlike the horrid ground-weaver it is also found outside Britain. It gets its name from the mohawk of spines running across its back, making it truly unlike any other British harvestman. Harvestmen are arachnids but form a separate order to the spiders. They can usually be easily identified by their fused one-part body, in contrast to the two-part body-plan of spiders.

The first pile of stones yielded only a tiny, red, non-native invertebrate called the many-eyed flatworm, *Marionfyfea adventor*, which was new to Finley and Louis.

The second pile yielded nothing of note. As we carefully turned stones, Finley told me about a new species of jumping spider that had been found on Penryn Campus this year during a bioblitz.

'A couple of members of the public found these tiny spiders and brought them to me and I had no idea what they were. I showed them to Tylan Berry, a proper spider expert, and he had no idea either. Turns out it's new to science.'

'A new endemic spider?' I asked.

'Well, the expert at Manchester Museum, Dmitri Logunov, says that its closest relatives are from the Caribbean, so it's an alien, just one that hasn't been discovered in its home range yet. It's called *Anasaitis milesae*.'

Another false endemic!

The third pile of stones was by some shaded stone steps to the right of the path. 'This was the best spot last time I was here,' said Finley, 'and John Walters said on Twitter he had found 13 last weekend.'

This spider is so rare and infrequently seen that John keeps a running tally of all the individuals ever recorded. He had recently posted *only 180 have ever been seen in the world!* I hoped we could make it 181.

Finley carefully turned over each stone from the pile by the steps individually, diligently inspecting the undersides. Louis was in the belt of woodland behind us, flipping over rocks and logs like an inquisitive bear.

'How easy are they to spot?' I asked Finley.

'They're easy to see,' he replied, turning over a stone in his hands. 'They're distinctly orange-coloured.'

He picked up the next rock and let out an 'Oh!'

I leant in, eagerly, expecting to see a tiny spider. Instead, there was a miniscule mite with two gangly forelimbs scurrying across the craggy surface. 'Have you seen one of these before?' asked Finley. 'This is *Linopodes motatorius*, it's the only soil mite with those distinctly long front legs.'

I had seen mites like this before when rummaging under logs but had assumed that mite identification was an arcane skill practised only by elite naturalists. We watched it skitter across the stone, tip-tapping with those lanky legs, before it disappeared over the side of the rock.

We turned over all the stones in this heap by the steps with no success. 'There's more,' said Finley, 'don't worry.'

Louis emerged from the trees, similarly unsuccessful. We continued along the path, passing an abandoned shopping trolley that did much to enhance the atmosphere of the home of one of the rarest species on the planet. As we walked, I told Louis and Finley about some of my previous endemic trips; when I got as far as the York groundsel Louis piped up, 'I've seen that!'

'Where?' I asked, and Louis laughed. Earlier that year he had taken a Field Identification Skills Certificate (FISC), a test of botanical field skills run by the BSBI. Part of the assessment is in the field where candidates identify as many species as possible, and part is a lab test inside where they are tested on a range of specimens from a range of habitats. Alex Prendergast of Natural England organised this FISC and decided, deviously, to include York groundsel in the lab test. Can you imagine being presented with an 'extinct' plant to identify? It was an impish inclusion, but Louis found it amusing. 'I got a level four,' he told me. 'I want to take another and aim for level five.'

We stopped and turned over another pile of stones. Nothing. It was then I realised we were only 10m from the end of the path, where it right-angled under a bridge and alongside a busy road. On this last corner was a final pile of stones, nestled between two tree trunks. Finley, detecting my tension, told me that he thought we'd missed one pile by the start of the path, so this wasn't necessarily our last chance. Still, the line between success and failure was feeling pretty thin.

Louis turned over a couple of stones and solemnly set them to one side. Then, on the third stone: 'Err, there is a spider here. It's a bit orange.'

Finley, being the only one of us who'd seen the species before, squeezed into the gap by the pile to have a look. 'Yeah!' he said, 'that's it!'

I stood behind them on the path, almost bouncing with excitement, eager for a view of the 181st horrid ground-weaver ever seen. Finley started to back out between the trees but then stopped. 'There's a punk harvestman on this stone too!'

A chorus of appreciative noises emerged from the pair of them whilst I bit my tongue, trying not to imagine the horrid ground-weaver disappearing whilst all attention was focused on its punk cousin.

Finley turned briefly and handed me a damp chunk of wood – 'There you go!' – then turned back to the harvestman.

On this stub of broken branch was a tiny, brown-orange spider, smaller than the common shiny woodlice that also clung to the wood. The body of a spider is made up of two parts: the abdomen, the big 'bum' of the spider as my sister called it when we were kids; and the cephalothorax, the 'head' section of the spider. This head section was a hairless, translucent, glossy citrine-orange with an almost flame-like intensity at its edges. The abdomen was more orange-brown, almost mousey, an effect heightened by its neat swept-back clothing of hairs. In total, these two body segments were around 3mm long. It was sitting tight for the moment, its legs – transparent with a hint of cocoa colour – hugged close to its body, its 'knees' gathered together above it, like a folded umbrella without the fabric. I turned the piece of wood gently, seeing how the long bristle-like hairs on its legs gleamed pale in the sunlight. Having had enough of this, the spider stretched out its legs delicately, like a cat, paused for a moment, and set off briskly for the edge of the wood. I turned it in my hands, keeping the spider on top.

All this time my attention had been distracted from Finley and Louis, who announced they'd found another ground-weaver in the stone pile – the 182nd ever seen. I was passed the new spider in a little glass tube. This one shared the same orange 'head' as the first one, but its abdomen was much darker, almost black, with the pale hairs distinct against it. The legs were of the same coffee-tinted transparency, though this one had subtle areas darkened, giving it the merest hint of banding.

I know spiders are rarely seen as beautiful. In fact, I'm minimising the issue. Spiders are often dreaded, and even I suffer from a touch of arachnophobia when a palm-sized house spider skitters along a skirting board in my home. But the horrid ground-weaver,

Nothophantes horridus, is not a horrid spider. It's tiny, orangey, utterly inoffensive and harmless. But I think that because it's a spider, that most maligned of creatures, it takes *such an effort* to conserve it. If a bejewelled butterfly was endemic to this tiny area of Plymouth, I'm sure it wouldn't have seen repeated efforts to build over its habitat. But when it's a *spider*, something deemed creepy and unappealing, then it's easier for people to justify destroying its only home on Earth for another industrial unit. Surprisingly, much of conservation works this way – cute fluffy species attract funding, whilst less obviously charismatic species end up hanging by a thread (or a strand of silk). Isn't it shallow that a species' existence can hinge on whether we find it attractive enough to save?

I have endless respect for Buglife. They see straight through the 'pretty-privilege' of conservation and put their efforts into saving the species that need it most. Without Buglife the development around the path I was standing on might have blitzed the horrid groundweaver, and their other sites may have been built over. It's not much of a stretch to say that this species only exists thanks to their efforts.

Nothophantes horridus is a member of the spider family Linyphiidae, the 'money spiders'. As a child I was told that these spiders were good luck. Perhaps it's good luck that it's managed to survive so long given the repeated efforts to destroy its habitat? I think they need a lot more than luck – they should be celebrated as one of our very few endemic invertebrates and a jewel in Plymouth's crown. Maybe the city could change its tagline from the bland 'Britain's Ocean

City' to the much more valuable and enigmatic 'City of the Spider'?

It may be tempting to think that *finally* we live in a more enlightened time, but 700 miles north on the coast of Sutherland there are repeated efforts to develop part of Coul Links as a golf course. This is one of the last remaining undisturbed dune systems in Scotland and is the only known site on the planet for the endemic Fonesca's seed-fly. This species has only ever been found along approximately five miles of the coast here, and the planned development of the golf course would impact around half of it.

After five years of campaigning, including by Buglife and the RSPB, the plans were formally refused permission by the Scottish Government in February 2020, the sand dunes and the fate of their endemic fly now safeguarded forever.

No, sorry, I'm *totally* joking. In February 2023 plans for a golf course on the same site were submitted. They received objections from Buglife, NatureScot, the RSPB and Butterfly Conservation; as a result, the Highland Council ... voted to approve the application. The application is now back with the Scottish Government for a final decision. Again.

It's clearly an emotive and complex issue. On one hand, by declining the application, we can protect one of the rarest species on the planet and the habitat that it and thousands of other species rely on. On the other hand, the land can be developed for the world's most boring game. It truly is an agonising choice.

And I *know* that isn't the real argument. There are people talking about job creation and reversing depopulation – but destroying the irreplaceable isn't worth it. We wouldn't be justifying the destruction of half the world's habitat of tigers, rhinos or pandas for a golf course; this is only happening because of a shallow, human perception of value.

The 2020s truly are a cruel and unusual time.

In the days leading up to my trip to Plymouth to see the horrid ground-weaver I had tried to work out if there was a back-up endemic to look for in case the spider refused to participate. Checking the list of endemic invertebrates I had compiled with Craig back in February 2022, I realised our only known endemic millipede – *Anthogona britannica* – was found less than an hour from Plymouth on the south Devon coast.

Having successfully seen the horrid ground-weaver, I didn't really need to rely on my back-up species. However, the day I was meant to be driving home dawned sunny and surprisingly warm for December and it seemed churlish to pass up the chance to spot a bonus endemic.

For every species I'd tried to track down up until now, I had done all I could to try to ensure – as much as you can guarantee anything with nature – that I would be able to find the plant, animal or fungus I was looking for. This had meant contacting the wide variety of passionate and skilled experts that have helped me across these pages, or, when working solo, dedicating significant time to preparatory research so that I had the best possible chance of succeeding. In the case of the millipede, however, I would simply be making it up as I went along.

Part of the reason this wasn't originally considered as one of my target species was that I could barely find any information about it. The website of the British Myriapod and Isopod Group (BMIG) didn't have any photographs of it but did tell me that it was described as new to science as recently as 1993.

Before setting off from Plymouth I read the original paper, which gave me a description of the species: 7mm long (so, tiny), light brown, and with ten to 12 eyes, or 'ommatidia', on each side of its head. With millipedes, the number of eyes can vary within a species, or even on different sides of an individual's head. The 'holotype' (original specimen) of *Anthogona britannica* had 11 eyes on one side and 12 on the other. The paper also included diagrams, but only of the genitalia, which was way more intimate than I was intending to get with this millipede. It also gave grid references for the initial discovery. This was the best information I could find, so I set off to Slapton Ley.

Much of the drive took me down single-lane country roads with steep hedge banks and fun was had with back-and-forth reversing into shallow passing places when meeting traffic head-on. Eventually I reached the car park at Slapton Sands. I parked up at the northern end, near a monument commemorating the D-Day practice exercises that took place here in 1944. Ahead of me the beach sloped down to the sea, which shone blue-gold from the morning winter sun. I stood for a moment, savouring the warmth on my face, before turning in the opposite direction. The place I had parked was on a narrow ridge of shingle, only a few tens of metres wide, that improbably separates the sea from Slapton Ley, the largest natural lake in the South West. The proximity of the sea to this 1.5mile-long lake and the skinniness of the divide between them forces you to assume that it must be a saltwater lagoon, or at least strongly brackish, but it is entirely freshwater. This National Nature

Reserve is incredibly rich and biodiverse, being home to an estimated 3,000 species of fungi, the only remaining native site in Britain for a white-flowered plant of shingly margins called strapwort, and, most excitingly for me, being the site where *Anthogona britannica*, our only endemic millipede, was first discovered.

In February 1992, Steve Gregory, millipede and centipede expert (and in the present day the organiser of the centipede recording scheme) undertook a survey at Slapton Ley. Amongst his samples he found three tiny, light-brown millipedes that matched no known British species. Steve passed them on to Dick Jones, the millipede recorder at the time, who realised that he had actually found one of these at Slapton almost 10 years earlier, back in 1983, but had assumed – given that it was so diminutive – that it was just a baby millipede and thus nigh on impossible to identify.

Under close examination they turned out to be very small adult millipedes, and they appeared to be a species that had never been seen in Britain before: *Anthogona variegata*. This diminutive millipede is found from the north-east of Spain, through southern France, and up to Normandy, which is a mere 140km across the sea from Slapton.

However, despite looking incredibly similar, the genitalia of the Devon millipedes were clearly distinct from those in France. As with a lot of invertebrates, many millipedes can look very similar externally but have remarkably different reproductive anatomy, which reflects their divergence into different species. These Slapton millipedes were named as a brand new species, *Anthogona britannica*, and the 1993 paper describing them states that it 'is likely to turn up in other sites in south-west England and in all probability it is common on the French side of the Channel'. Nearly 30 years later this line has proved only very slightly true. The millipede *has* been found at other sites in Devon, but all are within 10km of Slapton, and it has never been found on the French side of the Channel or, indeed, anywhere else on the planet.

Standing in the corner of the car park I glanced at my phone. I had grid references for the 1992 specimens and one of those locations wasn't far from where I'd parked. I crunched across the shingle, crossed the road to the landward side of the ridge, and walked north along a narrow footpath along the edge of Slapton Ley for a few metres, squinting at my phone until the translucent GPS dot representing me synced up with the pin I'd dropped on my map.

The habitat around me was unremarkable. I'd imagined lightly vegetated, sandy shingle, based on my mental image of Slapton, but instead it was dense grass, 30cm tall, now drooping with the onset of winter. I knelt down on the path and began my search. I had no clear technique in mind, but I assumed that the millipedes – if they were here – would be down amongst the soil level. I parted the tussocks of grass until I was down to the layer of litter, the fragments of leaves and thatch that find their way to the ground and slowly decay into the soil. I was wearing fingerless gloves and I began to gently dig through this litter layer with my fingertips. It didn't take long for me to find my first millipede, and, pulling a pair of delicate forceps from my pocket, I gently picked it out from the soil.

It wasn't the species I was looking for. Firstly, it was too long, and secondly it was the wrong shape. The two most common body-plans of millipedes are the 'snake millipedes', which are the quintessential millipede shape, a neat cylindrical tube with many tens of legs; the other common shape is the 'flat-backed', which has fewer pairs of legs and each body segment is distinctly flattened, looking perhaps more like a typical centipede. *Anthogona britannica* is sort of in between; it isn't distinctly flat-backed but it does have a noticeable 'shoulder' on each body segment, hence its (rather bland and wordy) English name of 'British false flat-backed millipede'. The millipede I was holding was distinctly cylindrical, and so I gently placed it on the ground to allow it to wander off whilst I continued searching.

The next 20 minutes yielded various finds, though none were what I was looking for: a lesser crucifix ground beetle, named after the black cross on its striking orange wing cases; a spindly bug called a water-measurer that looks like a minute stick insect; and plenty more snake millipedes of a species called *Enantiulus armatus*. My hopes were just beginning to fade when I spotted the tiny pale coil of a snail shell stark against the dark soil. I gently picked it up, wondering if it would be some interesting species I hadn't seen before, and then immediately realised it wasn't a snail at all – it was a tiny, coiled millipede. I fumbled a hand lens out of my pocket and looked closer; each body segment had two distinct little shoulder-bumps. This had to be it, right?

I gently placed it in a tiny glass tube with a few strands of grass and by awkwardly holding my hand lens to my phone I was able to take a few reasonably clear photos of it. The problem was that, despite it matching the description, I wasn't completely certain – maybe there were other species it could be confused with? When this species was first discovered it was thought to be the juvenile of something else, so could I have just found the young version of a bigger millipede? I just couldn't be sure.

I searched for another 40 minutes and found two further millipedes of the same size, shape and colour. This gave me a bit more confidence that they were probably the right species, but I decided to take them home with me so I could check more thoroughly. I made sure each tube had some soil, moss, and grass fragments so the millipedes had a microcosm of habitat to keep them fed and hydrated, and set off from Slapton.

As soon as I got home, I sent one of my photos to Steve Gregory, the original discoverer of the species. His reply wasn't entirely positive:

> *What's the body length?* Anthogona *is short – up to 7mm and with c. 12 ocelli. I suspect this may be* Anamastigona pulchella *– to 11mm long and with 15–17 ocelli.*

I wasn't sure exactly how big they were; undoubtedly they were tiny, but tiny enough? I placed one of my tubes over a tape measure and waited for one of the millipedes to walk over it. It looked to be exactly 7mm. I then placed the tube under a high-powered microscope to try and count its eyes.

This was the first time I was able to see one of them in full detail. I watched as it busied its way through the soil and leaf fragments in the tube. Whereas it had appeared simply light brown before, up close it was marked with alternating rings of pale tan and warm cinnamon. Each ring of its body had bulging humps, like shoulder pads, on each side, as well as three long bristle-like hairs, which caught the light with a silvery gleam (technically these are called 'macrochaetae', meaning, essentially, big bristles). I watched as it walked, the sequence of motion passing through its 50-or-so pairs of legs like a Mexican wave. Its eyes, however, were almost impossible to focus on. From above, all I could get a good view of were its furry, slightly clubbed antennae, which waggled endearingly as it navigated the terrain. Occasionally I'd catch a glimpse of the triangular block of eyes on the side of its head, but never for long enough for me to get them in focus to count them. All I could do was wait.

It took a long time for the millipede to stand still, and when it did it was at the wrong angle to see its face. I gently rotated the tube but only managed to disturb the millipede, which then wandered around again before disappearing into the soil I'd provided. After much patient waiting, I finally got a decent view of the side of its head where I could see its ommatidia. I stared deeply into the millipede's eyes. They were black, shiny and round, like the drupes of a blackberry, arranged in a blunt triangle. I could count 11 of them … or maybe 12; it was hard to get everything in focus at the same time. But it certainly wasn't in the range of 15–17 eyes.

I messaged Steve to tell him, and he replied:

> *That looks good for* Anthogona. *I'd forgotten just how small they were! I've not seen this species since 1994. I was looking for a male* Chordeuma [another species of millipede] *back in 1992 and had been told males were the small ones so I picked this species up in error!*

Success! As the BMIG website didn't have any pictures of this species I offered Steve my photos (not that they're particularly good). Steve's response caught me off guard:

> *Any images will be the first ever images of this species!*

What? I was stunned. I suppose it made sense in a way – I hadn't been able to find a single photograph anywhere online but I didn't think it was because they simply didn't exist. It turns out that my clumsy phone picture taken awkwardly through a hand lens is the first ever photograph of this species. But there was a further surprise to come. Trying to understand how this species had avoided photography for so long, I asked Steve how often people recorded it.

> *8th December 1995 is the latest date I can see. I'm not aware of anything more recent – but there must be!*

I was sure there must be later records too, but even after further searching I couldn't find anything after 1995.

This species, the British false flat-backed millipede, is found nowhere else on Earth other than a 20km stretch of the Devon coast. It was overlooked until 1992, described in 1993, and then seemingly last seen in 1995. No one had ever photographed it. If it had gone extinct then all we'd have left in the world would be a few specimens in the Paris Natural History Museum and diagrams of its genitals. How can we have something so rare and precious on our own doorstep and not check in on it for more than a quarter-century? Not celebrate it?

There is a silver lining here. If I – and I am, to be honest, basically an enthusiastic idiot – can spend an hour on the Devon coast, find a species that no one has seen in almost 30 years and take the first-ever photographs of it, then think what *any of us* can do.

I'm not a millipede expert, I'm not an expert in anything, and yet we now have photographs of this species so that future searchers can at least picture what they're looking for, and so that anyone can look up our only endemic millipede and appreciate its miniscule fragility.

This was the very last species I saw in the course of exploring Britain's unique wildlife, and it feels meaningful that at the very end I made my own contribution to the knowledge and stories of our endemic species. I think the world is a slightly better place for knowing that the British false flat-backed millipede still exists.

Epilogue

Ten months prior to my trip to Plymouth, in February 2023, Andy Shaw invited me to join him in York. Andy had successfully harvested thousands of seeds from his resurrected York groundsel at his nursery in 2022 and the time had come to reintroduce back into the wild. I met him and his brother Martin on a cold and clear winter day; the sun was bright and the energy was optimistic.

Andy was as chatty as ever as we wandered the streets of York, keeping up a running stream of conversation about the new species in his collection, the funding he was hopefully getting to grow on plants for new conservation projects, and his future plans for the York groundsel. Martin was his brother's opposite – quiet, chiming in only occasionally with an insightful comment.

We meandered through the city, visiting some of Andy's choice locations to return the groundsel to, eventually ending up on a footpath running down the southern bank of the Ouse, the river that cuts its way through the heart of York. There was a steep bank that sloped down from the footpath to the river below at a 45-degree angle. This bank had a thin layer of sediment, deposited by high waters, and despite it being only early February it was already greening up with seedlings.

Andy knelt, poking some emerging leaves. 'Common groundsel,' he said, 'loads of it.' He eyed down the slope. 'And Oxford ragwort too.'

These are the two parent species of the York groundsel.

'If they're both doing well here then it should be perfect for York groundsel too,' said Andy, excitement rising in his voice.

After walking a strip of footpath running from Scarborough Bridge to Lendal Bridge, Andy was satisfied.

'This is the spot,' he said, gesturing to a stepped area of the bank leading down between the limes that edge the footpath. 'We can stand on the steps and throw the seed onto the slopes either side.'

He stood back, taking in the view like a director. 'And you can see the top of York Minster over there, just beyond the buildings on the other side of the river. Perfect.'

He peeled off the flexible lid of the bucket and looked inside. 'People are probably going to think we're scattering ashes, aren't they?'

Martin and I looked at each other. They might. Andy shrugged.

'We can tell people it's our uncle. He loved York and was a very big man.' He laughed, shaking the heaped bucket of mixed sand and seed.

He offered it to me. 'Go on,' he said, 'you can throw the first handful, be the person to put this back into the wild.'

I demurred, saying that Andy should do it after all the effort he'd put in. Andy wouldn't hear of it, and so I found myself halfway down the steps with a handful of the most precious sand I'd ever held, primed to cast it onto the slope.

Andy had his camera out, and called directions so he could get the perfect photograph of me, the river and the

Minster behind. Eventually he was happy. 'Go!' he called, and I threw my handful, scattering a neat arc of sand and seeds that briefly shone gold in the low winter sun.

More than a year later I was back in York. It was early May 2024 and I was wrapping up my writing, but there was one thing I still needed to see. I had returned to the city twice in 2023, once in summer and again in autumn, each time hoping to find a flowering York groundsel. They *had* flowered – I'd seen pictures posted online – but luck wasn't on my side during those visits. I failed to find them down by the river where I'd thrown the first handful of seed, or anywhere else where Andy had scattered them.

I saw plants that *might* have been young York groundsel – plants with narrow, jagged leaves unlike the abundant groundsel or Oxford ragwort – but without a flower I just couldn't be certain.

I was back again, a new year and a new opportunity, and this time I had expert advice. Andy had recently been back to check on the reintroduction and had messaged me the location of plants at sites across the city, telling me that he had spotted a single plant in flower.

With that in mind, I made my way back down the river again, following the south side of the Ouse to Scarborough Bridge. Around the base of trees that line the path I saw young plants that looked suspiciously like York groundsel but none were in flower. No problem. I had faith that the plant Andy had told me about would be holding on for me.

I crossed Scarborough Bridge and went down the ramp at the other side, heading towards Marygate car park. Before entering you pass through a paved area with four small trees, their trunks surrounded by neat black cages. It was in the small untended patch of earth around these trees where the first York groundsel of 2024 had chosen to flower.

I wasn't sure which of these tree pits was home to York's prodigal son, so I walked slowly, checking each pit as I passed. Nothing. Nothing. Nothing. For a moment I feared I'd missed it, that the weedkiller patrol or some tidy-minded individual had torn out these Lazarus flowers, but no. The fourth and final tree was surrounded by an oasis of urban greenery, half a dozen flowering York groundsel in pride of place.

After 20 years, the York groundsel was back.

As I close this final chapter of my travels across Britain, seeking out the unique and irreplaceable endemic species that call this island home, I am struck by the tremendous variety in their fates. The rare and threatened Catacol and Menai Strait whitebeams stand in stark contrast to those thriving comfortably in Watersmeet. New discoveries that expand the known ranges of the Celtic woodlouse, Chater's bristletail, and the British cave shrimp inspire hope, contrasting with the precarious existence of the York groundsel and interrupted brome which remind us of the effort required to prevent their extinction. These 20 species, along with the unexpected bonus encounters along the way, offer a mere snapshot of the total diversity and complexity of our endemic species.

If there is one lesson to be drawn from this exploration, it is the profound need for understanding. Many of our endemics are shrouded in mystery, their ecology, range and requirements often unknown, making their conservation a daunting task. Think of Turk's earth centipede, discovered in 1988 and never seen again since; or the Manx shearwater flea, missing since 1966. Equally pressing is the public's awareness – or lack thereof – of these unique species. How can we expect people to care about or protect a species they don't know exists? We must do more to celebrate and raise awareness of our endemics; people only care about what they know, and only save what they care about.

Throughout this experience, I have met remarkable individuals whose dedication and passion astounded and inspired me: people like Mark Lynes, Alan Leslie, and Jonathan Revett, who have painstakingly distinguished and described species; naturalists like Alex Prendergast, Brian Eversham, and Lee Knight, who push the boundaries of our understanding of our endemics; and conservationists such as Linda Robinson, Craig Macadam, Ashley Arbon, Richard Moyse, Kathy Friend, Joe Alsop, Sally Pidcock, Robbie Blackhall-Miles, and Andy Shaw, who work tirelessly to protect and secure the future of these species. And then there are the budding natural historians and scientists, Finley Hutchinson, Louis Parkerson and Francesca Toccaceli, whose knowledge and enthusiasm fill me with hope for the future.

Back when the initial idea of this endemic journey was taking shape, I considered myself a naturalist and a conservationist, though these words always felt a bit grandiose for my skills. I could identify a variety of plants, moths and birds, but I was not an expert in any one area. My work in conservation often felt one step removed, confined to desks and meetings rather than out in the field. But this exploration of our endemics has changed my perspective; my broad, jack-of-all-trades approach being precisely what was needed. My ability to understand the terminology of trees and millipedes, fungi and woodlice, speak semi-intelligently with experts, or track down species myself was invaluable.

I found myself drawn into direct conservation actions almost by accident: helping to preserve Baker's hawkweed and South Stack fleawort in Andy's ark; recognising the existence of the third Catacol whitebeam on Earth; and re-finding the British false flat-backed millipede after more than a quarter-century. This is not to say that I see myself as exceptional; instead, it demonstrates that any one of us, with dedication and interest, can make a difference. We can all advocate for our local wildlife, provide more space in our gardens, streets and lives for nature, learn to identify species, submit biological records, and support organisations dedicated to conservation.

Each of us has the power to make an impact and to safeguard the unique natural heritage of Britain. Together we can rise to the challenge of protecting and championing our incredible endemic species for generations to come.

FINAL NOTES, 2024

In March Andy emailed me to tell me that Richard Abbot who, along with Andrew Lowe, first discovered the York groundsel back in 1979, had passed away in February. Andy told me that Richard was pleased with the return of this species to the city.

Andy also sent me a picture of a truly enormous South Stack fleawort in his polytunnel, told me that he had grown 'massive plants' from the Baker's hawkweed seed I had sent him, and that Connie the Barton Road comfrey was now vast and he was ready to take cuttings from her – all of these being valuable 'ark' populations in case of disasters at wild sites.

In April I spoke to Alex Prendergast, who told me that a false fen dandelion had been found in north Norfolk in 2023, and that this year it had been discovered in mid Norfolk and at a site in Suffolk. This doesn't herald some dramatic change in the circumstances for this species, but it shows that there are a growing number of dedicated people tackling dandelions and putting serious effort into recording our most threatened species. At least if we know where they are persisting then focused effort can, hopefully, be put to their conservation.

Later that month I stopped off in Chirk on the way to a BSBI meeting and found a dozen flourishing plants of Welsh groundsel around the car park of the town hall and the neighbouring furniture and carpet showroom. Trevor Dines – author, conservationist and BSBI trustee – has spoken to the council about protecting and celebrating this special species.

In May I went for a walk in Grass Wood with Natasha Foxford, who has created the beautiful chapter illustrations you've seen between these pages. I managed to find and identify my own false-toothed lady's-mantle – but I also spotted a single plant of the dreaded *Alchemilla mollis* along a path. I hope it doesn't get a foothold there.

In June I rang Ashley Arbon to see how his population of interrupted brome was faring after the incident in 2022. It had recovered and was doing well, and he emailed some pictures so I could see for myself. I also got an email from Alan Leslie, who told me that the Backs goldilocks buttercup, which was thought to be solely found around the Backs of a few Cambridge colleges, had since been discovered in the grounds of Milton Hall just outside the city. It's still a Cambridgeshire endemic, but no longer a Cambridge endemic.

I spoke to Craig Macadam, who had published his report on endemic invertebrates at the end of 2023. The 20 species we had discussed were included, but not the Lundy cabbage weevil whose status is still foggy. Craig also told me about a 'new' endemic, a caddisfly called *Rhyacophila septentrionis*. It's not really new; it was described in 1865 but was then synonymised – falsely, it turns out – with a more widespread species called *Rhyacophila fasciata*. It seems that the Victorians had it right all along, and this caddisfly is restored as our 21st endemic invertebrate. If the Lundy cabbage weevil ever gets sorted out and formally named, then we'll have 22.

Back in March 2022 when I met Craig in Scotland the best identification guide to stoneflies was a book from the 1950s that had been reprinted in the 1970s. Since then, a brand new guide has been published, *British and Irish Stoneflies (Plecoptera)*, by Hugh B. Feeley, Jason Doe, and Craig Macadam himself. Hopefully this will help raise the profile of stoneflies and encourage more stonefly recording.

Whilst finalising my write-up and fact-checking about the British earthstar, I discovered a paper published in 2022, which announced the discovery of *Geastrum britannicum* in the Czech Republic. They consider it a recently arrived species, rather than an overlooked native, and think it's most likely a non-native species in Europe originally from elsewhere in the world. They also mention its discovery in Slovakia, and other sources online suggest it has also been found in Finland, the US and Madagascar. Native status in Britain seems unlikely, and as it is being increasingly found across the world it doesn't even count as a false endemic. Jonathan was right – I was being overly hopeful!

A recently published book, *The Marsh Tit and the Willow Tit*, by Richard Broughton, discusses willow tit subspecies. Not everyone is fully convinced with the classification of British willow tits as an endemic subspecies as it's based on evidence from a rather limited range of specimens. Whereas it would be heartening to know that we, in Britain, aren't at risk of losing something completely unique, would its possible relegation mean that even less conservation attention is paid to one of our fastest-vanishing species? More research is needed.

And finally, Matt Harding, a colleague of mine who knew about my trip to Arran, sent me a link to a blog post from the Royal Botanic Garden Edinburgh (RBGE). In the post, Max Coleman wrote about collecting seed for the conservation of Arran's endemic whitebeams and showed photographs of the last two Catacol whitebeams. One was the big, spreading tree that Jack and I had seen, the other was a small sapling – but not the same as the deer-ravaged sapling found by Robbie and belatedly recognised by me. It turns out that whilst there was a general understanding that there were now two Catacol whitebeams, people weren't talking about the *same* two trees. I've spoken to RBGE and NatureScot and everyone now knows there are three Catacol whitebeams – and hopefully NatureScot can do something to improve the grazing situation and safeguard them. It is certainly no longer *quite* the world's rarest tree!

Acknowledgements

This book would have been simply impossible without the time dedicated by the following experts: Craig Macadam, Christian 'Sparrow' Owen, Alex Prendergast, Alan Leslie, Joe Alsop, Ashley Arbon, Richard Moyse, Kathy Friend, Lee Knight, Rosie Ellis, Alan and Sandra Rowland, Andy Shaw, Martin Shaw, Robbie Blackhall-Miles, Sally Pidcock, Mark Lynes, Brian Eversham, Linda Robinson, Jonathan Revett, Steve Gregory, Finley Hutchinson and Louis Parkerson.

There are also the experts who showed me species that I simply didn't have the space to include in this book, and so, agonisingly, I had to cut some adventures. Thanks to Lee Schofield and Rob Dixon for sharing Haweswater with me and showing me the endemic eyebright, *Euphrasia rivularis*. Thanks also to Andy Shaw who took the time to show me the stunning Ley's whitebeam and fat-leaved hawkweed. Thanks to Alex Prendergast who, in addition to taking me on a dandelion hunt, introduced me to an endemic sea lavender, an endemic bramble, and a few elms. Thanks also to Helena Crouch, BSBI Vice-County Recorder for Somerset, whose detailed instructions on the whitebeams of Cheddar Gorge helped me find several beautiful endemics.

Thanks to the experts behind the scenes who gave me advice and support: Roger Key, Fred Rumsey and

ACKNOWLEDGEMENTS

the BSBI Vice-County Recorders Sarah Cowan, John Crossley and Bob Hodgson.

Thanks also to James Lowen, Rich Vooght, the Botanical Society of Britain and Ireland, the Royal Society for the Protection of Birds, Buglife, the British Trust for Ornithology, Plantlife and the Lundy Field Society.

Thanks to my colleagues, old and new, who backed me: Kevin Walker, who planted the seed of an idea; Laurence Rose, who always supported me; Matt Goulson, who gave me the time to begin exploring this idea; Sam Thomas, whose photos of Arran whitebeams encouraged me to seek them out before we even met; Matt Harding, whose messages about endemics inspired the reveal of the three Catacol whitebeams; and my old boss, Richard Bashford, who thought it was a good idea.

Thanks to my friends who made this all possible: Lisa Jones, who believed in me before anyone else did – and thanks to the entire Jones clan; Ruth Lindley, who turned out to be a natural whitebeam-spotter and whose contributions were painfully cut; Heather Stuckey, whose energy, thirst for adventure, and provision of mammal traps made so much of this book possible; Robert Jaques, a snivelling worm; Mr Jack Plumb, who risked life and limb on our Arran expedition; and Natasha Foxford, whose illustrations enhance the book and who dedicated days of her life to keeping me on track. It wouldn't have been possible without any of them.

Thanks to my family, who I love: Phil, Deb, Jenny and Claire, and I'm sorry that our trips to see our endemic subspecies of the belted beauty moth, Pugsley's marsh orchid and Lindisfarne helleborine were cut. At least as consolation we have lovely memories of spending time together.

References

CHAPTER 2

Knox, A. 1990. Identification of Crossbill and Scottish Crossbill. *British Birds* 83: 89–94.

Lewis, M. & McInerny, C. J. 2022. SBRC position on Scottish Crossbill. *Scottish Birds* 42: 71–72.

CHAPTER 8

Pugsley, H. W. 1936. The Brassica of Lundy Island. *Journal of Botany* 74: 323.

CHAPTER 12

Morris, M. 1978. *Cotoneaster integerrimus* – a conservation exercise. *Botanical Society of the British Isles Welsh Bulletin* 28: 6–8.

CHAPTER 14

Peace, T. R. 1960. The status and development of elm disease in Britain. *Forestry Commission Bulletin* 33: 41

CHAPTER 17

Spada, C. D., Miserere, L., Blockeel, T. L., Guglielmo, F. & Tutino, S. 2022. *Thamnobryum angustifolium* (Holt) Nieuwl. in the Maritime Alps, new to Italy. *Journal of Bryology* 44(1): 62–69.

CHAPTER 20

Gregory, S. J., Jones, R. E. & Mauris, J.-P. 1994. A new species of millipede (Myriapoda: Diplopoda: Chordeumatida) from the British Isles. *Journal of Natural History* 28(1): 47–52.

BIBLIOGRAPHY

Carr, G., Lunn, J. & Pinder, S. 2024. The rapid extinction of Willow Tits in a post-industrial landscape. *British Birds* 117(4): 195–202.

Clapham, A. R., Tutin, T. G. & Warburg, E. F. 1952. *Flora of the British Isles*. Cambridge University Press, Cambridge.

Dvořák, D. 2022. Geastrum britannicum – a new species of the Czech mycobiota. *Mykologické listy* 151: 29–34.

Lowe, A. J. & Abbott, R. J. 2003. A new British species, *Senecio eboracensis* (Asteraceae), another hybrid derivative of *S. vulgaris* L. and *S. squalidus* L. *Watsonia* 24: 375–388.

Lynes, M. 2022. Alchemilla – *Lady's-mantles of Britain and Ireland*. Botanical Society of Britain & Ireland, Totnes.

Macadam, C. R. 2023. Britain's Endemic Invertebrates. Buglife – The Invertebrate Conservation Trust, Peterborough.

Porley, R. D. 2013. *England's Rare Mosses and Liverworts: Their History, Ecology, and Conservation*. Princeton University Press, Princeton and Oxford.

Rich, T. C. G., Houston, L., Roberts, A. & Proctor, M. C. F. 2010. *Whitebeams, Rowans and Service Trees of Britain and Ireland*. Botanical Society of Britain & Ireland, Totnes.

Rich, T. C. G. 2020. List of vascular plants endemic to Britain, Ireland and the Channel Islands. *British & Irish Botany* 2(3): 169–189.

Richards, A. J., Haworth, C. C. 1984. Further new species of *Taraxacum* from the British Isles. *Watsonia* 15: 85–94.

Richards, A. J. 2021. *Field Handbook to British and Irish Dandelions*. Botanical Society of Britain & Ireland, Totnes.

Sangster, G., Collinson, J. M., Kirwan, G. M., Knox, A. G.,

McMahon, B. J., Parkin, D., Schweizer, M. & Höglund, J. 2022. The taxonomic status of Red Grouse. *British Birds* 115(1): 28–38.

Sell, P. & Murrell, G. 2018. *Flora of Great Britain and Ireland: Volume 1, Lycopodiaceae – Salicaceae.* Cambridge University Press, Cambridge.

Stace, C. A. 2019. *New Flora of the British Isles*, 4th edition. C&M Floristics, Totnes.

Tomlinson, I. & Potter, C. 2010. 'Too little, too late'? Science, policy and Dutch Elm Disease in the UK. *Journal of Historical Geography* 36: 121–131.

Usher, M. B. 1968. A new species of bird flea from the Manx Shearwater in Scotland. *Entomologist's Gazette* 19: 173–180.

Index

Abbot, Richard 322
Abernethy National Nature
 Reserve 25, 28–30
Alchemilla falsadenta 197–205
 filicaulis 195
 glabra 199–200
 mollis 196, 203, 205, 323
 monticola 197
 oxydonta 199
 sciura 195
 subcrenata 198
 wichurae 228
 xanthochlora 200
alder, hybrid 76
Alnus cordata x A. incana 76
Alsop, Joe 253–9
Anasaitis milesae 302
Anaspis septentrionalis 14
 thoracica 14
Anglesey 166–74
Anisantha diandra 88
 sterilis 88
Anoscopus albifrons 14
 duffieldi 14
Anthogona britannica 308–16
ant, narrow-headed 83, 301
 wood 28
Apodemus sylvaticus fridariensis 264
 sylvaticus hirtensis 263
apomictic reproduction 76–7, 213, 214
arable plant decline 91–2
Arbon, Ashley 86–7, 323
Archaeognatha 46–7
Argonemertes australiensis 52
Armidillidium pictum 148
Arran, Isle of 117, 250, 280, 281–96, 325
Arvicola amphibius 273
assortative mating 27

Back from the Brink conservation
 project 8, 37, 55, 83, 87
Baker, John Gilbert 226
Baker's Pit cave, Devon 101–8
bats, horseshoe 99
beardmoss, Scottish 252
beetle, dung 14, 46
 elm bark 208
 Lundy cabbage flea 117, 120, 123–5, 127
 northern dune tiger 83
 tumbling flower 14
bellflower, clustered 90
berry, Great Orme 55, 186–93
Berry, Tylan 302
Betula pendula x utilis 76
birch, hybrid silver 76
Blackhall-Miles, Robbie 166–74, 282, 296
blewit, wood 238
bluebells 8
bonnetcap, bleach 238
bonxies (great skuas) 264–5, 270–1
Bradshaw, Margaret 198, 203
Bristletails, Chater's 14, 46–7, 53–4, 215
 southern 47
British Birds 26, 33–4, 37–8
British Myriapod and Isopod Group
 (BMIG) 41–2, 49, 309, 314
brome, great 88, 323
 interrupted 8, 55, 83–95
 soft 84, 85, 88
 sterile 88
Bromus hordeaceus 88
 interruptus 88
Bryoerythrophyllum caledonicum 252
bryophytes 250–62
Bryum dixonii 252
 lawersianum 252

BSBI (Botanical Society of Britain and
  Ireland) 9–10, 55, 57–8, 69, 85, 134,
  138, 160, 189, 194, 211, 223, 267,
  283, 303
BTO (British Trust for
  Ornithology) 39
Buglife 13, 22, 98, 300, 306, 307
buttercups 55, 65, 68–82
  Backs goldilocks 75, 80–1, 323–4
  goldilocks 68–82, 323–4
  Pertenhall goldilocks 68, 69–74, 80,
    208
  Tandridge goldilocks 81
  Toft goldilocks 80–1
butterflies 182–4
butterfly, silver-studded blue 182–4

cabbage, Lundy 55, 115–33
caddisflies 324
Caledonian Forest 38
Cambridge Botanic Garden 85
Carlton Marsh, South Yorkshire 35–7
Cat Specialist Group 264
Catacol Glen, Isle of Arran 281,
  285–96
cave pearls 103–4
celandines 70
Centetostoma bacilliferum 301–2
centipedes 41
  Turk's earth 15, 321
Centranthus ruber 135–6
Cephaloziella nicholsonii 251
Ceratophyllus fionnus 131
Ceratosphys amoena 50–1
Ceutorhynchus contractus 121
  var *pallipes* 121
chamomile, stinking 92–3
charlock 92
Chater, Arthur 47, 180, 215–16
chickweed, Edmonton's 117
choughs 176
cinquefoil, shrubby 229
climate change 22
Coincya wrightii 124
Coleman, Dr Max 211, 325
colonisation, British elm 216–17
comfrey, Barton Road 'hybrid' 143–7,
  322–3
  Russian 143
  white 143–4
Commidendrum rotundifolium 281
'Connie the Comfrey' 145–7, 322–3
Constable, John 206–7
Convolvulus tricolor 136
copperwort, greater 251
cord-grass, American smooth 153–4

common 154
  small 153
  Townsend's 154
corncockle 91
cornsalad, narrow-fruited 92
Cotoneaster
  cambricus 188–93
  integerrimus 187–8
cotula, alpine 31–2
Coul Links, Scotland 307–8
Covid-19 global pandemic 227
crossbill, common 25–9
  parrot 26–9
  Scottish 25–9, 38
Crossley, John 267
crustaceans 41, 45, 96–8
curlew, Eurasian 7–8
cycad, Wood's 281
Cylindroiulus 49
  pyrenaicus 50

dance-flies 15
dandelions 56–67
  Bertha's 63, 65
  cut-leaved 63–4
  dark-green 63
  false fen 57–67, 323
  Nordstedt's 64
Dasiphora fruticosa 229
Dearne Valley wetlands, South
  Yorkshire 38, 39
Derbyshire Dales National Nature
  Reserve 252–3
Dilta chateri 14, 47
  hibernica 47
Dines, Trevor 323
disease, Dutch elm *see* Dutch elm disease
DNA 26, 31, 34, 227, 247
Dunkel, Franz 81
Dutch elm disease 206–8, 213–14, 215,
  218–19
DYCs (damned yellow
  composites) 224–5

earthstar, arched 244
  British 237, 243–9, 324
  crowned 241–2
  rayed 'four-footed' 243, 245
Eden Project, Cornwall 52
elms 55, 206–20
  Assington 215
  Chater's 215–16
  colonisation of British 216–17
  Cornish 215
  English 211
  Hatley 218, 220

Hayley 219–20
  rhombic-leaved 215
  wedge-leaved 212
  wych 213
Enantiulus armatus 312
endosperm 77
Eversham, Brian 73, 208–9

'false endemics' 51–3, 85, 251, 302
'false marriage' 77
Felis silvestris
  grampia 264
  silvestris 264
fertiliser 91
Field Identification Skills Certificate (FISC) 303–4
flatworm, many-eyed 302
flea, Manx shearwater 131–2
fleawort, field 176, 177, 180
  South Stack 176–81, 215, 322
Flora of Great Britain and Ireland (Sell & Murrell) 211, 212, 213, 215, 216, 217
fly, Fonesca's seed- 307–8
fossil bones 99–100
Foulden Common, Norfolk 59
Fuchsia magellanica 135
Fumaria capreolata 138
  occidentalis 136
  pupurea 134, 136–41
fungi 208, 235–49
  see also earthstars
fungus, honey 238
funnel, chicken-run 241

Gabunillo aridicola 52
  coecus 52
  sp. Eden A 52
gamebird shooting licenses 39
Gammarus 107–8
Geastrum britannicum 244–9, 324
  quadrifidium 243, 245
genetic testing 26, 34, 52, 125, 247, 273–4
gentian, spring 222
Glennie, Brigadier E.A. 111
goat, Kashmir 191
good-king-henry 223
Grass Wood reserve, Yorkshire Wildlife Trust 195–205, 323
grasses 83
grayling 184–5
grazing 38, 228–9, 233, 286
Great Orme Country Park, Wales 181–93
Gregory, Steve 310, 313, 314–15

Griffith, John Wyne 186
groundsel, common 152, 156, 318
  Welsh 155–7, 323
  York 151–5, 157, 303–4, 317
grouse, red 32–5, 38–9
  willow 32–4

Haplophthalmus mengii 43, 44
Harding, Matt 325
Hartet, Ernst 26
harvestman, punk 301–2, 304
hawkweed, Baker's 225–8, 229, 230–4, 322–3
Hayley Wood, Cambridgeshire 217–20
Hazelton, Mary 111
'heat islands' 135
Herbertus borealis 251
herbicides 86, 91, 92
Hieracium bakeranum 225–6
Hipparchia semele 184–5
  ssp. *thyone* 184–5
hoglice, freshwater 41
Holt, George Albert 255
Howarth, Chris 65
Hutchinson, Finley 298–306
hybrid plant reproduction 152–4
Hyophorbe amaricaulis 281

Ice Age, last 98, 125, 263, 273
'ice flowers' 222
Ingleborough 9–11
ink-cap, shaggy 237
International Ornithological Committee (IOC) 38
invertebrates
  and elms 211–12, 214–15
  endemic 13–24, 298–307, 308–12, 324
isopods 41

Jacob's ladder 147
Joint Mitnor Cave, Devon 99
Jones, Dick 310
Jones, Emma 70–4, 79–80
Jones, Vincent 226
Journal of Bryology 260–1

Kew Gardens *see* Royal Botanic Gardens, Kew
Key, Dr Robert 127
Kleinschmidt, Otto 36
knawel 8
Knight, Lee 96–114
Knox, Alan 26

lady's-mantle 55
  Cairnwell 195

false-toothed 197–205, 323
  garden 196, 197
  hairy/slender 195
  least 194–5
  pale 200–1
  rock 228
  sharp-toothed 199
  smooth 199, 201
  velvet 197
Lagopus
  lagopus 32–3
  lagopus scotica 33
  scotica 32, 254
Lawers, Ben 252
Lawley, Mark 260
leafhoppers 14
Leiocolea fitzgeraldiae 251
Leslie, Alan 69, 74–81, 144, 154, 323–4
Linnaeus, Carl 151
Linopodes motatorius 303
Linyphiidae 306
little robin 149–50
liverworts and mosses *see* bryophytes
Logunov, Dmitri 302
Longworth mammal traps 266
  see also voles, Orkney
Lophocolea 251
  brookwoodiana 251
love-in-a-mist 136
Lowe, Andrew 322
Loxia curvirostra 25
  scotica 25
Lundy 115–33
Lundy Field Society 119, 120
Lynes, Mark 194–205
Lynford Arboretum, Norfolk 235–42

Macadam, Craig 13–15, 46, 324
Marine Conservation Zones,
  British 119
Marionfyfea adventor 302
Maurieseuma nontronense 50–1
Melville, Ronald 210–11
Meotica anglica 14
  moczarskii 14
Merthyr Mawr Nature Reserve,
  Wales 40–6
Metatrichoniscoides celticus 41
mouse, house 275–6
  St Kilda field 263
  St Kilda house 263, 276
  wood 263, 264
Microtus agrestis 273
  arvalis 273
  arvalis orcadensis 264
milkcap, mild 238–9

Millennium Seed Bank, Kew 89, 153
millipedes 41, 48–50, 308–16
  British false flat-backed 312–16
  'Celtic ghost' 51
  'Maerdy monster' 51
  Portuguese 49
  snake 312
  Telfer's 50–1
  Welsh silk 50–1
  Welsh two-tail 50
Mills, J.N. 226
mites, elm 211
  soil 303
morning glory, dwarf 136
Morris, Maurice 187–8, 190, 192–3
Mortehoe, Devon 134–5
moss, Arisaig crisp- 252
  Cornish path 8, 251–2
  Derbyshire feather- 252–62
  Dixon's thread- 252
  fox-tail feather 257–8, 261
  Scottish thread- 252
  Skye bog- 251–2
  yellow crisp- 252
  Yorkshire feather- 252
mosses and liverworts *see* bryophytes;
  moss
moth, white-spotted pinion 215
Moyse, Richard 87–94
Myodes glareolus 273
  glareolus alstoni 264
  glareolus erica 264
  glareolus skomerensis 263
myriapods 41

Naevosa 64
Nantporth Nature Reserve 167–8
Natural England 227, 303
NatureScot 307, 325
'Nectaries' 78
nemerines, land 52
New Flora (C. Stace) 210–11
Nicotiana sylvestris 76
Nigella damascena 136
Niphargus 96
  aquilex 101, 105–7, 112
  glenniei 97–8, 109–14
  No Take Zones, British 119
Norton, Tristan 138–9
notchwort, Fitzgerald's 251
Nothogeophilus turki 15
Nothophantes 299
  horridus 299–307

Obliqua 58
Ogmore-by-Sea, Wales 40–6

INDEX

Ommatoiulus moreleti 49
orchid, fly 83
  man 94
Orkney islands 117, 264–77
Orthotrichum cambrense 252
Owen, Christian 42–67
Oxford Botanic Garden 151

palm, loneliest 281
Palustria 58
parasol, stinking baby 237–8
Parkerson, Louis 298–306
Parry, Tom 190
Peace, Dr Tom 207–8
Pengelly Cave Studies Trust 98
Pengelly, William 98
pesticides 56–7
Phagocata vitta 122
Pidcock, Sally 185–93
pine, ground 90
Plantlife 83
Platyarthrus hoffmannseggii 43
Plebejus argus 182–4
  ssp. *caernensis* 183–4
Plecoptera *see* stoneflies
Plumb, Jack 283–97
Poecile montanus 36
  montanus kleinschmidti 36
Poecilobothrus majesticus 15
Pohlia scotica 252
pollution 20, 119, 258–9
poppy, common 90, 92
  long-headed 90
  prickly 90, 91
  rough 91, 93
  yellow-juiced 90
Potter, Clive 208
Poyner, John 29, 30–1
Prendergast, Alex 57–67, 303–4, 323
Pridhamsleigh Cave 111
primrose, Scottish 55, 267–71, 277–8
Primula scotica see primrose, Scottish
prongwort, northern 251
Psammoporus insularis 14, 46
pseudogamous apomixis 77
Psylliodes luridipennis 120–1
  napi 121
ptarmigan, willow 33
puffins 130
Pugsley, Herbert William 124, 225–6, 232

ragwort, Oxford 151–3, 155–6, 318
ramping-fumitory, purple 134, 136–41
  western 136
  white 138–9

Ranscombe Farm 83, 87
Ranunculus auricomus 68
  cantabrigiensis 75, 80
  leslieanus 81
  multidens 81
  waltersii 78
rat eradication 130, 131
Red List 14, 113
Reed's Cave 104, 109–14
Revett, Jonathan 237–49
rhododendrons 127–8
Rhyacophila fasciata 324
Rich, Tim 55–6, 158, 194, 226
Richards, A.J. 58
Richens, Richard 210–11, 216
River Eden 260
River Tees 223–33
Robinson, Linda 223–33
rocket, sea 125
Rousay 267–71
rove beetle 14
rowan 284, 295
Rowland, Alan 119–23
Royal Botanic Garden Edinburgh (RBGE) 325
Royal Botanic Gardens, Kew 89, 153, 245, 248
RSPB (Royal Society for the Protection of Birds) 39, 307
South Stack 175–81
Ruderalia 59
Rum, Isle of 131–2
rupturewort, fringed 150

sainfoin 85
sandwort, Yorkshire 10–11
saxifrage, Irish 149
Schoenus-fen 59
Schoenus nigricans 59, 66
Scottish Birds Records Committee 30
sea anemone, Ivell's 14–15
sea slaters, marine 41
Sell, P.D. 226
Senecio cambrensis 156
  eboracensis 151–6
  squalidus 151–3
  vulgaris 152–3
  x *baxteri* 152
service-tree, Arran 284–5, 287–8
sexual reproduction, elm 213, 214
Shaw, Andy 146–56, 233–4, 317–20
shearwater, Manx 129–32
Shetland 117
shooting, grouse 39
shrimp, British cave 96, 97–8
Skara Brae, Orkney 272, 273–4

skuas, great 264–5, 270–1
Slapton Ley, Devon 309–13
Smith, Dr Philip 85
sonograms 27–8
Sorbus 158
  admonitor 159–62, 163
  arranensis 284
  arvonicola 168
  devoniensis 159
  fennica 288
  pseudofennica 284–5, 287
  rupicola 284
  subcuneata 162
  vexans 162–6
Spartina anglica 154
  maritima 153–4
spider, horrid ground-weaver 298–307
  jumping 302
  money 306
Stace, Clive 194, 210–11
stiltball, sandy 246
stonefly, northern February red 15–24
storm-petrels 130
strapwort 310
Styles, Joshua 58
suckering, reproduction-by- 213–14
Sulber Pasture 9–10
Symphytum orientale 144–5

talus cones 100
Taraxacum 61
  anglicum 63
  berthae 63, 65
  bracteatum 62
  lacistophyllum 63
  palustrisquameum 57
Teesdale assemblage 221–2
Thamnobryum alopecurum 257–8
  angustifolium 257
  cataractarum 252
thrift, tall 149
tit, marsh 36, 37
  willow 35–7, 39, 325
Tomlinson, Isobel 208
Tortella limosella 252
Trichoniscoides saeroeensis 43

Ulmus chaterorum 215–16
  cornubiensis 215
  crenata 219
  procera 211

  rhombifolia 215
  serrata 215
  sylvatica 218
uropods 45

valerian, red 135–6
vetch, wood 116
vocalisations, crossbill 27–8
voles 117
  bank 263–4, 273
  common 273
  field 273
  Orkney 250, 264–7, 271–6, 278–80
  Skomer 263
  water 273
Vooght, Rich 100

Walker, Kevin 9–10
Walters, John 301, 302
Walters, Max 78, 194–5
Warburg, Edmund 163
wasp, digger 83
weevil, Lundy cabbage 117, 121, 125–6, 132–3, 324
whitebeams 55, 117, 155, 158–74, 250
  Arran 284, 286
  bloody 162–6
  Catacol 281–96, 325
  common 169, 171
  Devon 159–60
  Leys 170
  Menai Strait 166–74
  Motley's 155
  'no parking' 159–62, 163
  rock 284
  slender 162, 165
  Watersmeet 166
Widewater Lagoon, Essex 14–15
wildcats 264
Wildfowl and Wetlands Trust (WWT), Welney 243
witch's egg 239–40
woodlice 40–6, 148
  ant 43
  Celtic 40–6, 54
  spurred ridgeback 44–5
woundwort, limestone 149
Wright, Frederick Elliston 124

yellow-rattle, greater 148–9
York 317–20